The Story of the Q

The Story of the Qur'an

Its History and Place in Muslim Life

INGRID MATTSON

Blackwell
Publishing

BLACKWELL PUBLISHING
350 Main Street, Malden, MA 02148-5020, USA
9600 Garsington Road, Oxford OX4 2DQ, UK
550 Swanston Street, Carlton, Victoria 3053, Australia

First published 2008 by Blackwell Publishing Ltd

2   2008

Library of Congress Cataloging-in-Publication Data

Mattson, Ingrid.
   The story of the Qur'an : its history and place in Muslim life / Ingrid Mattson.
      p. cm.
   Includes bibliographical references and index.
   ISBN 978-1-4051-2257-3 (hardcover : alk. paper)—ISBN 978-1-4051-2258-0 (pbk. : alk. paper)
1.   Koran—Theology. 2.   Koran—History. 3.   Koran—Criticism, interpretation, etc. I.   Title.

   BP132.M39 2008
   297.1'2261—dc22

                                                    2007010745

A catalogue record for this title is available from the British Library.

Set in 10.5/13pt PhotinaMT
by SPi Publisher Services, Pondicherry, India
Printed and bound in the United Kingdom
by TJ International Ltd, Padstow, Cornwall

For further information on
Blackwell Publishing, visit our website at
www.blackwellpublishing.com

Contents

Preface

I chose to write this book after teaching an introductory, graduate-level course on the Qur'an at Hartford Seminary for a number of years. To that end, it reflects my interest in having an academically grounded but accessible introduction to the Qur'an. I have tried to not burden the general educated reader with too many specialized terms and concepts. At the same time, by referencing a number of important Islamic thinkers and providing annotations to specialized research, I have sought to make this book a starting point for those interested in a deeper study of the Qur'an and Islam. I have included both English-language studies and original Arabic sources in the Bibliography. When available, I have referred to English-language translations of Arabic sources to facilitate further study by a broader readership.

In many ways, this book reflects my personal perspective on the Qur'an. In an introductory work like this, the author can select only a small number of Qur'anic verses to discuss, refer to only a fraction of the important Muslim thinkers and writers in this field, and highlight only a handful of significant historical incidents and cultural developments. At the same time, the reader might notice that I approach the Qur'an from the perspective of a Western academic who is also trying to live as a faithful Muslim. This is not the only perspective on the Qur'an, but it is one that, perhaps, has been underrepresented in the literature.

The Qur'an has been a topic of great interest on the part of Western media and the general public in recent years. Unfortunately, many people take liberty to speak about the meaning of the Qur'an without having studied it. What is most remarkable is the rise of what I will call the "non-Muslim Islamic fundamentalist." These are people who (perhaps because they read their own scripture in a literal and decontextualized fashion) open an English translation of the meaning of the Qur'an and, plucking a verse out of context, declare that this is proof that "Muslims believe (this) or (that)." Some of these individuals might honestly be interested in knowing what the Qur'an says. I hope that this book will be of some assistance to those people. Others, who are ideologically opposed to Muslims and Islam – whether because of religious intolerance or for political reasons – will continue to try to reduce the breadth and diversity of the Islamic experience to the views of an extremist, militant minority.

Citing the Qur'an

Passages of the Qur'an are cited throughout this book with two distinctive features. First, most passages are set apart in italics and block quotes. I have chosen to distinguish the verses I cite in this manner to slow the reader down, and to give him or her the opportunity to reflect individually on these citations. In the end, the context provided for each citation is of my own choosing. But each of these verses can be found in other, often drastically different contexts throughout Muslim societies. Thus, a verse the reader encounters in my chapter on "culture," where it serves as a decorative or sacred feature of an architectural space, might be alternately found as proof for a legal judgment in a medieval text. In structuring this book in a way that allows the reader to randomly and independently skim through the chapters and reflect on the Qur'anic verses scattered throughout, I hope to replicate an aspect of the way in which Muslims can decontextualize and recontextualize verses they encounter throughout their lives.

Secondly, in most cases when citing a Qur'anic passage, I give the name of the sura in which it is found, not simply the number of the sura. Although the numbering of Qur'anic suras and verses in the text of the Qur'an (the *mushaf*) is not new, until very recently, in scholarly works, suras were always referred to by their name, not their number. In my experience, it is far easier to remember the name of a sura than its number when trying to recall the location of a specific verse. Consequently, I believe that it is more advantageous to readers generally, and to students specifically, to identify the name of the sura in which cited verses are found.

Arabic Transliteration

There are a number of different systems for transliterating the Arabic language. In a complete system of transliteration, diacritics (dots or lines under or over letters) are used to distinguish a number of Arabic phonemes. For the sake of simplicity, I have not used any diacritics except for ' and ' to signify *'ayn* and *hamza*.

To avoid confusion, throughout the book, wherever an author I am citing uses a different transliteration for *Qur'an* (i.e., "Koran," "Qoran," "Quran," etc.) I have changed it to "Qur'an." I have done the same with *muslim* and other common Islamic terms.

Dates

The Islamic calendar begins in 622 CE with the emigration (*hijra*) of the Prophet Muhammad to Medina. The Islamic *hijri* year is comprised of twelve lunar months of 29 or 30 days each. This means that an Islamic calendar is approximately 11 days shorter than a year of the Gregorian (solar) calendar. January 1, 2007 falls within the year 1427 AH ("after *hijra*"). In this book I will generally give both dates, *hijri* first, "common era" (CE) dates second. Sometimes biographical literature cites only the year of death; in such cases, converted dates are approximate and might be off by one year.

Acknowledgments

Many people have helped me in small and large ways to complete this book. I am particularly grateful to Ian Markham, Dean of Hartford Seminary, for encouraging me to write it, and for giving me helpful advice to ensure its completion. I also want to thank Heidi Hadsell, President of Hartford Seminary, for agreeing to my sabbatical leave to work on the book, and for supporting me in many ways.

I am grateful to Hisham al-Talib at the International Institute of Islamic Thought for providing some research funding for this book. Thanks to Omer Totinji for helping things along.

I am deeply grateful to Reem Osman for sharing the story of her journey to memorize the Qur'an. I pray that this will be an act of *sadaqa jariya* (perpetual charity) for her.

I am humbled by the generosity of Sheikh Abdullah Adhami who shared with me his research about Sheikh al-Kurdi's *isnad* and took the time to answer my questions. I pray that God continues to increase his ability to benefit students of sacred knowledge. Any errors I have made or incorrect information I have conveyed are solely my responsibility.

Thanks are owed to Valerie Vick for reading and editing the manuscript and to Bilal Ansari for research assistance. Thanks to Ahmed Hashim for helping to draw the *isnad* (although I had to change it in the end). Thanks to everyone at Blackwell, especially Rebecca Harkin.

Thanks to dear friends and family who have provided much needed encouragement, advice, and companionship along the way: my mother, Jacqueline Mattson; my teacher, Sheikh Muhammad Nur Abdullah; my friends, Nour Akhras and Heba Abbasi. My children, Soumayya and Ubayda Aatek, continually inspire me. They are kind and thoughtful individuals who have generously encouraged their mother to spend much of her time engaged in teaching and public education. Finally, there is no one who has sacrificed more for this book than my husband, Amer Aatek; he is my best advisor, my partner, and supporter. May God bless and reward him for all he has done.

1

God Speaks to Humanity

God Hears and Responds

Before God mentioned her, Khawla bint Tha'laba was apparently an ordinary woman living in seventh-century Medina in the Arabian Peninsula. For every person in this tribally organized sedentary community, dignity and honor were, to a large extent, commensurate with the status of his or her group. Descent (*nasab*) or affiliation (*wala'*) with a powerful clan was, for many people, a decisive factor in determining physical security and material success. Still, every individual had opportunities to prove the strength of his or her own character (*hasab*). For men, politics and war were arenas of particular distinction. Most women had little chance of significantly contributing to these areas of public life, although there were notable exceptions.[1] Rather, most women distinguished themselves by establishing and maintaining beneficial relationships with family, neighbors, and guests. Beauty, an energetic spirit, generosity, loyalty – these were the hallmarks of a noble woman. As the charms of youthful beauty faded, a woman could expect to earn increasing respect and gratitude for the relationships she had cultivated over the years.

It may have been anger that made Aws ibn Samit reject his wife with the vulgar expression, "To me, you are like the backside of my mother."[2] Whatever the reason, after so many years of marriage, these words reduced Khawla to the status of his mother's behind (completely devoid of sensual attraction). Moreover, according to Arab custom, there was no way to revoke the declaration of *zihar*. Henceforth, it was prohibited for Aws to touch Khawla, yet she was not free of the marital bond. Sympathetic family and friends had no power to override such norms and customs. Khawla's only chance was

to appeal to a power higher than social custom and patriarchal authority. And so, Khawla complained to God.

Complaining to God is not difficult; the challenge is eliciting a
satisfactory response. In what Marshall Hodgson termed the "Irano-
Semitic" tradition, the expected response from God entailed not only
spiritual comforting but also social transformation.[3] At the individual
level, God could send a sign: a kind stranger with food and comforting
words, the sun breaking free of the rain clouds, a heavenly vision
appearing in a dream. Transforming society, on the other hand,
required a different kind of intervention. It is for this purpose that
God sent prophets with authority to speak on his behalf, empowered
to overturn the existing social order.

When Khawla first went to the Arabian prophet to complain of the
injustice done to her, she was disappointed. Muhammad[4] indicated
that existing customs remained normative unless God revealed a new
ruling, and the Prophet had received no revelation about this issue.
Khawla did not give up hope, for she knew that this custom was
unjust; she continued to complain to God, and waited near his Messenger, expecting him to receive a revelation. Then the answer arrived:

> God has heard the words of she who disputes with you regarding
> her husband and made her complaint to God. God hears your
> conversation. Verily God is All-Hearing, All-Seeing.
>
>   Those of you who shun their wives by zihar – they are not their
> mothers. Their mothers are only those women who gave birth to
> them. Indeed they utter words that are unjust and false; but God is
> Absolving of Sins, All-Forgiving.
>
> (Mujadila; 58:1–2)

With these verses God confirmed Khawla's conviction that what had
been done to her was unjust and was to be prohibited by law. Upon
hearing this revelation, 'A'isha, the Prophet's wife who later would
herself desperately need God to hear and respond to unjust claims
made against her, declared, "Blessed is He whose hearing encompasses
all things!"[5]

Defining the Qur'an

Khawla's story shows the Messenger of God to be a man deeply
involved in the lives of those around him. More importantly, Khawla's

story shows that God's speech can be elicited by the concerns of ordinary people. The Qur'anic revelation, although transmitted through the Prophet, is not a response to his concerns alone. From an Islamic theological perspective, God created a community of men and women to whom he wanted to speak, in a manner that would have universal and eternal significance for people of other times and places.

This ruling on a form of divorce customary among pre-Islamic Arabs is one of a number of specific rulings that were revealed to Muhammad to rectify injustices present in his community. Other rulings deal with more general evils present in all societies, such as murder, theft, and betrayal of trust. Exhortations to strengthen the bonds of community are also found in abundance in the Qur'an. Honoring parents, sheltering orphans, giving charity, and fighting oppression are among the duties and hallmarks of the righteous. The foundation of all these legal and ethical pronouncements is faith in the one true God, the creator and sustainer of all creation.

Much of the Qur'anic revelation, however, is not, as is the case with Khawla's story, obviously related to any historical event or legal dispute. The Qur'an is also infused with invocations, supplications, and doxologies:

> Blessed is He in whose hand is the dominion, and He has power over all things.
>   He who created death and life to test which one of you is best in deeds, and He is the Eminent, the All-Forgiving.
>
> (Mulk; 67:1–2)

Perhaps these were the words God spoke to the Prophet in his solitary moments, as he stood praying deep into the night. Other passages in the Qur'an are clearly directed to the Prophet individually, commanding him to rise and warn his people or to listen carefully to the revelation (74:1–7). Many passages of the Qur'an narrate incidents in the lives of pre-Islamic Hebrew and Arabian prophets and show how the resistance and hardship Muhammad faced in his mission to guide others to God is mirrored in the righteous struggles of his ancestors in faith:

> We sent messengers before you to the communities of old; and we never sent a messenger but that they mocked him.
>
> (Hijr; 15:10–11)

Together, these legal judgments, prayers, and narrative passages form a unity by virtue of their status as God's words, revealed to the Prophet Muhammad.

In later chapters, we will explore these themes in more depth and we will describe how the Qur'an became a textual unity that encompassed numerous discrete revelations addressing diverse issues. In this chapter, we will describe the historical context of the revelation, show how Muhammad received God's message, and consider how the Qur'an describes itself in relation to other forms of God's speech and guidance to humanity.

Ancient Origins of the Meccan Sanctuary

The story of the Qur'anic revelation begins in Mecca, a desert town located in the Hijaz, the northwestern region of the Arabian Peninsula. In the sixth century CE, Mecca was poor in natural resources and comforts; it was not a pleasant oasis, rich in date palm groves, like Yathrib, a city almost 300 miles to the north where Muhammad would eventually establish his community of believers. Mecca was sparse and dry, made habitable only because mountain springs provided enough water to sustain a town of merchants and tradespeople.

According to the history of the pre-Islamic Arabs, Mecca was founded as a settlement by Abraham, his concubine-wife Hajar, and their son Isma'il. It was Abraham and his son who built a simple structure, the Ka'ba (literally, "the cube"), as a center for the worship of God. Other traditions traced the founding of Mecca as the primordial and most holy of sacred sites to Adam, the father of humanity, but credited Abraham and his family with establishing a permanent settlement there.

In an early Islamic report, rich in symbolism and detail, the Prophet Muhammad tells the story of how the unwavering faith and determined effort of Abraham and Hajar opened the way for divine intervention to secure the establishment of this sacred site:

> The first woman to use a belt was the mother of Isma'il. She used a belt so that she might hide her tracks from Sarah. Abraham brought her and her son Isma'il while she was suckling him, to a place near the Ka'ba under a tree on the spot of Zamzam, at the highest place in the mosque. During those days there was nobody in Mecca, nor was there any water. So he

made them sit over there and placed near them a leather bag containing some dates, and a small skin containing some water, and set out homeward. Isma'il's mother followed him saying, "O Abraham! Where are you going, leaving us in this valley where there is no person whose company we may enjoy, nor is there anything here?" She repeated that to him many times, but he did not look back at her. Then she asked him, "Has God ordered you to do so?" He said, "Yes." She said, "Then He will not neglect us," and returned while Abraham proceeded on-wards, and on reaching the Thaniya where they could not see him, he faced the Ka'ba, and raising both hands, invoked God saying the following prayers: *"O our Lord! I have made some of my offspring dwell in a valley without cultivation, by Your Sacred House in order, O our Lord, that they may offer prayer perfectly. So fill the hearts of people with love towards them, and provide them with fruits, so that they may give thanks."* (Ra'd; 13:47)[6]

Isma'il's mother went on suckling Isma'il and drinking from the water she had. When the water in the water skin had all been used up, she became thirsty and her child also became thirsty. She watched him tossing in agony and she left him, for she could not endure looking at him, and found that the mountain of Safa was the nearest mountain to her on that land. She stood on it and started looking at the valley keenly so that she might see somebody, but she could not see anybody. Then she descended from Safa and when she reached the valley, she tucked up her robe and ran in the valley like a person making a great effort (*majhud*),[7] until she crossed the valley and reached the Marwa mountain where she stood and kept looking, expecting to see somebody, but she could not see anybody. She repeated that (running between Safa and Marwa) seven times.

The Prophet Muhammad said: This is the source of the tradition of the running of people between (the mountains of Safa and Marwa). When she reached Marwa (for the last time) she heard a voice and she said "Shush" to herself and listened attentively. She heard the voice again and said, "O, (whoever you may be)! You have made me hear your voice; have you got something to help me?" And behold! She saw an angel at the place of Zamzam, digging the earth with his heel (or his wing), till water flowed from that place. She started to make something like a basin around it, using her hand in this way, and started filling her water skin with water with her hands, and the water was flowing out after she had scooped some of it.

The Prophet added: May God bestow Mercy on Isma'il's mother! Had she left Zamzam (to flow freely), Zamzam would have been a stream flowing on the surface of the earth. The Prophet further added: Then she drank and suckled her child. The angel said to her, "Do not be afraid of being neglected, for this is the house of God which will be built by this boy and his father, and God never neglects His people." The house at that time was on a high place resembling a hillock, and when torrents came, they flowed to its right and left.

She lived in that way till some people from the tribe of Jurhum or a family from Jurhum passed by her and her child, as they were coming through the way of Kada'. They landed in the lower part of Mecca where they saw a bird that had the habit of flying around water and not leaving it. They said, "This bird must be flying around water, though we know that there is no water in this valley." They sent one or two messengers who discovered the source of water, and returned to inform them of the water. So, they all approached. The Prophet added: Isma'il's mother was sitting near the water. They asked her, "Do you allow us to stay with you?" She replied, "Yes, but you will have no right to possess the water." They agreed to that. The Prophet further said: Isma'il's mother was pleased with the situation as she used to love to share the company of the people. So, they settled there, and later on they sent for their families who came and settled with them so that some families became permanent residents there. The child (i.e., Isma'il) grew up and learned Arabic from them and (his virtues) caused them to love and admire him as he grew up, and when he reached the age of puberty they had him marry a woman from amongst them. . . .

Then Abraham stayed away from them for a period as long as God wished, and called on them afterwards. He saw Isma'il under a tree near Zamzam, sharpening his arrows. When he saw Abraham, he rose up to welcome him (and they greeted each other as a father does with his son or a son does with his father). Abraham said, "O Isma'il! God has given me an order." Isma'il said, "Do what your Lord has ordered you to do." Abraham asked, "Will you help me?" Isma'il said, "I will help you." Abraham said, "God has ordered me to build a house here," pointing to a hillock higher than the land surrounding it. The Prophet added: Then they raised the foundations of the House (i.e. the Ka'ba). Isma'il brought the stones and Abraham was building, and when the walls became high, Isma'il brought this stone and put it for Abraham who stood over it and carried on building, while Isma'il was handing him the stones, and both of them were saying, *"O our Lord! Accept (this service) from us, Verily, You are the All-Hearing, the All-Knowing."* (Baqarah; 2:127)

The Prophet added: Then both of them went on building and going round the Ka'ba saying: *O our Lord! Accept (this service) from us, Verily, You are the All-Hearing, the All-Knowing.*

With this narrative of the founding of Mecca, the Prophet Muhammad reaffirms the ancient sanctity of the site for his contemporaries. At the same time, Muhammad's message is that Islam is not a renunciation of the traditions of the Arabs. He shows that their revered ancestors, Abraham, Hajar, and Isma'il, did not worship the idols with whom the Arabs had since populated the Ka'ba; rather, they had worshipped the One true God. Thus it is Islam, not idol worship, that is the original belief and most authentic carrier of Arab tradition. We shall see in a later chapter that this idea, that Islam is a revival of *their* original beliefs, is a message that the Qur'an will also direct to Christians and Jews.

The Arabian Context

In the late sixth century CE, Mecca was ruled by the tribe of Quraysh, the tribe into which Muhammad was born. Tribes across Arabia, both settled and nomadic, were not united in any political body nor were they ruled by a common authority. For centuries, various powers, including the Byzantines, the Persians, and the Ethiopians, had ventured into the Peninsula to secure their interests. The Byzantine and Persian empires, at war with each other, at times engaged the services of nomadic tribesmen living in the northern regions of the Peninsula to protect and expand their borders. Money, honorary titles, and other incentives were bestowed upon tribes that, in spite of the best hegemonic efforts of the empires, remained fickle and were inclined to switch sides whenever they felt it served their interests.[8] In Yemen, the southernmost area of the Peninsula, the sixth century witnessed struggles for power in the wake of the collapse of centralized authority. In the early sixth century, a Jewish ruler who persecuted Christians was overthrown by armies sent by the Christian ruler (the "Negus") of Ethiopia.[9] Near the end of that century, Persian troops occupied the south.

Within the Peninsula, alliances among tribes were always shifting, but they brought a measure of stability and predictability. Alliances were made for mutual protection and to facilitate trade and travel. Weak and depopulated clans could easily be forced into concessions, for the alternative was a life of constant insecurity, death, and captivity by stronger groups.[10] In the late sixth century, the Quraysh seemed to have been able to develop enough lasting alliances to allow them to engage in caravan trade across the Peninsula, especially between Yemen and Syria.[11] That Mecca was held sacred by many tribes throughout Arabia gave the Quraysh a distinct advantage.

Mecca was seldom directly affected by the political and military struggles occurring along the periphery of the Arabian Peninsula. However, around the year 570 CE, the year in which Muhammad was reported to have been born, Mecca's sanctuary was almost destroyed. Muslim historians report that Abraha, an Abyssinian general ruling Yemen, built a magnificent church in Sana' to rival the Ka'ba and to divert the Arab pilgrimage to it. One or more Meccans reacted by defiling the church, making Abraha determined to destroy the Ka'ba. The Abyssinian army prepared for war, and marched towards Mecca with an elephant who would help them reap destruction upon the temple. According to Islamic sources, the elephant refused to march upon the Ka'ba, despite being beaten, and the army was destroyed by a flock of birds that filled the sky and pelted them with stones.[12]

The Meccans understood the outcome of the "Battle of the Elephant" to be a clear indication that God protected and blessed the Ka'ba. This was confirmed in the Islamic period with a Qur'anic revelation about the incident:

> Have you not seen how your Lord dealt with the companions
>   of the Elephant?
> Did We not disrupt their plans?
> And send against them flock of birds ?
> Hitting them with hard clay stones;
> Leaving them like a field of grazed crops.
>
> (Fil; 105)

The pre-Islamic Arabians were not surprised that supernatural forces could disrupt the normal course of human affairs. They were particularly aware that certain places and particular times had special significance to unseen forces. In their journeys they passed through haunted valleys, they rested by blessed trees, and they sought advice from soothsayers. Scattered throughout the desert were oasis sanctuaries (*haram*), where local holy families maintained shrines and mediated disputes.[13] But the greatest and most widely honored sanctuary in Arabia was the Ka'ba of Mecca.

By the time Muhammad was born, it seems that the Quraysh and other local tribes had for generations deemed the Ka'ba and the hills of Safa and Marwa to be sacred. Historical sources indicate, however, that the Quraysh developed Mecca as the premiere pilgrimage site for the Arabs just a few decades before the birth of Muhammad.[14] It was Muhammad's grandfather, 'Abd al-Muttalib, who is credited with rediscovering the well of Zamzam.[15] By the end of the sixth century, tribes from across the Arabian Peninsula made annual pilgrimage to Mecca, where they engaged in a diverse set of rituals. The use of stone and wooden idols in worship is said to have been common, and the veneration of ancestors and animal sacrifices made in their names widespread.[16] Pilgrimage was conducted during certain months deemed sacred and, during these times, strangers and even enemies could mix in Mecca without fear. No weapons were allowed in the Meccan sanctuary and violent actions were prohibited. The Quraysh hosted the pilgrims, providing water and other amenities to the guests of "the House of God," as the Ka'ba was known.[17]

The major religions of Africa and Western Asia – Christianity, Judaism, and Zoroastrianism – were also not unknown to the residents of Mecca.[18] There were a few Christians living in and around Mecca and a significant settlement of Christians in the southern city of Najran. A number of Jewish tribes lived in the city of Yathrib, with which Muhammad had ancestral ties.[19] Yathrib would later become "Medina," the "City of the Prophet," when Muhammad established his Islamic community there in the thirteenth year of his mission.

In their travels and trade, the Quraysh were exposed to Christian, Jewish, and Zoroastrian communities from Syria, Iraq, Yemen, and Ethiopia. The Quraysh, perhaps because they were so deeply attached to the Ka'ba, did not adopt any of these religions. It would be the mission of Muhammad to reconcile the particular sanctity of the Ka'ba with a universal monotheism through the Abrahamic model. Muhammad would criticize the use of these idols and their presence inside the Ka'ba as a violation of the monotheistic principles established by their ancestor Abraham. Until that time, those few Meccans who were troubled by idol veneration were said to have sought the true religion of Abraham (*al-hanifiyya*), some eventually adopting Christianity, others remaining independent, unaffiliated monotheists.[20] These individuals are reported to have abstained from eating meat sacrificed to idols and to have shunned rituals they deemed idolatrous.

The Arabic Language

Although the pre-Islamic tribes of the Arabian Peninsula were not united under a common political or religious authority, they did share many important aspects of culture. By the seventh century, the Arabic language especially had emerged as a vehicle for the transmission of values and identity that distinguished the Arabian tribes from other groups. At this time, the written language was incipient and little used, but oral communication was highly sophisticated.

Poetry was the greatest cultural production of the pre-Islamic Arabs, who developed multiple genres and regional variations of poetic forms. Poems were recited orally, and their rhyming verses and internal meters gave them a musical feel – sometimes they were even accompanied by music or at least the beat of a staff. Poets boasted of romantic liaisons and military conquests, and lamented departed lovers and fallen comrades. In the *qasida*, a form of epic poetry held in the highest esteem by the pre-Islamic Arabs, group solidarity was emphasized and reinforced by poets who praised loyalty to kinsmen and lambasted the enemy. Great warriors and tribal chiefs were praised for showing kindness to widows and orphans in acts of *noblesse oblige*. That the wealth they distributed among themselves came from raiding and plunder was not problematic. Labid, one of the great pre-Islamic poets, represents this view in the following selection from one of his poems:

> Every indigent woman seeks the refuge
>   of my tent ropes,
> Emaciated, rag-clad, like a starved she-camel hobbled
>   at her master's grave.
> When winter's winds wail back and forth
>   her orphans plunge
> Into streams of flowing gravy which
>   my clan crowns with meat.
> When tribal councils gather,
>   there is always one of us
> Who contends in grave affairs
>   and shoulders them,

> A divider of spoils who gives
>   each clan its due,
> Demanding their rights for the worthy,
>   the rights of the worthless refusing
> Out of superior might; a man munificent,
>   who with his bounty succors,
> Openhanded; a winner and plunderer of all
>   that he desires –[21]

Among the pre-Islamic Arabs, mercy and forgiveness towards enemies were disdained. Manliness (*muruwwa*) was proven by boldly pursuing revenge for fallen kin. Only bloodshed could restore the integrity of a group attacked by an outsider. Even women had their own genre of poetry in which they encouraged their men to seek revenge for fallen kin, and belittled any man willing to accept compensation or reconciliation. In lines typical of this genre, one pre-Islamic woman challenges the virility of the men of her tribe if they do not seek retribution for their slain kinsman:

> If you will not seek vengeance for your brother
> Take off your weapons
> And fling them on the flinty ground
> Take up the eye pencil, don the camisole
> Dress yourselves in women's bodices
> What wretched kin you are to a kinsman oppressed![22]

Upholding martial virtues did not prevent pre-Islamic Arabs from expressing a range of emotions, and poets of this period described their natural environment with great sensitivity and beauty. However, whereas the Qur'anic revelation would draw attention to natural elements as signifiers of the Creator, and proof that God would recreate life after death, the pre-Islamic poet had no such basis for hope. Separated from his kin, the mood of the poet was nostalgic and melancholic. For him, the landscape was scattered with traces of an irretrievable past and with portents of a certain and final departure. Khansa', a celebrated female poet of the pre-Islamic period, describes how after the death of her beloved brother Sakhr, the world signified to her only loss and despair:

> The rising sun reminds me of Sakhr
> and I remember him each time the sun sets.[23]

Mecca was a prime location to hear the best Arab poets recite their verses. In the decades before the birth of Muhammad, as increased trade enabled the Quraysh to establish a more secure position for themselves in the Arabian Peninsula, Mecca's importance as a cultural center also increased. It was here in the 'Ukaz market that the finest poets gathered every year to recite their epics in a lively competition. Over the years, some poems were deemed so extraordinary that they were hung (mu'allaq – hence they were known collectively as the "Mu'allaqat") with honor on the Ka'ba. Muhammad grew up in a sanctuary in which the House of God was literally draped in eloquent language.

The *Jahiliyya*: A Time of Lawlessness and Immorality

Conversion narratives are important in most religious traditions. These narratives show the way faith transforms individuals by taking them out of the darkness of disbelief to the light of truth. These narratives also show the way that faith can dramatically transform a society mired in immorality and corruption to become a moral and just community of believers.

Early Muslims called the pre-Islamic period the *Jahiliyya*, a word signifying immaturity, immorality, and ignorance. In a speech that Muhammad's cousin Ja'far ibn Abi Talib is said to have made to the Negus of Abyssinia when a group of early Muslims sought his protection from the religious persecution of the Quraysh, Ja'far describes the *Jahiliyya* and the change brought about by Islam thus,

> O King, we were an uncivilized people, worshipping idols, eating corpses, committing abominations, breaking natural ties, treating guests badly, and our strong devoured our weak. Thus we were until God sent us an apostle whose lineage, truth, trustworthiness, and clemency we know. He summoned us to acknowledge God's unity and to worship him and to renounce the stones and images which we and our fathers formerly worshipped. He commanded us to speak the truth, be faithful to our engagements, mindful of the ties of kinship and kindly hospitality, and to refrain from crimes and bloodshed. He forbade us to commit abominations, to speak lies, to devour the property of orphans, to vilify chaste women. He commanded us to worship God alone and not to associate

anything with Him, and he gave us orders about prayer, almsgiving, and fasting....[24]

Early Muslims did recognize that before Islam, the Arabs had some laudable qualities, such as generosity and nobility; however, group partisanship mostly prevented the development of a commitment to moral responsibility beyond the tribe. Similarly, although the Quraysh had established some valuable agreements for furthering the economic and political stability of Mecca, a commitment to individual rights was absent. For example, early Muslim sources mention the Treaty (hilf) of Fudul as an important achievement of the pre-Islamic Quraysh. The treaty was devised after a visiting merchant to Mecca had been robbed, and a group of the city's notables gathered to bind themselves "by a solemn agreement that if they found anyone, either a native of Mecca or an outsider, had been wronged they would take part against the aggressor and see that the stolen property was returned to him."[25] The Prophet Muhammad would later praise this treaty and say that he would sign it even if it were compacted in Islamic times, showing that Muslims should embrace justice wherever it was found. The Treaty of Fudul demonstrated that it was possible to develop a rule of law that transcended tribal loyalties. At the same time, the treaty benefited the Quraysh above anyone else, since it ensured that their city would be secure for trade. The security of poor free and slaves, on the other hand, was clearly not one of the merchants' concerns. 'Abdullah ibn Jud'an, the very man who called for the Treaty of Fudul and hosted the oath-taking ceremony in his home, made his living before Islam selling the children of prostitutes he kept in his brothel.[26]

The Qur'an (24:33) would forbid the practice of forcing slave women into prostitution, as it would forbid many of the pre-Islamic practices that subjected women to all manner of indignities. Perhaps the most disturbing of such practices was female infanticide, which seems to have been practiced not just because of poverty, but out of fear of dishonor.[27] Among the nomads especially, women were vulnerable to kidnapping and forced marriage if their group was attacked. It was a terrible dishonor for a man to fail to guard his female relations. For weak and vulnerable groups, the risk of violation was great, and for this reason, they turned to female infanticide rather than see their daughters whom they could not protect captured and taken away. Strong tribes like the Quraysh could deliberately shun these practices with the confidence that they would be able to protect themselves from such humiliation. Still, the Qur'an (16:58–59) indicates that old habits die hard, and that a negative reaction to the birth of a daughter was the cultural norm among the pre-Islamic Arabs.

It would be reductionist to explain social-cultural changes in Mecca before Islam as simply serving the cause of economic stability or resulting from expanding trade, as some authors have done.[28] Assessing other motives, however, is almost impossible, since early Islamic sources are sometimes unreliable in this respect. On the one hand, early Muslims wanted to show how bad the pre-Islamic period had been, and consequently, how greatly Islam had improved society. On the other hand, there clearly was a desire on the part of some narrators to refrain from portraying their ancestors in a purely negative light. Nevertheless, it is worth mentioning that some sources indicate that the Quraysh banned female infanticide just before the rise of Islam because they found it "shameful."[29] This shows that there was a moral dimension to this prohibition.

Furthermore, this prohibition was enacted in the context of the establishment of a new ritual identity declared by the Quraysh sometime around the "Year of the Elephant" – the year Abraha tried to attack the Ka'ba and the year in which Muhammad was reportedly born.[30] Studies have shown that around this time, the Quraysh developed successful trade alliances that allowed them to take up a purely sedentary lifestyle in Mecca; previously, the city was inhabited mostly during the pilgrimage season.[31] The Quraysh called themselves and all tribes who settled with them in Mecca the "Hums," a word said to signify their "zeal" in promoting Mecca as the most important Arabian sanctuary. They are reported to have said, "We are the sons of Abraham, the people of the holy territory, the guardians of the temple and the citizens of Mecca. No other Arabs have rights like ours or a position like ours."[32]

The Early Life of Muhammad

The Qur'an and Islamic tradition ascribe significance to the fact that prophets are often born in unusual circumstances or have difficult childhoods. Adam, recognized as the first prophet of Islam, was created without a father or mother. Moses was taken from his family to be raised in the house of the Egyptian tyrant. Joseph was betrayed by his brothers and sold into slavery. Jesus was born without a father.

Muhammad lost his father, 'Abdullah ibn 'Abd al-Muttalib, while he was still in his mother's womb. Muhammad came from a respectable Meccan family, and had a grandfather who could care for him, so his situation was not dire. However, in a patriarchal society, a fatherless child was at a distinct disadvantage and was called an "orphan" (*yatim*).

The Quraysh had a custom of sending infants to live with bedouin tribes for the first few years of their lives. They believed that the desert air was healthier, and that the bedouin would teach their children the customs and pure language of their ancestors. For the bedouin who accepted the children, the advantages were more than monetary. According to Arab (and later Islamic) custom, wet-nursing created a relationship similar to that established by birth. The wet-nurse was respected as a mother, and her children were brothers and sisters to the nursed child. Establishing such a relationship with the future leaders of a powerful tribe like the Quraysh was a strategic move for impoverished nomads. According to early Islamic narratives, because Muhammad was an orphan, he was passed over by a group of bedouin women who came to Mecca looking for sucklings. In the end, a kindly woman named Halima took pity on the child. That Muhammad was blessed became immediately apparent to Halima, as her worn-out donkey suddenly sprang to life and carried her and the child back to drought-stricken lands that now became verdant.

Muhammad was returned to the custody of his mother and grandfather when he was a toddler. But his childhood was marked by the repeated loss of close family members. His mother died when he was six years old and his grandfather died when he was eight. The boy was then taken in by his paternal uncle, Abu Talib, who remained dedicated to protecting Muhammad throughout his life. When Muhammad became a prophet and faced threats from some members of the Quraysh, Abu Talib, who never became a Muslim, still defended his nephew.

Muhammad learned the art of trade from his uncle, and probably accompanied him a number of times to Syria to buy and sell his goods there. Islamic sources narrate the story of one trip in particular, in which portents of Muhammad's future prophethood became manifest. When the trade caravan stopped near a monastery, a Christian monk noticed a cloud miraculously shading the young Muhammad as he worked around the camp. Examining the boy, the monk found the "seal of the prophet" – a mark on Muhammad's back proving his special status.[33] This is one of a number of Islamic narratives that show pious Christians supporting or confirming Muhammad's position as a prophet sent by God.

At the age of twenty-five, Muhammad was hired by a widow, Khadijah bint Khuwaylid, to conduct trade on her behalf. Impressed by the young man's comportment and charm, Khadijah had a friend convey the message that she would not refuse Muhammad if he proposed marriage. Muhammad married the forty-year-old woman with whom he lived monogamously for the next twenty-five years until her death. Khadijah was Muhammad's closest companion, the first to believe in his mission and the mother of his children, including a few boys who died in infancy and four girls who lived to adulthood. Until the end of his life, Muhammad would remember Khadijah with immense gratitude and love.

Islamic sources say that before he became a prophet, Muhammad was not distinguished with political or economic power in Mecca. He was, however, known among the Quraysh as a man of honesty and integrity and was called "the trustworthy" (al-amin). About five years before Muhammad received his first revelation, the leaders of Quraysh relied on his sound judgment to resolve a particularly sensitive dispute. They were rebuilding the Ka'ba after having discovered some rot in its foundation. After they completed the reconstruction, the only task remaining was to reinsert the sacred "Black Stone" in the corner of the building.[34] The leaders could not agree on who should have this honor, so when Muhammad appeared, they decided he should resolve the dispute. Muhammad's ingenious solution was to place the stone on his cloak which was lifted by all the leaders gathered, then he himself positioned the stone in its final resting place.[35]

Whatever its historical value, this story is rich with symbolism. The religious life of the Quraysh, like the Ka'ba, had rotted at the foundation. It would take the Prophet Muhammad to unite the Quraysh and lead them in a project of spiritual renewal.

Muhammad as the Messenger of God

Muhammad was called to be the Messenger and Prophet of God around age forty, although he reported that for some time before the angel Gabriel first appeared to him, he had experienced a change in his spiritual state. 'A'isha, a later wife of Muhammad, reported what he had told her about this change: "The first thing that came to the

Messenger of God at the beginning of the revelation were good dreams in his sleep. He never saw a dream except that it came to him like bright daylight. Then seclusion became dear to him and he began to seclude himself in the cave of Hira' distancing himself from idols and praying.... "[36]

Like other seekers of God, Muhammad experienced the paradox of first entering a spiritual awakening in his sleep. Many centuries later, the great scholar Abu Hamid al-Ghazali (d. 505/1111) would explain both the possibility of prophecy through dreams and the way in which the experience of dreaming might help us understand something of the experience of prophecy:

> God most high...has favored His creatures by given them something analogous to the special faculty of prophecy, namely dreams. In the dream-state a man apprehends what is to be in the future, which is something of the unseen; he does so either explicitly or else clothed in a symbolic form whose interpretation is disclosed.
>
> Suppose a man has not experienced this himself, and suppose that he is told how some people fall into a dead faint, in which hearing, sight and the other senses no longer function, and in this condition perceive the unseen. He would deny that this is so and demonstrate its impossibility. "The sensible powers," he would say, "are the causes of perception (or apprehension); if a man does not perceive things (sc. the unseen) when these powers are actively present, much less will he do so when the senses are not functioning." This is a form of analogy which is shown to be false by what actually occurs and is observed. Just as intellect is one of the stages of human development in which there is an "eye" which sees the various types of intelligible objects, which are beyond the ken of the senses, so prophecy also is the description of a stage in which there is an eye endowed with light such that in that light the unseen and other supra-intellectual objects become visible.[37]

To be awake to God, while awake to the world, is the goal of seekers of the Divine. Like other men of God, Muhammad was drawn to retreat to a mountain cave, where the quiet darkness might allow the experiences of the night to pass into the day. We do not know what words, what prayers Muhammad uttered in the cave. Historical sources give little detail on the way in which the Quraysh in general and Muhammad in particular practiced seclusion (called *tahannuth*). What is reported is that Muhammad would spend one month a year in seclusion, giving food to any poor person who came to him during that time.

Ibn Ishaq records the following account in which Muhammad describes his experience in the cave:

> While I was asleep (Gabriel) came to me with a (coverlet of brocade) upon which was some writing. He said, "Read." I said, "What shall I read?" He squeezed me so tighly that I thought it was death, then he released me and said, "Read!" I said, "What shall I read?" He squeezed me again until I thought I would die, then he let me go and said, "Read!" I said, "What shall I read?" He squeezed me a third time until I thought I would die and said "Read!" I said, "What then shall I read?" I said this only to save myself from him, in case he would do the same thing to me again. Then he said,
>
> > *Read in the name of your Lord who created –*
> > *Created the human from a suspended (embryo).*
> > *Read! And your Lord is most bountiful.*
> > *The One who instructed using the pen.*
> > ('Alaq; 96:1–5)
>
> So I recited it, and he left me. When I woke up, I felt as though those words were written on my heart.[38]

Muhammad was shaken by the dream, so he left the cave and began heading down the mountain. But like a vision that burst out of his dreams, the angel Gabriel suddenly appeared in the form of a man standing on the horizon saying, "O Muhammad, you are the messenger of God and I am Gabriel." Muhammad remained transfixed for a long time, and when he returned to his wife, she comforted him when he told her what had happened. Khadijah played an important role in building Muhammad's confidence during his transition into prophethood. Ibn Ishaq, who wrote a comprehensive biography of the Prophet about a century after his death, said about Khadijah, "She was the first to believe in God and His apostle, and in the truth of his message. By her God lightened the burden of His prophethood. He never met with contradiction and charges of falsehood, which saddened him, but God comforted him by her and he went home. She strengthened him, lightened his burden, proclaimed his truth, and belittled men's opposition. May God almighty have mercy upon her!"

Immediately after Muhammad told Khadijah about his vision of Gabriel, she sought confirmation of the authenticity of her husband's experience by consulting with her cousin Waraqa, a Christian monk. After speaking with Muhammad, Waraqa said, "You are the prophet of this people. There has come unto you the greatest *namus* who came to Moses. You will be called a liar and they will treat you with scorn and cast you out and fight you."

The words recited by Gabriel to Muhammad in the cave are the first verses of the Qur'an revealed to Muhammad. The first word, *'iqra'*, meaning "read" or "recite," indicates both what is to be the continuous manner of revelation and the basis for naming the collected words. For the next twenty-three years, until his death, Muhammad will receive words from God. He will listen to these words and recite them to his community. The Prophet and his followers will then recite these words back to God in their prayers and devotions. Collectively and individually, these words are called "the Qur'an" – "the Recitation."

After his first few encounters with the angel, which the Prophet seems to have experienced as awesome, even frightening, Gabriel's presence became less unsettling to him, and he describes their later encounters in a way that suggests an almost easy familiarity: "Gabriel met me by the side of the road and said...."[39] The Prophet told his followers that God's words were also revealed to him in other ways.[40] In particular, he said that sometimes the revelation came to him "like the ringing of a bell, after which he grasped what was revealed to him."[41] This mode of revelation, said the Prophet, was the most difficult for him. The strain placed on Muhammad as he received the revelation was sometimes evident to those present. 'A'isha, the wife of the Prophet, is reported to have said, "Sometimes the revelation would descend upon the Messenger of God and although it was a cool morning, his forehead would glisten with perspiration."

In a later chapter, we will explore what the Qur'an as the speech of God signifies to various Muslim thinkers. For now, it is important to understand that at times, the Prophet conveyed to his followers divine guidance from Gabriel that was not "Qur'an." That is, sometimes Gabriel came to the Prophet with divine instructions that were binding, but were not articulated as Qur'an.[42] In some cases, Gabriel delivered these instructions publicly, appearing in the form of a man who was visible to the Prophet's companions. The following narrative, for example, is one of the most widely cited sources used by Muslim scholars to show the core principles of Islamic faith and spirituality:

> ('Umar, a Companion of the Prophet reported:) One day while we were sitting with the Messenger of God (may God's peace and blessings be upon him), there appeared a man with very white clothing and very black hair; no sign of travel could be seen on him and none of us knew him. He sat next to the Prophet so their knees were touching and placed his hands on his thighs. He said, "O Muhammad, tell me about Islam." The Messenger of God replied, "Islam is to testify that there is none worthy of worship except God and that Muhammad is the Messenger of God, to establish prayers, to pay the zakat, to fast the month of Ramadan and to make pilgrimage to the House (the Ka'ba) if you have the means to do so." (The man) said, "You have spoken truthfully." We were amazed that he had asked a question and then said that (the Prophet) had spoken truthfully. (The man) said, "Tell me about faith (*iman*)." (The Prophet) replied, "It is to believe in God, His angels, His scriptures, His messengers, the Last Day and to believe in divine decree (*qadr*), both the good and the evil of it." He said, "You have spoken truthfully." Then he said, "Tell me about excellence (*ihsan*)." (The Prophet) answered, "It is to worship God as if you see Him, and even though you do not see Him, you know that He sees you." He said, "Tell me about the Hour (the end of time)." (The Prophet) said, "The one being questioned does not know any more about it than the questioner." He said, "Then tell me about its signs." (The Prophet) answered, "The slave-girl shall give birth to her master and you will see the poor barefoot and unclothed shepherd competing in constructing tall buildings." (The man) went away and I stayed for a long time. Then (the Prophet) asked, "O 'Umar, do you know who the questioner was?" I replied, "God and His Messenger know best." He said, "That was Gabriel who came to teach you your religion."[43]

This narrative, although central to Islamic teachings, is not part of the Qur'an because the angel's words were not "God's speech"; rather, they were God's instructions delivered in the angel's own words. The story is therefore found among another body of writings known as *hadith* ("reports"), which record the Prophet's words and actions, known as the Sunna ("the way"). The Prophet consistently maintained a distinction between his words and God's words; nevertheless, the Qur'an mandates obedience to the Prophet and declares that he is the role-model chosen by God for the believers. Consequently, Muslims have always understood that the Sunna is the best source for understanding and implementing the Qur'an.

For twenty-three years, from the time the angel first appeared to him in the cave until his death in 632 CE, the Prophet Muhammad would receive revelations addressing all aspects of the relationship between humanity and God. Some revelations would address fundamental questions of the human condition, such as the meaning of life and death, while other revelations would address particular moral and social problems, like infanticide and economic injustice. The fact that much of the Qur'an was revealed to the Prophet when he was in the company of others highlights the importance of his contemporary community in the process of revelation. Although Muslims consider the Qur'an universal in its application, they have generally believed that an accurate understanding of the scripture is contingent in large part on an understanding of the historical and social context of the revelation. It is this context we shall explore further in the next chapter, focusing particularly on the way in which the revelation responded to specific concerns of the Prophet's community with rulings and principles that had lasting significance for later generations of Muslims.

Notes

1   This does not mean that women were passive and voiceless. Among others, Asma' bint Yazid was one of the most eloquent and forceful female Companions to express a desire for greater recognition in society. See Mohja Kahf, "Braiding the Stories: Women's Eloquence in the Early Islamic Era," in *Windows of Faith: Muslim Women Scholar-Activists in North America*, ed. Gisela Webb (Syracuse: Syracuse University Press, 2000), 168–171. One woman who was able to overcome the common limitations on women's activity in a dramatic fashion was Umm 'Umara Nusayba bin Ka'b. She was one of two women who, with seventy men from Yathrib, pledged allegiance to the Prophet at 'Aqaba the year before the *hijra*. Defense of the Prophet was a condition of the pledge, a condition Nusayba fulfilled at the Battle of Uhud where she employed sword and shield with astonishing dexterity to save the Prophet's life. Muhammad Ibn Sa'd, *al-Tabaqat al-Kubra*, 8 vols. (Beirut: Dar al-Kutub al-'Ilmiyya, 1958), 8:303–306.

2   *Tafsirs* (Qur'an commentary) of Sura Mujadila (58) narrate this story as the "occasion of revelation" of the early verses. See, for example, Abu Ja'far Muhammad ibn Jarir al-Tabari, *Jami' al-bayan fi tafsir al-Qur'an*, 30 vols. in 12 bks. (Cairo: Dar al-Hadith, 1987), 28:2–9.

3   Marshall G.S. Hodgson, *The Venture of Islam: Conscience and History in a World Civilization*, 3 vols. (Chicago: University of Chicago Press, 1974), 1:117.

4   Muslims have a religious obligation to invoke the peace and blessing of God upon the Prophet Muhammad when his name is mentioned. This supplication "God's peace and blessings be upon him" is fully written or signified by a sign in Islamic texts.

5   Tabari, 28:5.

6   Notice how Qur'anic verses are woven into this story.

7   From the Arabic root *j-h-d* "to struggle," the same root generates the word *"jihad"* – a righteous struggle involving physical and spiritual exertion, including, but not limited to, martial struggle.

8   Fred McGraw Donner, *The Early Islamic Conquests* (Princeton: Princeton University Press, 1981), 37–49.

9   'Abd al-Malik ibn Hisham, *al-Sira al-Nabawiyya*, 4 vols. (Beirut: Dar al-Khulud, n.d.); all future references to this work will be to the translation by Alfred Guillaume, entitled, *The Life of Muhammad: A Translation of Ishaq's Sirat Rasul Allah* (Oxford: Oxford University Press, 1955), 4–21; Irfan Shahid, "Pre-Islamic Arabia," in *Cambridge History of Islam*, 2 vols., ed. P. M. Holt (Cambridge: Cambridge University Press, 1970), 1:14.

10   Donner, 20–37.

11   R. Simon, "Hums et Ilaf, ou Commerce sans Guerre," *Acta Orientalia Academiae Scientiarum Hungaricae*, 23/22 (1970): 205–232.

12   Ibn Hisham, 21–30.

13   Donner, 34–37.

14   Abu Muhammad 'Abdullah ibn Muslim "Ibn Qutayba" al-Dinawari, *al-Ma'arif* (Beirut: Dar al-Kutub al-'Ilmiyya, 1987), 312.

15   Ibn Hisham, 62–63.

16   Joseph Henninger, "Pre-Islamic Bedouin Religion," in *Studies on Islam*, ed. Merlin L. Swartz (New York: Oxford University Press, 1981), 3–22.

17   Ibn Hisham, 55–56.

18   There are many good studies on the pre-Islamic religions of Arabia, including A. F. L. Beeston, "Judaism and Christianity in Pre-Islamic Yemen," in *L'Arabie du sud: histoire et civilisation*, ed. Joseph Chelhod (Paris, 1984), 271–278; the Qur'an makes reference to the pre-Islamic practice of sacrificing animals in the name of ancestors in Sura Baqara 2:200.

19   His great-grandfather, Hashim, married a woman from Yathrib who gave birth to the Prophet's grandfather, 'Abd al-Muttalib. Ibn Hisham, 59.

20   Ibn Hisham, 98–103.

21   Suzanne Pinckney Stetkevych, *The Mute Immortals Speak: Pre-Islamic Poetry and the Poetics of Ritual* (Ithaca: Cornell University Press, 1993), 16–17.

22   Stetkevych, 196.

23   Jaroslav Stetkevych, *The Zephyrs of Najd: The Poetics of Nostalgia in the Classical Arabic Nasib* (Chicago: University of Chicago Press, 1993); M. M. Bravmann, " 'Life after Death' in Early Arab Conception," in *The Spiritual Background of Early Islam* (Leiden: Brill, 1972), 288–295.

24   Ibn Hisham, 151–152.

25   Ibn Hisham, 57.

26   Ibn Qutayba, 319.

27   Ingrid Mattson, *A Believing Slave is Better than an Unbeliever: Status and Community in Early Islamic Society and Law* (University of Chicago doctoral dissertation, 1999), 200.

28   W. M. Watt, *Muhammad at Mecca* (Oxford: Oxford University Press, 1953); see also Donner, 3–9.

29   M. J. Kister, citing al-Jahiz in "Mecca and Tamim (Aspects of their Relations)," *Journal of the Economic and Social History of the Orient*, 8 (1965): 135–136.

30   Abu'l-Walid Muhammad ibn 'Abdullah al-Azraqi, *Ta'rikh Mecca*, ed. Rushdi Malhas (Mecca: Dar al-Thaqafa, 1965), 179–183; Muhammad ibn Habib, *Kitab al-Muhabbar* (Hyderabad, 1942), 179–180; Ibn Hisham, 87–89.

31   See Simon.

32   Ibn Hisham, 87.

33   Ibn Hisham, 79–81.

34   Abraham is said to have told Isma'il that the angel Gabriel brought him the Black Stone from heaven. See Tabari, *Ta'rikh al-rusul wa'l-muluk*, translated in 39 volumes by multiple translators as *The History of Prophets and Kings*, series editor Ehsan Yar, vol. 2 translated by William M. Brinner as *Prophets and Patriarchs* (Albany: State University of New York Press, 1987), 70–72.

35   Ibn Hisham, 85–86.

36   (Because there are so many editions of the major hadith collections, in addition to citing the particular books I use, I will also indicate the name of the chapters in which the hadith are found.) Abu 'Abdullah Muhammad ibn Isma'il al-Bukhari, *Kitab al-Jami 'al-Sahih* (Riyadh: Dar al-Salam, 1998), "*Kitab Bad' al-Wahy*," 1–2.

37   Abu Hamid Muhammad al-Ghazali, *The Faith and Practice of al-Ghazali*, translation of *al-Munqidh min al-dalal and Bidayat al-hidaya* by W. Montgomery Watt (1953; reprint, Oxford: Oneworld, 1994), 68–69.

38   Ibn Hisham, 106.

39   Muslim ibn al-Hajjaj, *Sahih*, 18 vols., published as *Sahih Muslim bi sharh al-Nawawi* (Beirut: al-Dar al-Thaqafa al-'Arabiyya, 1929), "*Kitab al-Zakat*," 7:76.

40   Two main modes are cited in the hadith below, but Qur'an scholar al-Suyuti (d. 911/1505) mentions some other modes, including revelation while sleeping and direct revelation to the Prophet during his "heavenly ascent" (*al-isra'*). See Jalal al-Din 'Abd al-Rahman ibn Abi Bakr al-Suyuti, *al-Itiqān fī 'ulūm al-Qur'an*, 2 vols., ed. Fawwaz Ahmed Zamarli (Beirut: Dar al-Kitab al-'Arabi, 1999), 1:168–171.

41   Bukhari, "*Kitab Bad' al-Wahy*," 1–2.

42   Suyuti, 1:167.

43   Muslim, "*Kitab al-Iman*," 1:144–165.

2

The Prophet Conveys the Message

Historicizing the Qur'an

The Qur'an contains over six thousand verses (*ayat*) that were revealed singly and in groups over twenty-three years. Verses are collected into *suwar* (*sing. sura*), a word meaning "enclosure" that is usually translated as "chapter." The 114 suras of the Qur'an are of greatly unequal length – the shortest (Kawthar; 108) is comprised of three verses, the longest (Baqara; 2) is 286 verses. For reasons we will discuss in greater detail later, the suras are roughly ordered according to length, not chronology. One reason why the Qur'an cannot be organized chronologically is that the exact timing of the revelation of each verse is unknown. In addition, many suras are composed of verses that were revealed at different times, so a chronological ordering of verses could not be done without dismembering the suras.

That the Qur'an was not ordered chronologically does not mean that early Muslims were uninterested in the history of the revelation. Indeed, they had two different but related reasons for wanting to know this history. The first was the wish to retain and recover information about the Prophet to whom the sacred words were revealed. For early Muslims, such reports were cherished like oral relics connecting them to his blessed presence. The second reason was that the historical context in which the Qur'an was revealed was often a key to understanding its meaning. The Qur'an refers to specific individuals and groups, like the *Ansar* (the "Helpers" – 9:117) and a man named Abu Lahab (111) as well as specific places like "Hunayn" (9:25) and "the farthest mosque" (17:1). It is natural that Muslims who were not familiar with these names would want to know about them and their connection to the story of Islam.

More generally, the social and cultural context of the revelation was important for those wanting to implement rules and norms articulated in the Qur'an. Without hearing the story of Khawla, for example, a Muslim living in Iran at the end of the first century of Islam might not understand the implication of these verses dealing with *zihar* – a practice that seems to have been peculiar to a segment of Arabs in the pre-Islamic period. Of course, many levels of context are necessary to draw meaning from any text, oral or written. Not only proper names, but even general words need to be understood according to their historical and cultural usage. The word *qawa'id*, for example, is used in Modern Standard Arabic to signify "foundations" or "principles," a usage that is also found in the Qur'an (i.e., 16:26), but would make no sense in Qur'an 24:60, where it signifies "elderly women." We discover this meaning by conducting a historical-linguistic analysis of the term.

In a later chapter, we will examine the hermeneutical devices employed by Muslim scholars to understand the Qur'an in all its fullness of meaning. For now, we are interested in limiting ourselves to exploring the twenty-three-year history of the unfolding of the revelation. That is, we wish to understand the relationship between the development of the Prophet's community and the Qur'an. For a number of reasons, this is not a simple exercise.

The most immediate problem is that the Qur'an itself does not narrate the life of the Prophet or the history of the community. References to individuals and events as well as allusions to conflicts and victories are scattered throughout the Qur'an; however, the Qur'an contains no detailed or coherent historical narrative about the first Muslim community. In this way, the Qur'an is very different, for example, from the Gospels that narrate the life of Jesus. Early Muslims did gather and preserve reports (*hadith*) about the life of Muhammad and his community, but it took time for the emergence of authored biographies of the Prophet and histories of his community to emerge.

The books produced near the end of the second century of Islam were compiled from shorter narratives found in small books and collections and took a variety of forms. The first is a chronological biography called a *sira* (literally meaning "the way traveled"). Most notable among the *Sira* literature is Ibn Hisham's (d. 218/834) redaction of Ibn Ishaq's (d. 150/767) *Biography of the Messenger of God (Sirat Rasul Allah)*. Another important kind of Islamic historical text is the biographical dictionary (the *tabaqat* literature), in which profiles of many individuals are collected and organized according to historical period. Ibn Sa'd's (d. 230/845) *The Great Generations* (*al-Tabaqat al-Kubra*) is particularly important for the early Islamic period and life of the Prophet. Another kind of historical text focuses on individuals and events important to a particular city during a specific period of time. 'Umar ibn Shabba's (d. 261/875) *History of Medina the Radiant* (*Ta'rikh al-Madina al-Munawwara*) is an important text of this genre for the latter period of the Prophet's life.

There is controversy among contemporary scholars about when the earliest texts were written because primary documents from the first century of Islam are scarce. Until now, historians have not discovered a major collection of papyri, vellum or parchment contracts, letters or tax registers from the first century, although some scattered documents have been found.[1] This is not surprising given the fragility of such materials, the relocation of the capital of the Islamic empire three times – from Medina to Damascus to Baghdad, with corresponding changes in political leadership – in the first hundred years or so following the Prophet's death, and the number of times in which major cities were overrun by invaders (including, perhaps most devastatingly, by the Mongols in the thirteenth century CE). The historian is not without resources, however, for there are many early documents and reports reproduced in later historical texts. Obviously, claims that such documents and reports are authentic need to be examined according to a sound historiographic methodology because witnesses can forget or lie, stories can be embellished or selective, and documents can be forged or copied inaccurately.

What is quite unique about the Islamic tradition is that concerns about the accuracy and authenticity of reports were expressed relatively early in its historical development. Within the first century of Islam, some Muslims raised concerns that reports about the Prophet were being fabricated. The culprits were mainly individuals who wanted to justify their political positions in the wake of conflicts over the consolidation of centralized rule and the legitimization of religious authority.[2] According to Sunni tradition, it was at this time that individuals making claims about the Prophet's life were now required to name their sources. From this early attempt to verify reports, a sophisticated science of hadith analysis developed over the next two centuries. It was a commitment to this science that largely defined the Sunni Muslim community as it developed a distinct identity during this period.[3]

The science of hadith is based on filtering reports for obvious fabrication or error by analyzing their content (the *matn*), as well as scrutinizing the chain of transmission of the report (the *isnad*). The *isnad* is a chain of individuals beginning with the contemporary narrator and ending with the individual who originally articulated the report. For example, the following hadith, with the *isnad* rendered in italics, begins with the early third-century Andalusian jurist Yahya ibn Yahya al-Laythi (d. 234/848) and ends with 'A'isha, who is witnessing to her personal experience with the Prophet; the hadith reads:

> *Yahya related to me from Malik from Abu'l-Nadr the client of 'Umar ibn 'Ubaydallah, from Abu Salama ibn 'Abd al-Rahman that* 'A'isha, the wife of the Prophet, may God bless him and grant him peace, said, "I was sleeping in front of the Messenger of Allah, may Allah bless him and grant him peace, and my feet were in the direction in which he was praying (his *qibla*). When he prostrated, he nudged me and I pulled up my feet, and when he stood up I spread them out." She added, "There were no lamps in the house at that time."[4]

According to hadith methodology, each person in this *isnad* – Yahya, Malik, Abu'l-Nadr, Abu Salama, and 'A'isha – must be scrutinized to ensure his or her probity and ability to memorize and articulate such statements, in addition to making sure that each person in the chain would have had the opportunity to hear the report from the other. Analysis of hadith involves many other factors, and over the first few centuries of Islam this became an expansive, sophisticated field of study.

The success of the Sunni science of hadith in identifying "authentic" (*sahih*) reports from "weak" (*da'if*) or even "fabricated" (*mawdu'a*) reports has been questioned by scholars outside Sunni Islam, most vigorously by some "Orientalists" (i.e., non-Muslim Western scholars). After almost a century of extreme skepticism towards hadith literature on the part of many Western academics, in the last few decades a new generation of scholars has employed innovative research techniques to support the claim of the early origin of many hadith.[5] At the same time, as we shall discuss in a later chapter, many Muslim modernists have also expressed doubts about the ability of traditional Sunni hadith criticism to fully distinguish authentic from fabricated hadith.[6]

For our purposes, it is important to realize that most of the contested reports involve legal and theological issues, not reports about the simple facts of the life of Muhammad as prophet. If we consider the differences between Sunnis and Shi'ites, for example, we see that the two communities developed sharply divergent positions on many historical events of the first century, as well as on scriptural interpretation and matters of law and theology. What is remarkable, however, is that despite these serious differences, the two communities are united not only on the authenticity of the Qur'anic text (a topic to which we shall return in the next chapter), but also on most of the details of the life of the Prophet Muhammad and the role of his community in the period of revelation. That is, although Shi'ites interpret some events in the Prophet's life differently than Sunnis, they mostly agree with the facts of his mission as a prophet. That the Prophet received the Qur'an around forty years of age, that he faced opposition from his own tribe, that he emigrated from Mecca to Medina and continued to struggle for the security of his community in that city, that he ultimately returned victorious to Mecca – all of these details and many more about the life of the Prophet are agreed upon by both Sunnis and Shi'ites. The main point of divergence is the emphasis put on the role of the Prophet's daughter, Fatima, and her husband, the Prophet's cousin 'Ali; Shi'ites elevate their status and accept some reports about them that are not present in the Sunni narratives. Because Shi'ites believe that after the Prophet's death the early caliphs prevented 'Ali from taking his rightful place as his successor, they subsequently developed a movement based on resistance to political oppression and glorification of the descendents of the Prophet. These, then, are themes Shi'ites might emphasize more than Sunnis in narrating the life of the Prophet; nevertheless, the main story is the same.

In his book *Narratives of Islamic Origins*, Fred Donner argues that this consensus about the outlines of the Prophet's life exists "because events actually did happen in the way described by our sources." This does not mean that every hadith claimed to be "authentic" by Muslim scholars must be accepted; indeed, until today, hadith scholars debate among themselves the merits of reports found in various collections. What this does mean, however, is that the major events of the Prophet's life collected in early Islamic narratives are, more likely than not, historical facts.

These narratives, however, cannot easily be separated from the way events were perceived and interpreted by later Muslim communities. In the first half-century of Islam, for example, a period Donner calls the "Pre-Historic Phase" of Islamic historiography, personal memories of events were "evanescent." In this primarily oral phase, as long as memories "were not linked to some framework (pietistic, genealogical, lexicographical) that made them worth remembering by others, they were in danger of simply being forgotten as their witnesses died off."[7] Donner identifies a number of issues that were of concern to the early Muslim community after the death of the Prophet and provided frameworks for remembering and collecting narratives. These issues include prophecy, community, political hegemony, and leadership.

With these considerations in mind, we must realize that any narratives we use to provide a historical context for the Qur'anic message will be inadequate for allowing us to grasp the full significance of the Qur'anic revelation.[8] They are inadequate not primarily because of fabrication or inaccuracy of individual reports, although this is a possibility in some cases, but because even the best historical narrative, even the most vivid memory, collective or individual, is necessarily selective. In engaging these narratives, we will consequently be somewhat limited by the concerns and perspectives of those whose narratives have survived. Indeed, as we discuss in later chapters, because the Qur'an is considered to be a perfect preservation of the revelation to the Prophet, while all hadith and narratives are incomplete attempts by imperfect individuals to capture events, there are Muslims who have rejected applying any historical context to the Qur'an when using it as a source of guidance. Such attempts inevitably flounder, if only because of the concern we raised earlier, namely, the impossibility of ascribing meaning to the Arabic words of the revelation without a historical context. Nevertheless, as we shall discuss later, contemporary Muslims in particular are often keen to deconstruct paradigms early Muslims imposed on the Qur'anic message in order to allow the construction of alternative paradigms.

In any case, for the vast majority of Muslims, early Islamic narratives are essential for contextualizing the Qur'an, even if they draw different conclusions from that context. Historical narratives about the period of the revelation can therefore provide perspective on two distinct but related issues: first, they can give us insight into the way the Qur'an affected a significant segment of the seventh-century population of the Arabian Peninsula. Second, these narratives create a context for the revelation that has influenced the way later Muslims relate to the Qur'an. In every generation, Muslims have referred to the various stages of revelation and discussed what this unfolding of God's word in time implies for individual spiritual growth, as well as for the development of an upright community. Even more compelling for many Muslims is the way in which these narratives show how the Qur'an demanded a response from those who lived in the society in which it was first revealed. Those who heard the Qur'anic message had to make a choice: to believe and stand up for that belief – or to reject the message and fight it. These stories of the tremendous spiritual and moral transformation of the community to first receive the Qur'an continue to challenge Muslims today.

In addition to *Sira* literature, the context for many Qur'anic verses is found in a class of hadith reports known as "occasions of revelation" (*asbab al-nuzul*). These reports link a specific verse or set of verses of the Qur'an with a historical event. Early Muslim scholars organized these reports in different ways: they made lists of verses revealed by day and those revealed by night, verses revealed during the summer and those revealed during the winter, verses revealed when the Prophet was traveling and those revealed when he was at home, verses revealed on earth, and those revealed in heaven (when the Prophet ascended to God).[9] The categorization that became most important was the division into Meccan and Medinan verses. Despite the fact that Mecca and Medina are places, this is more of a chronological than spatial division. Meccan verses are those revealed during the first thirteen years of the revelation, when the Prophet preached Islam in Mecca. During this period, Islam gained many converts, but Muslims also faced harsh opposition from the ruling Quraysh. The persecution of Muslims increased until the Prophet's own life was in danger. At this point, the Prophet accepted an invitation to move to Yathrib with his companions and rule as political authority of the city and spiritual leader of his people. Yathrib became know as "al-Medina" – "the City (of the Prophet)" – and the Medinan period lasted ten years until Muhammad's death in 632 CE.

Our goal in this chapter is to trace the path of the Qur'anic revelation as it has been understood by most Muslims. We will not give a detailed narrative of the *Sira*, but will explore themes and ideas found in passages revealed mostly in Mecca and then discuss how new challenges faced by the Muslim community in Medina are reflected in verses revealed during that period. Throughout our discussion, we will identify themes and stylistic devices that provide unity and coherence to the diverse passages under consideration. When relevant, we will take note of the ways in which the particular contexts of the Meccan and Medinan communities are important to the revelatory process. In later chapters we will return to this subject, because later generations of Muslims have struggled to understand the way in which their interpretations of the Qur'an must take into account this historical context and, consequently, the extent to which the Qur'an continues to be relevant to their own society and concerns.

The Medium and the Message

According to Muslim scholars, many of the first Qur'anic verses to be revealed relate to Muhammad's inner state as he began his prophetic mission. We have already mentioned how the first revelations had a powerful psychic and physical impact on Muhammad. Describing one of these encounters, the Prophet is reported to have said, "While I was walking I heard a voice from the sky. I raised my head and behold, there was the angel who had come to me in the cave of Hira'; he was sitting on a throne that was between heaven and earth. I was so frightened by him that I returned home and said 'Wrap me up, wrap me up,' so they covered me. Then God, exalted is he, revealed:

> *O you who are wrapped up:*
> *Rise and give warning,*
> *And glorify your Lord,*
> *And purify your garments,*
> *And shun all idols!"*[10]
> (Mudaththir; 74:1–5)

Muslim scholars say that with these verses, Muhammad was commissioned to take his message to the world. This revelation would not be for his spiritual enrichment alone, but was to be brought to warn others to leave their erring ways and embrace the purity of faith.

What is impossible to convey when translating these verses is the way their sound when recited accords so well with their meaning. Perhaps it is not even enough to say that the sound of the recitation is in harmony with the meaning of the words, but that the sound itself conveys meaning. Those who appreciate music know that it can be meaningful without lyrics; many would even say that music can transmit meaning that cannot be signified with words. The Qur'an is not music; however, when it is recited, it can have a similar aural impact. Apart from melodic techniques reciters may employ in their recitations, Qur'anic verses are imbued with rhyme, assonance, and rhythm. In this way, the Arabic of the Qur'an draws on some aural patterns of pre-Islamic poetry, yet it is not poetry. In the words of one scholar, the Arabic of the Qur'an is a unique blend of rhymed prose (saj') and unrhymed free prose, "with an important contribution by assonance, couched in a variety of short and long verses dispensed in suras of various lengths. The different patterns of rhymes, assonances and free endings in the verses, as well as the different lengths and rhythms of these verses and the varying lengths of the suras themselves, are all literary structures related to the meaning offered. In the final analysis, they comprise an essential element of the effective delivery of the total message of the Qur'an."[11]

Because the sound of the Qur'an is so important to its meaning and impact, we will highlight various aspects of the aural dimension of some passages as we discuss the import of their words. To do otherwise risks diminishing the significance of the extent to which Muhammad's contemporaries were affected by the style, eloquence, and overall impact of the recited Qur'an. This does not mean that listening to the Qur'an was simply an aesthetic experience for some of these people, and the Qur'an itself vigorously denies that it is a kind of poetry. Instead, the Qur'an claims for itself that it is unique and irreproducible (17:88), but Muslims have understood that a significant aspect of the "inimitability" of the Qur'an is the way in which its message is so well expressed in its linguistic medium. To completely separate the medium and the message in our analysis would give us a poor understanding not only of the Qur'an, but also of the way it has been able to affect its listeners/readers over the centuries.

With these considerations in mind, we return to the passage above to note that these first five verses of Sura al-Mudaththir are all short commanding statements. God is ordering the Prophet to proclaim his message, so the words are simple and blunt, conveying the sense that it is time to stand up for what is right. In Arabic, the verses all end with a sharp short syllable and consonantal rhyme: muda-_thir_, an-_dhir_, kab-_bir_, tah-_hir_, fah-_jur_. This is God speaking in what some Muslim theologians characterize as his "majestic" (jalili) mode – the voice of God that emphasizes his power, sovereignty, and transcendence.

But God also speaks in a softer, more intimate tone that emphasizes his nearness to humanity; this scholars call God's "beautiful" (jamali) mode. We see this message and this tone in a sura revealed sometime after Muhammad had publicly proclaimed his mission. Reports say that after receiving a number of initial revelations, there was a pause, and

Muhammad became anxious that he had done something wrong. Some reports say that a neighbor mocked the Prophet that his "muse" had abandoned him. Then God revealed the following sura:

> *By the bright morning light;*
> *By the night when it is quiet;*
> *You have not been abandoned by your Lord, nor is He displeased.*
> *Know that the end will be better for you than the beginning;*
> *And your Lord will give to you, then you will be pleased.*
> *Did He not find you an orphan, then shelter you?*
> *And did He not find you wandering, then guide you?*
> *And did He not find you in need, then provide for you?*
> *So as for the orphan, do not disdain him,*
> *And as for the beggar, do not repulse him,*
> *And as for the blessings of your Lord, proclaim them!*
>
> (Duha; 93)

The message is primarily gentle and reassuring; God reminds the Prophet of the difficulties he has encountered before, and that it is God who has sustained him through those hard times. The Arabic rhythm is easy and gentle and the first eight verses end in a soft long rhyming vowel: *duhaa; sajaa; qalaa; ulaa; tar-daa; awaa; hadaa; aghnaa*. The voice then shifts in the final three verses back to a command; now that the Prophet feels secure, he is reminded to return to his mission to proclaim God's word. Accordingly, these verses break the long gentle rhyme, ending instead with short syllables and consonants: *taq-har; tan-har; had-dith*. Here, as elsewhere in the Qur'an, the message is clear: God is loving, comforting, and forgiving, but God is also demanding; the believer must put faith into action.

In the early years of the revelation, those who rejected the Qur'an as the word of God struggled to find another way to characterize it and to explain Muhammad's ability to bring forth these powerful verses. The following report portrays the Quraysh as trying to find ways to diminish Muhammad's impact, fearful that their conflict with him would disrupt the peace of the annual trade fair, an event so important for the Meccan economy:

> When the fair was impending, a number of the Quraysh came to al-Walid ibn al-Mughira who was a man of some standing, and he addressed them with these words: "The time of the fair has come round again and representatives of the Arabs will come to you and they will have heard about this fellow of

yours, so agree upon one opinion without dispute so that none will give the lie to the other." They replied, "You give us your opinion about him." He said, "No, you speak and I will listen." They said, "He is a shaman (*kahin*)." He said, "By God, he is not that, for he has not the unintelligent murmuring and rhymed speech of the shaman." "Then he is possessed," they said. "No, he is not that," he said, "we have seen possessed ones, and here is no choking, spasmodic movements and whispering." "Then he is a poet," they said. "No, he is no poet, for we know poetry in all its forms and meters." "Then he is a sorcerer." "No, we have seen sorcerers and their sorcery, and here is no blowing and no knots." They asked, "Then what are we to say, O Abu 'Abd al-Shams (al-Walid)?" He replied, "By God, his speech is sweet, his root is a palm-tree whose branches are fruitful, and everything you have said would be known to be false. The nearest thing to the truth is your saying that he is a sorcerer, who has brought a message by which he separates a man from his father, or his brother, or his wife, or his family."[12]

The Qur'an, of course, explicitly rejects charges that Muhammad is a poet or a sorcerer or a man possessed (21:5; 36:69; 10:2; 51:52, etc.), but at the same time explains that the beauty of its recitation and its message will be veiled from those who consciously reject faith and arrogantly cling to their desires. Indeed, God, who is the creator of all things, will also create the means to block their understanding and appreciation of the Qur'an as long as their attitude does not change:

> *Among them are some who listen to you, but we have placed a veil over their hearts so they do not understand, and deafness in their ears. Even if they saw every sign they would not believe in it to the point that they come and dispute with you, saying, "This is nothing but tales of the ancients!"*
>
> (An'am; 6:25)

God is One

The foundation of Qur'anic theology is monotheism; the Arabic term is *tawhid*, whose root means "one." Muslims consider the very short Sura al-Ikhlas the finest expression of this doctrine:

Say: He is One,
God the Self-Sufficient,
He did not beget, nor was He begotten,
And unto Him there is equal no one.

(Ikhlas; 112)

This sura is remarkable for the doctrine it conveys within four short verses, where it defines God as a unity, self-sufficient and utterly unique. The Arabic is almost childlike in its simplicity; each word in the sura is only one or two syllables, the first and last verse end in the same word (*ahad* – "one"), and the other two verses rhyme with that word. A non-Arabic speaker could probably memorize the recited sura in a few minutes. The simplicity and accessibility of Sura al-Ikhlas accords with the Qur'anic and Prophetic message that belief in such a God is innate (*fitri*) and universal. No doubt for all these reasons, the Prophet Muhammad is reported to have said that Sura al-Ikhlas is equivalent to a third of the Qur'an.[13]

Here, as elsewhere in the Qur'an, the primary name used to refer to God is "Allah." The Arabic word *Allah* is a cognate of the Hebrew *Elohim* and the Syrian and Aramaic *Alaha*. In English, the word that signifies this eternal, self-sufficient creator is "God," and this is the term into which Muslim theologians therefore do not hesitate to translate the Arabic *Allah*.[14]

The pre-Islamic Arabs knew of Allah as the Creator, but the Qur'an argues that their understanding of the nature of God was incomplete and a deviation from the original Abrahamic teaching. In this respect, Abraham plays an important role in the Qur'an as the most credible authority to define the nature of God. The Qur'an implies that since the Arabs believed they were descended from Abraham and that he had first established the Ka'ba (often called "the House of God," "the Ancient House" or just "the House") as a pilgrimage site, they should concede that his understanding of God must be the correct one. These connections are made in the following passage:

When We established the site of the House for Abraham (We commanded:) Do not associate anything with Me, and purify My House for those who circle round it and stand and bow and prostrate therein.
And announce the pilgrimage to the people; they will come to you on foot and on every lean animal traveling through deep mountain passes,

*So they will witness its benefits for them and during the appointed
days they will pronounce the name of God upon the domestic cattle
with which they have been provided; so eat from it and feed the
downtrodden poor.*
*Then let them complete their rites and fulfill their vows and circle
round the Ancient House.*

(Hajj; 22:26–29)

The Qur'an criticizes the Meccans for their blind emotional attachment to the traditions of their forefathers, yet, at the same time, the
Qur'an tries to redirect this sentiment to engender a stronger attachment to their even more distant ancestor Abraham. Still, the Qur'an
does not want the Meccans to exchange one unthinking belief for
another. The Qur'an explicitly rejects the claim that "we found our
fathers doing this" is a valid reason for embracing a particular belief
or ritual practice. Abraham is therefore engaged as an authority in the
Qur'an, but as an authority who demonstrates that individual struggle
and a sincere commitment to the truth are required for guidance.

*When Abraham said to his father Azar, "Do you take idols as gods?
I see that you and your people are clearly in error,"*
*Then we showed Abraham the kingdom of the heavens and the earth
so that he might be among those who are firmly convinced.*
*When darkness covered the night he saw a star and said, "This is
my Lord," then when it set he said, "I do not love things that set."*
*Then when he saw the moon ascending he said, "This is my Lord,"
and when it descended he said, "If my Lord does not guide me I will
be among the people who are astray."*
*Then when he saw the sun rising he said, "This is my Lord – this is
greater," and when it set he said, "O my people, I am free from that
which you associate (with God)."*
*Indeed I have turned my face towards the One who created the
heavens and the earth, as a hanif and I am not a polytheist.*

(An'am; 6:74–79)

Abraham begins his spiritual journey by rejecting the idols, but does
not immediately arrive at a true understanding of the nature of God.
His faith is shown, rather, to be the fruit of a sincere struggle in which
he employs his powers of logic and observation. Just as importantly,
Abraham is willing to admit when he has erred, and, in his humility,
confesses that without God's guidance, he will be unable to arrive at
ultimate truth even through his own powers of reasoning.

The Qur'an employs the narrative form in this passage to great effect. The story encourages the listener to identify with Abraham's struggle, which is important for Muhammad's contemporaries, many of whom associated celestial bodies with the Divine. Where a simple direct command or condemnation might elicit a defensive response, the narrative form encourages empathy and, ideally, greater self-awareness. In terms of aural effect, even here where narrative is the dominant style, the verses generally rhyme, giving the passage harmony and unity.

The story of Abraham conveys the message that although reason is not capable of arriving at ultimate truth alone, it must still be willfully engaged in a struggle to achieve guidance. Logic, then, is a necessary, albeit not sufficient, instrument to be employed by the seeker of the Divine. This is shown by a number of passages in which the Prophet Muhammad's contemporaries are criticized for claiming that God has daughters:

> They ascribe daughters to God – exalted is He – while they give to themselves what they desire.
> When one of them is brought the good news of the birth of a female, his face darkens and he is filled with anger.
> He avoids his people because of the evil news given him – shall he keep it despite the contempt he feels, or shall he bury it in the dust? What an evil judgment they make.
>
> (Nahl; 16:57–59)

In this passage, the Qur'an uses logic to undermine the belief held by some of the Prophet's contemporaries that God has daughters. Elsewhere (17:40, 37:149–153, 43:16–20, 52:39, 53:19–23) the Qur'an indicates that these "daughters of Allah" were thought to be angelic or celestial beings who acted as intercessors between God and humanity. The Qur'an juxtaposes this belief with the typical reaction of such men when they are brought news of the birth of a daughter: they become filled with rage, withdraw in shame from their friends and family, and brood in isolation until they make a decision either to commit infanticide or suffer to keep the child. The contrast between female angels flying towards heaven and a newborn baby girl being buried in the ground could not be more vivid. The Qur'an argues that it is not reasonable for people who hate daughters for themselves to believe that God would choose to have daughters.[15]

Lest one think that the Qur'an considers the association of females with God to be particularly egregious due to an underlying assumption of female inferiority, it is important to realize the Qur'an is equally emphatic in rejecting the belief that God has a son:

> *O People of the Book! Do not go to extremes in your religion nor say anything about God except what is true. Verily Christ Jesus the son of Mary is only a messenger of God and His word that He bestowed unto Mary and a spirit from Him. So believe in God and in His Messengers and do not say "Trinity." It is better for you to cease. Verily God is only one God; too exalted is He that He should have a son (walad). To Him belongs what is in the heavens and what is one earth, and sufficient is God as the Trustee.*
>
> (Nisa'; 4:171)

Here, as in the passage rejecting the ascription of daughters to God, is the exclamation, "too exalted is He (*subhanahu*)" to have a son. In fact, the word *walad* is a general term signifying "child," although it can specifically signify "male child." The real problem with believing that God has sons or daughters, then, has nothing to do with the gender of the child, but that it is a false concept that has been projected onto God. Perhaps this is sometimes the result of a desire to appropriate God to justify human relationships or for some other emotional or social need. In the case of the Trinity, however, the Qur'an asserts that this mistaken doctrine is the inevitable result of the limitations of human imagination. If theologians do not recognize that no matter how deeply they probe, no matter how sophisticated their discourse, they will never truly understand the nature of God, they will always end up with concepts that restrict God in a way that is not in accord with his nature. Thus, the claim that Jesus is God's son is criticized in the Qur'an as a kind of "exaggeration" in religion.[16]

In the above verse, the Qur'an addresses the "People of the Book" (*ahl al-kitab*), a group evidently quite distinct from the majority of Muhammad's contemporaries in Mecca, who are generally understood to be the group identified as "polytheists" (*mushrikun* – literally, "those who ascribe partners (to God)") or "disbelievers" (*kafirun* – literally, "those who cover up (the truth)"). The People of the Book include both Christians and Jews, although it is likely that the former are primarily intended in passages dealing with the position of Jesus. Scholars agree that verses addressing the People of the Book were revealed in Medina and so this is a topic we will explore in more depth later in this chapter.

Although the Qur'an vigorously upholds God's transcendence over doctrines of incarnation or divine immanence, God is not unapproachable. Indeed, the Qur'an says:

> *It is We who created the human being and We know what his inmost self whispers to him, for We are nearer to him than his jugular vein.*
>
> (Qaf; 50:16)

God can be close to his creation without being immanent in it because his being is not constrained by the laws of creation, such as those governing space and time. Simply put,

> *There is nothing like unto Him.*
>
> (Shura; 42:11)

The Qur'an uses some language that might be considered anthropomorphic, for example, speaking about God's "hands" or "face." However, these terms are used in a way that is metonymical; for example,

> *The one most God-conscious will be far from (the fire),*
> *He who gives his wealth in purification,*
> *Not wanting from anyone for a favor to be repaid,*
> *Only seeking the Face of his Lord Most High,*
> *And he will be well-satisfied.*
>
> (Layl; 92:17–21)

The Qur'an, therefore, does not generally allow the listener/reader to approach God by associating him with corporeal images and indicates that human imagination simply cannot comprehend the reality that is God. At the same time, the Qur'an does not refrain from describing God, but it does so mostly by invoking his "names" or "attributes" (*asma'*):[17]

> *He is Allah; there is no god but He: the Knower of what is hidden and what is manifest; He is the Merciful, the Compassionate.*
> *He is Allah; there is no god but He: the Sovereign, the Holy, the Flawless, the Faithful, the Guardian, the Eminent, the Almighty, the Supreme; God is highly exalted above what they associate with Him.*
> *He is Allah the Creator, the Producer, the Shaper; to Him belong the most beautiful names. All that is in the heavens and on earth praise Him, and He is the Exalted, the Wise.*
>
> (Hashr; 59:22–24)

The Prophet Muhammad is reported to have said that God has ninety-nine attributes. These attributes are found throughout the Qur'an; in most cases only one or two attributes are mentioned in any one passage, although the above passage lists fifteen. Lists of God's ninety-nine attributes became important teaching tools for Muslim theologians and teachers of Islamic spirituality. Sufism, in particular, has promoted the recitation of and reflection upon these attributes as a way of approaching God.

All of this developed, however, in later generations; during the time of the revelation, the attributes of God were encountered primarily in their context in the Qur'an. Here the attributes serve an important rhetorical and theological purpose. In the first place, the attributes provide a unifying thread, functioning almost like a refrain as they punctuate, in particular, the endings of verses. Hundreds of verses throughout the Qur'an end with references to some of God's attributes, usually in a variation of the phrase "And God is (one attribute) and (another attribute)." For example, a common pairing of just two of the attributes (All-Hearing, All-Knowing) is found in over thirty combinations, examples of which include the following:

> *Verily God is All-Hearing, All-Knowing.*
> > (2:181, 244; 8:17; 22:75; 31:28; 49:1; 58:1)
> *And God is All-Hearing, All-Knowing.*
> > (2:224, 256; 3:34, 121; 9:98, 103; 24:21, 60)
> *Verily You (O Lord) are the All-Hearing, the All-Knowing.*
> > (2:127; 3:35)

Variations of these phrases appear especially in longer and medium-length suras where they create a sense of harmony among longer narrative, legalistic, and didactic passages. This harmony is both thematic and auditory because many of the attribute terms are assonant, having the same Arabic morphology (the *fa'eel* form): *'aleem, hakeem, qadeer, baseer, azeez, hameed*, etc. Repetition and assonance support the relative ease with which motivated individuals can memorize the Qur'an. This is true even in cultures in which oral learning has been replaced by textual learning. Qur'anic memorization would have been that much easier, then, for individuals like the Prophet Muhammad's companions, who lived in an oral culture and were accustomed to memorizing lengthy poems, genealogical lists, and other information. At the same time, given that discrete passages of the Qur'an were revealed over a twenty-three-year period, unifying and refrainic elements like these attributes phrases reinforced the sense that this "recitation" (the *qur'an*) is, in fact, one "book" (*kitab*).

Because they describe God in diverse ways, the attributes phrases also convey the important theological message that the divine reality cannot be contained by a single or even a combination of concepts. Passages of admonition, for example, generally invoke God's attributes of knowledge, sight, and hearing to emphasize that wrong actions cannot be hidden from God. But such passages are almost always followed by verses invoking God's attributes of forgiveness and mercy. This invocation of God's different attributes at various times conveys the message that God exceeds our expectations and that any one perspective of God is not even close to the complete reality that is God.

The use of multiple perspectives to reflect one divine reality is also achieved in the Qur'an through the use of a rhetorical device called *iltifat*. A grammatical shift in perspective, *iltifat* (literally, "turning") is found in pre-Islamic Arabic poetry and is extensively employed in the Qur'an.[18] For example, the first sura of the Qur'an, Sura al-Fatiha, begins:

> *All praise is for God the Lord of the Worlds,*
> *The Merciful, the Compassionate,*
> *The Sovereign of the Day of Judgment,*
> *You alone do we worship and You alone do we ask for aid.*
> (Fatiha; 1:1–4)

In the first three verses of this passage, God is spoken about in the third person. This perspective on God conveys a sense of his majesty and dominance over creation. The fourth verse then startles the listener/reader with its use of the second person singular to address God; suddenly the relationship becomes intimate and personal. The grammatical shift employed in this passage not only serves a stylistic purpose but also conveys a theological message: that God is in complete command over all of creation, yet in his majesty is immediately accessible to those who turn to him in worship and supplication. By employing a grammatical device to convey this concept, the Qur'an also teaches that the reality of God is beyond even the most perfect engagement of human language to reflect God's word. Similarly, sometimes the Qur'an uses the first person plural, the majestic "We," to identify God, but at other times, uses the first person singular, "I."

The Qur'an places great emphasis on another way the individual can approach God, which is by contemplating his signs. The Qur'an repeatedly asks the listener/reader to turn his or her attention to various aspects of creation – to look at the sky, the trees, the clouds, and to consider the complexity and beauty of creation; all these "signs" (*ayat*) point to the existence of the Creator.

Among the most complex and beautiful of creatures are human beings themselves; if people would only reflect upon their own abilities and perceptions, they will become aware of God:

> *Among His signs is that He created you from dust, then behold, you are humans scattered far and wide.*
>
> *And among His signs is that He created mates from your own selves so that you may dwell in tranquility with them, and He has created love and mercy among you; verily in that are signs for people who think.*
>
> *And among His signs is the creation of the heavens and the earth and the diversity of your languages and colors; verily in that are signs for the knowledgeable.*
>
> *And among His signs is the sleep you take during the night and the day and your seeking His bounty; verily in that are signs for people who listen.*
>
> *And among His signs is that He shows you lightening, invoking fear and hope, and He sends down from the sky water by which the earth is enlivened after it has been dead; verily in that are signs for people of intellect.*
>
> (Rum; 30:20–24)

The repetition of the phrase "and among His signs" at the beginning of each verse gives the passage a pleasing rhythm and enhances its otherwise lyrical quality. The passage is also highly dynamic in that each *aya* of the Qur'an pushes the listener/reader to pay attention to an *aya* outside of the Qur'an. Attention and intellect are forced to move between the *ayat* of recited verses and the *ayat* of created signs; that an awakening of the senses and the intellect to the power of God is intended is evident in the fact that each verse ends in a call for thinking, listening, and reasoning. The message is that God is to be approached by a multifaceted perceptive engagement with His creation.

In the context of seventh-century Arabia, this passage recalls the lyrical middle sections found in the *qasidas* – the great epic poems of the pre-Islamic period. The middle section of these tripartite poems generally describes a liminal state in which the hero is separated from his people and their settlements until he finds himself alone in the desert surrounded only by the natural world. In this state, the hero's awareness of the power of nature is awakened and, in nature, he sees signs of the path he must take to return to civilization, to his people, and to wholeness. At the same time, pre-Islamic poetry recognized the figure of the wanderer who never reintegrates into society. These *su'luk* arrogantly refused to accept their need for and responsibility to anyone other than themselves. Such figures, rather than returning to their people after a period of wandering, remained forever alone and were a danger to themselves and others.

The Qur'an draws on some of these same mythopoetic images, but arrives at a different conclusion: that apparent binary dichotomies (nature/culture, night/day, death/life) are in fact part of a larger coherent order that is given meaning by the sovereignty of God over all things. There is no place in the universe that is void of meaning. At the same time, although this transcendent meaning is "obvious," there are individuals who, because of their own arrogance, willfully deny their dependence upon God; such individuals have eyes that can see the signs, but have "hearts" that refuse to accept what is evident:

> *Have they not traveled through the land so they will have hearts that are wise and ears by which they can hear? Indeed, it is not their eyes that have gone blind but rather, it is their inner hearts that have become blind.*

> (Hajj; 22:46)

Moral Conduct and Its Ultimate Consequences

On an intellectual level, the Meccans may have been predisposed to accept Allah as the ultimate supernatural power because only Allah had something like a universal appeal to the Arab tribes. Although the Ka'ba was peopled with idols, the temple was said to be "Allah's house," and this was the major common pilgrimage site for most Arab tribes by the time of the rise of Islam. Further, in a land over which there was no governing authority, Allah was considered the guarantor of treaties and agreements.[19] Thus, Allah represented a moral authority who could be appealed to on occasion to transcend parochial tribal customs and authorities.

At the same time, to embrace Islam meant not only accepting Allah as the supreme creator but rejecting belief in any lesser deities and ceasing any rituals in which such deities were revered or worshipped. The Qur'an states very forcefully:

> God will not forgive the attribution of partners to Him, but He forgives anything else of those whom He wills. Whoever attributes partners to God has devised a tremendous sin.
>
> (Nisa'; 4:48)

No doubt it was difficult for many of Muhammad's contemporaries to let go of practices and rituals associated with their traditional deities and idols. As we have mentioned, the Qur'an frequently rebuts the claim that tradition (what "our forefathers" have done) is a legitimate reason for continuing a practice that violates revelation. It is therefore likely that there were those who opposed Islam, not for any strong ideological reason but simply because they were "conservative" in the sense of wanting to maintain the traditions of their ancestors. Indeed, the Prophet's own beloved uncle, Abu Talib, the man who sheltered him when he was orphaned and protected him from the harm of the Quraysh when he began his prophetic mission, is said to have refused to embrace Islam for this very reason. Abu Talib is reported to have said, "I cannot give up the religion of my fathers which they followed, but by God you shall never meet with anything to distress you so long as I live."[20] For many of the Meccans, however, resistance to Islam seems to have arisen mostly in response to its ethical and eschatological teachings, both of which work together to present a message that all humans act within a common moral framework that is divinely established and determines ultimate consequences.

The Qur'an makes frequent reference to the fact that the Meccans rejected the idea of the resurrection and judgment of the dead. At the rise of Islam, it seems that most Arabs believed that a measure of immortality could be gained only by performing heroic deeds for the sake of one's tribe, in the hope that later generations would continue to relate stories of these deeds after one's death. In this way, the hero's name might live on, and this was as much immortality as a man could hope for. The Qur'an indicates that the Meccans were not unaware of the concept of life after death; however, they simply did not find the idea compelling. Their response to the concept seems to have been based on a combination of pragmatism and materialism: although for generations the idea of the resurrection of the dead had been professed by some individuals, until now, no one had ever witnessed a person being resurrected; rather, all they ever witnessed was the physical decay and eventual annihilation of all traces of the dead. In response, the Qur'an tries to engage their imaginations to think beyond their material experiences and to show that in their rather detached belief in a transcendent God lay the possibility of a greater purpose for humanity

> *They say, "When we have died and become dust and bones will we be resurrected?*
> *This was promised to us and to our forefathers before and it is nothing but tales of the ancients."*
> *Say (in response), "To whom belongs the earth and everyone who is in it if you have knowledge?"*
> *They will say, "To God."*
> *Say, "Will you not then remember (Him)?"*
> *Say, "Who is the Lord of the seven heavens and the Lord of the great throne?"*
> *They will say, "(That is) for God."*
> *Say, "In whose hand is the dominion of all things, and He extends protection but there is no protection from Him, if you have know-ledge?"*
> *They will say, "God."*
> *Say, "Then how are you bewitched?"*
>
> (Mu'minun; 23:82–89)

It is impossible for the historian to estimate the number of Meccans who may have been opposed to Islam for intellectual reasons; there is simply no evidence to assess this. Certainly we cannot deny the possibility that among the Meccans were skeptics who refused to accept the idea of the resurrection of the dead; after all, later Muslim philosophers would question and reinterpret this doctrine[21] and there is no reason to believe that seventh-century Meccans were any less capable of consciously adopting a materialist or skeptical position on claims about transcendent matters.

At the same time, the Qur'an seems to indicate that the primary concern of those who rejected the idea of the resurrection of the dead was that this doctrine is concomitant with belief in the divine judgment of resurrected souls. In other words, what was most disturbing to the Meccans was the fact that this eschatology is connected with an imperative to ethical responsibility. In the following passage, for example, the Qur'an warns that those who defraud others will have to answer to God for their actions on the Day of Judgment:

> *Woe to those who deal in fraud!*
> *Those who demand full measure when they receive it from other people,*
> *but when they give measure or weight shortchange the others.*
> *Do they not think that they will be resurrected on a mighty day?*
> *A day when all people will stand before the Lord of the Worlds.*
>
> (Mutaffifin; 83:1–6)

Many of theses verses and suras revealed early in the Prophet's mission invoke dramatic and awesome images of the end of time and the last judgment. Fazlur Rahman remarks that "the basic idea underlying the Qur'an's teaching on the hereafter is that there will come a moment, 'The Hour (*al-sa'a*)', when every human will be shaken into a unique and unprecedented self-awareness of his deeds: he will squarely and starkly face his own doings, not-doings, and misdoings and accept the judgment upon them."[22] Michael Sells, who characterizes these early suras as "hymnic," says that they convey "a sense of directness and intimacy, as if the hearer were repeatedly being asked a simple question: what will be of value at the end of a human life?"[23]

In the following passage, the Qur'an invokes the image of a baby girl resurrected amidst the turmoil of the end of time to testify against the individual who buried her in an act of infanticide:

> *When the sun is folded up,*
> *When the stars are scattered,*
> *When the mountains vanish,*
> *When the pregnant camels are neglected,*
> *When the wild animals are gathered together,*
> *When the seas boil over,*
> *When the souls are sorted out,*
> *When the baby girl is questioned:*
> *For what crime she was murdered?*
> *When the scrolls are laid open,*
> *When heaven is unveiled,*
> *When the fire is stoked,*
> *When the garden is brought near,*
> *Each soul will know what it has prepared.*
>
> (Takwir; 81:1–14)

The style of this passage conveys the sense of urgency invoked with its stark end-of-time images. The verses are concise and end in a short rhyming consonant (-*at*). Like a persistent drum beat, the word "when" begins each verse, pounding home the message that despite the best attempts of humans to deny their own mortality and the consequences of their actions, indeed they will die and face a day of reckoning.

In these early passages, the Qur'an frequently returns to the theme of the arrogance of those who have a sense of entitlement to their wealth and social status. The unbeliever claims self-sufficiency when the reality is that everything he possesses, even his body and mind, were created by God:

> God brought you forth from the bellies of your mothers; you knew nothing and He gave you hearing, sight and minds so that you might have cause to be grateful.
>
> (Nahl; 16:78)

The great scholar of the Qur'an Toshihiko Izutsu showed the importance of this Qur'anic concept of "gratitude" (*shukr*) in defining the relationship between God and humanity.[24] He rightly pointed out that the word *kufr*, usually translated as "disbelief," also signifies "ingratitude." In this respect, the Qur'an draws a close connection between faith and gratitude towards God. Disbelief is a willful refusal to acknowledge God's favors to humanity. It is to be expected that someone who does not even acknowledge his responsibility to show gratitude to God will reject the idea that he has moral obligations towards humanity. Presenting himself as a "self-made man," the ingrate is arrogant and irresponsible towards God and humanity.

Servants of God

There is no doubt that the Qur'an places great emphasis on humanity's moral responsibility to exercise its power justly. At the same time, the Qur'an is not simply a call to social activism and political reform. Rather, the Qur'an indicates that such activity must be guided by divine norms and undertaken with a desire to obey God. The Qur'an does not present a dichotomy between the activities of this world and the next, but provides an ontological framework by which worldly engagement is made meaningful. The Qur'an states:

I have only created jinn and humans to worship me.
                                              (Dhariyat; 51:56)

The word "worship" (*'ibada*) literally means "servitude" or even "slavery" and defines the proper posture of humanity with respect to the Creator. The Qur'an addresses those who worship God as "Servant/s of God": *'Abd-Allah* (commonly rendered 'Abdallah; pl. *'Ibadallah*). Many religious traditions, including Christianity, as well as pre-Islamic Arabian religion expressed the notion of worship of the divine in terms of servitude. In pre-Islamic Arabian culture, individuals were often given names linking them in servitude and devotion to a number of gods, goddesses, and manifestations of divinity, including 'Abd al-Shams (Servant of the Sun) and 'Abd al-'Uzza (Servant of the goddess al-'Uzza), among others. This usage is common in other Semitic languages, and a near cognate for the Arabic 'Abdullah is found in the biblical Obadiah (Servant of the Lord). That the Prophet Muhammad's father was named 'Abdullah indicates his family's particular association with the Lord of the Ka'ba, but did not prevent Muhammad from recognizing that his father had been a polytheist. The Qur'anic message, then, is that it is not enough to recognize Allah as an object of worship, but that there is only one God and no others should be worshipped or revered.

This is the message of *islam* that all God's messengers brought to their people. The literal meaning of *islam* is "submission," and those who submit themselves to the One God are *muslims*. This is what the Qur'an means when it calls Abraham, Jesus, and other prophets *muslim*. In Meccan suras, it is this, what some scholars call a "primordial" sense of Islam, that is being promoted. Islam is to worship God alone, to honor the sacred, and to act kindly and honestly. The Qur'an says that God sent prophets to all people, some of whom have been named in the Qur'an and some of whom have not been named (40:78). The named prophets (usually called "messengers" in the Qur'an) include the pre-Abrahamic prophets, two of whom are mentioned in the Hebrew Bible – Adam and Noah – as well as two who are not – Salih and Hud. The latter are associated with the people of 'Ad and Thamud who lived in different parts of the Arabian Peninsula in ancient times. Scholars see this as an indication that "the Arabs had come to achieve a prophetology that was independent of the Biblical tradition."[25]

Figure 2.1   A man supplicates God during the performance of the Hajj to Mecca.
Early Muslim scholars reported that 10,000 Muslims from Medina joined the Prophet
Muhammad for his final pilgrimage in 10/632. By the beginning of the twenty-first
century, approximately 3 million Muslims were performing Hajj each year.

The Qur'an conveys the message that God is served both through
acts of charity and kindness and through prayer and other forms of
ritual worship. A common theme of Meccan verses is the arrogance of
wealthy disbelievers who refuse to share with the poor, even invoking
a distorted theological justification for their selfishness:

> And when it is said to them, "Spend on others out of what God has
> provided for you," the unbelievers say to those who believe, "Shall
> we feed those whom, if God had so willed, He would have fed
> himself? You are nothing but in manifest error."
>
> (Ya Sin; 36:47)

The believer, in contrast, recognizes that all he has – even his own
body – comes from God and that although it is not easy to give away
one's possessions and time to the needy, this is the path of righteousness:

> We have created man into a life of struggle.
> Does he reckon that no one has power over him?

He says, "I have squandered wealth in abundance!"
Does he reckon that no one beholds him?
Have we not made for him two eyes?
And a tongue and two lips?
And directed him to the two paths?
But he has not rushed to take the steep path.
And what will make you understand the nature of the steep path?
It is freeing the prisoner,
And giving away food on a day of scarcity,
To an orphan with ties of relation,
Or an indigent person lying in the dust,
And then to be among those who believe and encourage patience
and compassionate actions.

(Balad; 90:4–17)

Sira literature indicates that it was not until the end of the Meccan period (at least) that the five daily prayers were ordained for the Muslim community. In the early years of the revelation, Qur'anic recitation, especially at night, seems to have been the foundation of worship. One of the earliest suras begins with the verses:

O you enveloped (in garments):
Stand throughout the night, except for a little;
A half of it, or a little less;
Or a little more, and recite the Qur'an with a measured rhythm.

(Muzammil; 73:1–4)

It is possible that only small numbers of Muslims in Mecca were able to learn enough of the Qur'an to recite significant portions at this point. Fearing persecution, the Muslims generally refrained from gathering in large numbers to pray and new revelations were shared among believers in their homes, sometimes with great secrecy. When still a disbeliever, 'Umar ibn al-Khattab (later to become one of the most influential Muslim leaders) confirmed that his sister had secretly become a Muslim when he caught her and her husband in their home where they were learning some verses from another Companion. When 'Umar entered the house, his sister tried to hide the parchment with verses from Sura Ta Ha (20) that they had been reading. At first 'Umar was enraged, but then he calmed down and read the verses himself; at that moment, his heart opened to Islam and he became a Muslim.[26]

The division between the Muslim converts and the rest of the Meccans grew wider over time. This early Meccan sura is unequivocal in stating that Islam cannot be reconciled with the beliefs and practices of Muhammad's contemporaries:

> *Say: O you who reject faith:*
> *I do not worship what you worship,*
> *And you do not worship what I worship,*
> *And I will not worship that which you have worshipped,*
> *And you will not worship what I worship,*
> *To you your religion, and to me my religion.*
>
> (Kafirun; 109)

This sura sends a strong message that the worship of God cannot be compromised by allowing the worship of other deities. One hadith that describes the occasion of revelation for this sura says that a number of Meccan notables opposed to the message of the Prophet Muhammad approached him as he was worshipping at the Ka'ba and said, "Muhammad, come let us worship what you worship, and you worship what we worship. You and we will combine in the matter. If what you worship is better than what we worship we will take a share of it, and if what we worship is better than what you worship, you can take a share of it."[27] Here, the Meccans are depicted as though applying their business acumen to religion: why not pool their resources, invest in a few different kinds of worship, and all parties will come out with some gain?

Given this background, and given that the strong and clear message throughout the Qur'an is that God alone should be worshipped, many Muslim scholars have rejected the validity of the report about the so-called "Satanic Verses." This report claims that due to the distress the Prophet felt because of the severe persecution of his followers, he was susceptible to the suggestion of Satan to interject a verse into Sura al-Najm suggesting that the celestial goddesses al-Lat, al-'Uzza, and Manat are "high flying cranes whose intercession is approved." This validation of the beliefs of the Meccans was said to have pleased them so that they stopped their persecution of the Muslims. However, Gabriel appeared to the Prophet and made him aware of his mistake and revealed the verse,

> *We have not sent a prophet or a messenger before you except that*
> *when he longed for something Satan cast suggestions into his longing.*
> *But God will annul what Satan has suggested, then God will establish*
> *his verses; indeed God is All-knowing, Wise.*
>
> (Hajj; 22:52)

For the majority of Muslim scholars, this report does not meet the standards established by hadith criticism because it lacks a valid *isnad* and its content contradicts the fundamental Islamic belief that prophets are infallible. A minority of scholars, however, most notably the Syrian Hanbali scholar Ibn Taymiyya (d. 728/1328), accepted the validity of these reports. Ibn Taymiyya agreed with the majority that all prophets are infallible; however, he understood this infallibility not as preventing prophets from ever committing errors but as preventing them from persisting in them once committed. The commission of such errors is part of God's wisdom to allow them an opportunity to repent and perfect their character.[28]

In the end, the lesson all Muslim scholars derived from the above Qur'anic verses is that, one way or another, God promised and demonstrated that he would protect the Qur'an from any error, omission or addition.

Persecution of Believers Past and Present

The Meccan phase of the revelatory period was highly challenging for the Muslims. For thirteen years the Prophet stayed in his hometown of Mecca trying to convince his family and community to embrace his message. The Prophet had remarkable success winning converts in this period – many members of his family and others accepted Islam. Among the converts were the poor and disaffected, but also some wealthy and prominent individuals. Nevertheless, the Prophet was unable to convince those holding the reigns of power in Mecca to abandon their customs and practices that violated the monotheistic theology of the Abrahamic tradition, as well as to embrace a more ethical and just sociopolitical order.

In tribal Arabia, no individual was secure without the support and protection of a group. Despite the scorn and ridicule the Prophet received at the hands of some of his opponents, his physical security was ensured by the protection of his uncle, Abu Talib, a chief of the city. The Prophet was unable, however, to secure protection for any of his followers who occupied weak positions in the Meccan social structure. Slaves who embraced Islam, for example, could be killed with impunity by their owners. The first martyr (*shahid*, literally, "witness") of Islam was a slave woman named Sumayya who was tortured and murdered for embracing Islam without the permission of her owner. The only means the Muslims had to protect these slaves was to purchase them from their persecutors. One of the slaves freed by Abu Bakr – one of the first Muslim converts and a close friend of the Prophet

Muhammad – was Bilal, a man of African descent. Bilal's owner "used to bring him outside during the hottest part of the day, throw him on his back in the open valley and have a large rock placed on his chest, then he would say to him, 'You will stay here until you die or until you deny Muhammad and worship Al-Lat and al-'Uzza.' (Bilal) used to say 'One, One' while he was enduring this."[29]

One of the most violent opponents of Islam was the Prophet's own uncle, Abu Lahab. Very few individuals contemporary with the Prophet are named in the Qur'an, but this Meccan sura, which, when recited, almost has the sound of an incantation, condemns the former by name and tells of the terrible punishment awaiting him and his wife who participated in his harassment of the Muslims:

> *Perish the hands of Abu Lahab!*
> *No profit will he gain from his wealth or his earnings.*
> *He will burn in a flaming fire,*
> *And his wife will carry the wood;*
> *On her neck, a rope of twisted fibers.*
>
> (Masad; 111)

The most vigorous and active opponent of Islam among the Quraysh was a man positioned to assume leadership in the city and who, because of his unrestrained aggressiveness, became known as "Abu Jahl" ("The Father of Ignorance"). About Abu Jahl, the *Sira* narrates:

> It was that evil man Abu Jahl who stirred up the Meccans against them. When he heard that a man had become a Muslim, if he was a man of social importance and had relatives who would defend him, (Abu Jahl) would reprimand him and belittle him saying, "You have forsaken the religion of your father who was better than you. We will declare you an idiot and call you a fool and destroy your reputation." If (the convert) was a merchant, (Abu Jahl) said, "We will boycott your goods and reduce you to beggary." If (the convert) was a person of no social importance, he beat him and incited others against him.[30]

Failing any means to protect his followers from harassment and persecution, the Prophet encouraged them to seek asylum with a just Christian king in Abyssinia. Almost one hundred Muslims took this option and sought refuge there, where the Negus (the "ruler") welcomed them and allowed them to practice their religion freely. The Negus was said to have been especially moved by the recitation of a portion of Sura Maryam, in which the Qur'an gives a tender description of the Virgin Mary and her delivery of Jesus. A delegation of the Quraysh who wanted the Negus to surrender the Muslims to them tried to turn the Christian king against them by telling him that the Muslims considered Jesus to be a "slave." Ja'far, a son of Abu Talib, responded by giving the Qur'anic description of Jesus (drawing from various passages, including 4:171–172) saying, "he is the slave of God and his apostle and his spirit and his word which he cast into Mary the Blessed Virgin." The *Sira* says that in response, the Negus took a stick from the ground and said, "By God, Jesus the son of Mary does not exceed what you have said by the length of this stick," and he promised the Muslims his protection for as long as they desired to stay in his kingdom.

Meanwhile, the situation for the Muslims in Mecca had not improved. Because the Prophet was protected by most of the members of his clan Banu Hashim, the Quraysh decided that the only way they could seriously affect him was to punish his protectors. To achieve this end, they agreed to boycott Banu Hashim and their cousins, Banu Muttalib, who had refused to abandon them. The rest of the Quraysh agreed that they would neither buy from nor sell to members of the clans, nor would they intermarry with them. The boycott lasted over two years, during which time many of those boycotted suffered from severe deprivation. However, because many of the Quraysh were related to those suffering, they found it difficult to witness and, eventually, were able to get the boycott annulled.

As we have mentioned before, it is the *Sira*, rather than the Qur'an, that narrates these stories about the Prophet's community, but Meccan suras are replete with the theme of the persecution of the righteous. This early sura makes reference to a group of believers (some Qur'an commentators say they were Yemenite Christians) who were burned for their faith:

> *By the sky and its constellations,*
> *By the promised Day,*
> *By the witness and the witnessed,*
> *Destroyed were the keepers of the pit,*
> *Its fire supplied with fuel,*
> *They sat by the fire,*
> *And they witnessed what was done with the believers,*

They do not hate them for anything except that they believed in God,
the Eminent, the Praiseworthy,
The One to whom belongs the dominion of the heavens and the earth, and
God is a witness to everything.
Those who persecute the believing men and the believing women and do
not repent will have the punishment of Hell and the punishment of the Fire.
Those who believe and do good works will have gardens beneath which
rivers flow; that is the great reward.

(Buruj; 85:1–11)

Here, the Qur'an does not promise the believers that they will not suffer for their faith, nor does the Qur'an promise that they can always expect justice on earth. Rather, the comfort the Qur'an offers is that the suffering of the innocent will never be forgotten, for God witnesses all things. Those who persecute the righteous are offered the opportunity to repent – God's justice is not simple retribution. But unrepentant oppressors will suffer the punishment of fire, just as they had afflicted it on others. The persecuted believers can take comfort in envisioning a future life of peace and comfort.

This Qur'anic promise of a future reward was important to the Muslims in Mecca, where they helplessly witnessed the persecution of their brothers and sisters in faith. Even the Prophet Muhammad could do nothing more than remind the converts of God's promise. When he saw some Qurayshis torturing the married slaves Yasir and Sumayya and their son 'Ammar in the heat of the day, the Prophet could only say, "Patience O family of Yasir, your meeting will be in Paradise!"[31]

The Prophet and the believers are told by the Qur'an to find courage and hope in the struggles of earlier prophets. Again and again, the Qur'an tells stories of the difficulties the prophets endured when they called their people to worship God and to act righteously. Noah's people mocked him, Hud's people rejected him, Salih's people defied him, Abraham's people tried to burn him, Yusuf was betrayed by his brothers, Jesus' people abandoned him in his final hours. Nevertheless, these prophets persisted in their mission, so Muhammad should be persistent and patient as well:

We know that you are saddened by what they say, but they are
not repudiating you, rather it is the signs of God the oppressors
reject. Messengers before you were denied and they patiently bore
repudiation and injury until our assistance came to them. There is

no one who can alter the words of God; and indeed you have received
some news of the messengers.

(An'am; 6:34)

The Qur'an emphasizes the humanity of the prophets and that their mission is undertaken with the full engagement of their societies. This means that prophets are not isolated individuals, but men with families, who are the first people they evangelize. When their family members support them, it is a source of comfort to the prophets; when their family members reject them, it is an emotional burden they have to bear.

The first person to accept the prophethood of Muhammad was his wife Khadija; indeed, she is said to have played a critical role in encouraging the Prophet to embrace his mission. Characteristically, the Qur'an does not speak about Khadija by name, but the spiritual partnership of marriage is a theme of Meccan verses. We have already cited verses from Sura al-Rum describing the "love and mercy" that is shared by the married couple. In other verses, the believers are told that when they enter Paradise, they will be accompanied by their spouses (43:70) and family life is described as one of God's blessings:

God has made for you spouses from your own selves, and He has
given you, by means of your spouses, children and grandchildren,
and He has provided you with good things. Will you then believe in
vain things and deny the blessings of God?

(Nahl; 16:72)

Khadija was significantly older than Muhammad and now, about ten years after he began his prophethood, perhaps weakened by the boycott and old age, she died. This is described as a great loss to the Prophet, for not only was Khadija his marriage partner and mother to their four daughters, but "she had been a faithful support to him in Islam, and he used to tell her of his troubles."[32] Although the Prophet would marry again, he never forgot Khadija, his first love and his first wife, and he would honor her memory for the rest of his life.

In the same year, the Prophet suffered another terrible loss – the death of Abu Talib. This loss was difficult on a number of levels. First, Abu Talib had been a father-figure to Muhammad, acting as his guardian since he was a small child. Abu Talib had played an even more important role in protecting Muhammad from the harm of other Qurayshi leaders after he began preaching his message of Islam. With Abu Talib's death, the Prophet was now in a precarious position. Ibn Hisham says, "Abu Talib died some three years before (the Prophet) migrated to Medina, and it was then that Quraysh began to treat him in an offensive way which they would not have dared to follow in his uncle's lifetime." Finally, the Prophet was upset that Abu Talib had not declared himself a Muslim and had died staying true to the creed of his ancestors.[33] In connection with this incident, the following verses of Qur'an were revealed:

> *Verily you do not guide those whom you love, but God guides whom*
> *He wills, and He knows best those who receive guidance.*
>
> (Qasas; 28:56)

The Qur'an is clear that faith cannot be compelled and that the role of a prophet is to deliver his message; he has no power to convert others. Later, an even more explicit statement regarding this issue would be revealed:

> *There is no compulsion in religion. Guidance has been clearly*
> *distinguished from error. Whoever rejects evil and believes in God*
> *has grasped the trustworthy tie that has no weakness; and God is*
> *All-Hearing, All-Knowing.*
>
> (Baqara; 2:256)

The Qur'an certainly is not indifferent as to whether an individual chooses belief or disbelief; the Qur'an clearly indicates that some choices lead to the company of God and others lead to an evil end. At the same time, no person, not even a prophet, can compel belief; that is a choice God has given to each individual.

The year during which Khadija and Abu Talib died was known as the "Year of Sadness." The Prophet had lost his closest confidant, he no longer enjoyed the protection of his uncle, and he continued to witness the persecution of his followers. The Prophet was patient and persevering and he trusted in God, but there is no doubt that he was praying for a change for the better.

Around this time, the Prophet was given a strong indication that his situation would improve when he experienced a profound transcendent experience. This was the "Night Journey and Ascent" when the Prophet was taken by divine power from Mecca to Jerusalem and from there to heaven. Qur'an commentators believe that it is this miraculous occurrence that is referenced in the following verse:

> *Glory to the One who transported his servant by night from the Sacred Mosque to the Farthest Mosque – whose precincts we have blessed – in order to show him some of our signs; verily He is the All-Hearing, the All-Seeing.*
>
> (Isra'; 17:1)

Within a year of this remarkable spiritual experience, for the first time the Prophet would receive a positive response to his message. This came from some pilgrims from the city of Yathrib who embraced Islam. During the next pilgrimage season, a delegation of twelve men met the Prophet at a place called 'Aqaba and gave him a pledge of religious allegiance. When the delegation returned to Yathrib, the Prophet sent one of his companions to teach them their religious obligations. Islam spread in the community, and the next year a much larger delegation – about seventy-five people – again met the Prophet at 'Aqaba and gave him not only religious allegiance but also political allegiance. Upon completion of the second "Pledge of 'Aqaba," the Prophet immediately began encouraging his Meccan followers to emigrate to Yathrib. Within a year, the Prophet himself would join his followers in the city that now became known as "Medina" (the "City" of the Prophet).

Finally, in Medina, the Muslims were free to worship as they pleased and to shape society according to their norms. The *hijra* ("emigration") of the Prophet from Mecca to Medina marked the beginning of a new era, and for that reason, soon after the death of the Prophet, Muslims decided to establish a new calendar beginning the year of the *hijra* (622 CE).

Establishing a Viable State and a Just Political Order

One of the Prophet's first challenges in Medina was to establish a political and social order that would encompass the diversity of the groups living there. In Mecca, the vast majority of inhabitants had been from one tribe, the Quraysh, along with their dependents and slaves; Medina, on the other hand, was dominated by two large tribes that had been feuding for many years. The *Sira* indicates that the tribes looked to the Prophet as the leader who could bring peace to the city. Medina also had a significant Jewish population which was divided, like the Arabs, into tribes and clans. Finally, the *hijra* brought hundreds of Meccan Muslims into the city, further diversifying the population.

In order to promote the solidarity of the diverse community of Muslims, the Prophet established two projects immediately after arriving in Medina. First, he began construction of a mosque that would serve as the heart of the religious community. Although smaller mosques were allowed in the city, all Muslims had to attend the Prophet's mosque for congregational prayer on Friday, the "Day of Congregation" (Jumu'a; 62:9). Secondly, the Prophet established a pact of brotherhood between the refugees from Mecca (the *Muhajirun* – the "Emigrants") and the Muslims of Medina (the *Ansar* – the "Helpers"). Each brother from the Ansar was committed to helping his brother from the Muhajirun settle and establish himself financially. For a time, the brothers were even given a share of the inheritance designated for family members (Nisa'; 4:33).

Perhaps the greatest challenge for the Prophet once he arrived in Medina was to fulfill his new role as head of state. Although the Qur'an gives little specific direction on political governance, Medinan verses emphasize that the Prophet Muhammad is the ultimate human authority:

> *O you who believe, obey God and obey the Messenger and those in authority from amongst you. If you disagree about a matter then refer it to God and the Messenger if you believe in God and the Last Day; that is best and a better end.*
>
> (Nisa'; 4:59)

In addition to asserting the Prophet's overall authority, this verse assumes the existence and recognizes the legitimacy of lower levels of authority who represent sub-groups within society. It is this general power structure that is outlined in greater detail in the so-called "Covenant of Medina." The text of this remarkable document has been preserved in secondary sources and is widely considered, even by the most skeptical historians, to be authentic. According to the *Sira*, the Covenant was written by the Prophet when he arrived in Medina and addressed the reciprocal obligations of the people of the city. The Covenant primarily addresses the rights and responsibilities of large groups, including "the believers and Muslims of Quraysh and Yathrib" and "the Jews." Specific clans of Arabs and Jews are listed in various sections of the document and the Jews are affirmed in their religion. Some Jewish clans are described as being of "one community" with the believers, while at the same time having "their own religion."[34] In essence, the Covenant of Medina designates the Prophet Muhammad as Commander-in-Chief of the city-state and specifies that all groups work under his leadership to ensure the peace and protection of the city as a whole. The Covenant affirms the inviolability of the lives and property of all parties to the agreement as long as they abide by its terms for mutual defense.

As head of state, it was the Prophet's responsibility to protect Medina and its inhabitants. At the same time, once the Muhajirun had settled in Medina, they were committed to rectifying the injustices perpetrated upon them by the Meccan regime. The Qur'an therefore gives permission to engage in warfare (qital) to stop or prevent oppression:

> Permission (to fight) is given to those against whom war is waged because they are oppressed; and verily God is All-Powerful to help them – those who have been expelled from their lands without just cause, only saying, "Our Lord is God." If God had not allowed one group of people to defend themselves from another, certainly there would have been destroyed monasteries, churches, synagogues and mosques where God's name is extolled greatly. Surely God will help whoever helps Him; verily God is Strong, Eminent.
>
> (Hajj; 22:39–40)

In some respects, it is remarkable that this verse, considered to be the first and original Qur'anic permission for the use of military force, mentions Christian monasteries and churches and Jewish temples even before it mentions mosques. On the other hand, this inclusion is consistent with the Qur'an's presentation of Muhammad's mission as a continuation of the message and mission of earlier prophets. Accordingly, the Qur'an further supports the use of force for just cause by stating that earlier revelations recognize an ultimate reward for the ultimate sacrifice:

> God has purchased from the believers their souls and their wealth and they will be given Paradise. They fight in God's way: they slay and are slain. This is a promise which in truth He has bound Himself in the Torah, the Gospel and the Qur'an. And who is more faithful to his covenants than God? So rejoice in the deal you have contracted with Him – that is the supreme triumph.
>
> (Tawba; 9:111)

The parameters of "just cause" for engaging in warfare are not listed in one Qur'anic passage; rather, a number of verses refer to various justifications, including the protection of houses of worship mentioned above, as well as relieving oppression, according to the following passage:

> *Why should you not fight in the way of God when those who are helpless – men, women and children – are saying, "Our Lord, take us away from this oppressive town and its people and send us someone who will offer protection and send us someone who will offer assistance!"*
>
> (Nisa'; 4:75)

Once the decision has been made to go to battle, the believers must fight to win:

> *Slay them wherever you find them and drive them out of the places out of which they have driven you, for persecution is worse than killing. But do not fight them around the Sacred Mosque unless they attack you there. So if they fight you, fight them; that is the reward of those who reject the truth.*
> *But if they cease, then verily God is All-Forgiving, Compassionate. So fight them until there is no persecution and worship is for God, but if they cease, let there be no enmity, except against the oppressors.*
>
> (Baqara; 2:191–193)

Contrary to the impression this verse might give, that the Muslims were eager to wage war once it was sanctioned by revelation, in a number of places the Qur'an alludes to the fact that at least a significant number of Muslims were reluctant to go to war, fearing loss of their lives and property.

> *Warfare is ordained for you, although you dislike it. Perhaps you dislike something that is good for you, and perhaps you love something that is bad for you; God knows but you do not know.*
>
> (Baqara; 2:216)

Interestingly, the Qur'an makes reference to a similar problem faced by Moses when the Israelites feared fighting the Canaanites:

> *Recall when Moses said to his people, "O my people, remember the blessings that God has bestowed upon you in that he brought from your ranks prophets and kings and He gave you that which He never gave any one else in the world."*
> *"O my people, enter the holy land which God has ordained for you and do not turn back so that you will end up defeated."*

They said, "O Moses, but there are powerful people there so we will not enter (the land) until they are removed from there; when they are gone, then we will enter."

(Ma'ida; 5:20–22)

It is in this context that the Qur'an asserts the superiority of those who are willing to sacrifice for the good of the community by offering themselves for military service (the *mujahid/mujahidun*):

The believers who stay behind – except for those who are disabled – are not equal with those who struggle (al-mujahidun) in the way of God with their wealth and their lives. God elevates in rank those who strive with their wealth and their lives over those who stay behind. God has promised goodness to both, but God elevates those who struggle over those who stay behind with a great reward.

(Nisa'; 4:95)

That the Medinan revelations pay significant attention to situations of conflict is not surprising, given that the Muslim community was engaged in numerous battles during this period. Military force was used to secure the Medinan city-state, to protect its citizens and allies, to ensure the viability of trade, to recover property unjustly confiscated from the Muhajirun, and, finally, to overthrow the Meccan regime. In the battles of Badr, Uhud, Khandaq, and in other smaller skirmishes, many Muslims (and some of their non-Muslim allies[35]) lost their lives. The Qur'an reassures the community that such sacrifice, when made for a just cause, is one of the highest forms of witnessing to one's beliefs. Although he has lost his life, the believer who dies fighting for a righteous cause gains eternal life in the presence of God:

... And their Lord answers their prayers saying, "I shall never let the work of any laborer be lost – be he male or female – you are from one another. Those who emigrated or were exiled from their lands and suffered in My cause and fought or were killed – indeed I will efface their sins and admit them to gardens beneath which rivers flow." This is a reward that is with God; and God has with Him the most beautiful reward.

(Al 'Imran; 3:195)

Although the Qur'an permits the Prophet to engage in warfare to ensure the security of his community and to uphold justice, it does not prefer war over other means of achieving justice. In the following passage, the community is ordered to develop a viable and powerful military force as a deterrent to prevent aggression from known and unforeseen enemies. But even more preferable to the development of an effective deterrent force is to engage in peace negotiations with the enemy:

> *Make ready against them whatever force and war mounts you are able to muster so that you can use them to deter God's enemies and your enemies and others about whom you are unaware – but God knows about them. Whatever you spend in the path of God shall be repaid to you and you will not suffer injustice.*
> *But if the enemy inclines towards peace, then incline towards it also and trust in God; verily He is the All-Hearing, the All-Knowing.*
> (Anfal; 8:60–61)

During the years of conflict between the Quraysh of Mecca and the Muslims of Medina, the *Sira* indicates that some Jewish individuals and groups abided by the terms of the Treaty of Medina and aided in the defense of the city-state, or otherwise lived there peacefully. However, over the next few years, the largest Jewish tribes and clans conspired with the Qurayshi regime of Mecca to undermine and overthrow the new political order in Medina. Treasonous behavior was punished by confiscation of property, exile, and in some cases, execution. Despite extensive descriptions of these conflicts in the *Sira*, the Qur'an makes no explicit reference to military or political conflicts with Jews, but does refer to a group from the "People of the Book" who aided the "disbelievers" in a treacherous action (Ahzab; 33:25–27). In another passage, "many" of the "Children of Israel" are condemned for supporting the disbelievers in opposition to the believers of Medina; as a consequence of this action, among the worst enemies to this community are a group of Jews:

> *You will find that those who have the strongest enmity towards those who believe are the Jews and the pagans. You will find that those who are closest in affection to those who believe are those who say, "We are Christians." This is because among them are priests and monks and they are not arrogant.*
> (Ma'ida; 5:82)

Although the Qur'an recognizes the enmity that developed between the Muslims and many of the Jews of Medina and, further, puts this enmity in context by narrating a number of stories of past prophets who suffered from the disobedience of the Children of Israel, the Qur'an still recognizes the validity of Judaism as a path to God:

> *Verily those who believe, and those who follow the Jewish faith and the Christians and the Sabians – anyone who believes in God and the Last Day and does good deeds – will have their reward with their Lord and they will have no fear, nor will they grieve.*
> (Baqara; 2:62. Repeated in Ma'ida; 5:69 with slight variation)

In some instances, Medinan verses pertaining to the Jews or to the People of the Book appear to be directed at a particular group of Jews in Medina, while at other times the verses appear to be more general in nature. Although all scripture is open for interpretation, certainly the Qur'an's position on political and religious exclusivity or inclusivity is particularly susceptible to divergent interpretations. Although methodologies and theories of interpretation will be addressed in a later chapter, it is relevant here to mention a revisionist argument about the Jews of Medina made by some contemporary historians. These scholars have argued that communal identities separating Muslims and Jews during the time of the Prophet were much less fixed than they were to become in the decades after his death, and that the *Sira* exaggerates the conflicts with the Jews of Medina for historical and political reasons that developed over the first century of Islam, when it had become difficult to envision that any group of Muslims and Jews could ever have been, as the Treaty of Medina mentions, "one community."[36]

In the end, due to the historiographical challenges discussed at the beginning of this chapter, it is unlikely that a very clear picture of these events can ever be obtained. In any case, we should note the irony that the "politically correct" position on these events in the first century AH is apparently in direct opposition to that of the twenty-first century CE. In the former era, it was seen as desirable to emphasize communal distinctions and to prove divine favor through political dominance; in the latter era, what is desirable is to emphasize commonalities, connections, and an egalitarian political order.

Six years after the *hijra*, after many battles and losses on all sides, the Prophet implemented the Qur'anic recommendation for a negotiated peace and signed a truce with the Meccan regime at a place called Hudaybiya. The Treaty of Hudaybiya brought a cessation of hostilities between the Meccans and the Medinan state for about two years, until the terms of the treaty were violated when allies of the Quraysh attacked and killed allies of the Muslims. Once the treaty was violated, the Prophet ordered his troops to march upon Mecca.

According to the *Sira*, when one of the Muslims heard about the impending attack, he feared for some family members who were living in Mecca, so he secretly wrote a note warning them, perhaps so they could leave the city. When the note was discovered, the Muslims were angry because they had wanted to surprise the Meccans. The Prophet, understanding the concerns of the man, forgave him, but conveyed the following revelation he had received regarding this incident:

> *O you who believe, if you have come out to fight in my path, seeking my pleasure, do not take my enemies and your enemies as friends, offering them love when they have rejected what has come to you of the truth and have expelled the Messenger and all of you because you believe in God as your Lord. You secretly offer them love, and I know what you do in secret and what you do in public. Whoever among you has done this has strayed from the right path.*
> *If they were to get ahold of you, they would treat you as enemies, stretching out their hands and tongues against you to do evil, wishing you to disbelieve.*
>
> (Mumtahina; 60:1–2)

The message here is unambiguous: it is forbidden to subvert the interests of the community for personal desires and concerns, and most importantly, in times of war, sides need to be taken. It is characteristic of the Qur'an, however, that this stern and apparently exclusivist message is quickly followed by one that is gentle, forgiving, and offers hope for a peaceful future and an inclusive social order that is desirable in normal circumstances:

> *Perhaps God will put love between you and those whom you now consider enemies; God is All-Powerful, and God is All-Forgiving, Compassionate.*
> *God does not forbid you from dealing kindly and justly with those who do not fight you for your religion and who have not expelled you from your lands; verily God loves those who are just.*
> *Rather, God only forbids you from befriending those who fight you for your religion and expel you from your lands and help others in expelling you; whoever befriends such people become themselves oppressors.*
>
> (Mumtahina; 60:7–9)

Before the Muslims marched on Mecca, the Prophet announced a general amnesty and the city was taken peacefully. Despite the years of oppression the Muslims had suffered at the hands of the Qurayshi regime, revenge killings were prohibited and forgiveness was extended to those who sought it. Mecca now came under the sovereignty of the Muslim state, so the Ka'ba was cleansed of the idols and restored as a sacred house for the worship of God in the Abrahamic tradition. For the next two years, until the Prophet's death, the Muslims would continue to further the vital interests and security of their state by diplomatic and military means.

The Medinan revelations addressing the challenge of securing a viable and just political order are numerous and diverse. As an integral part of the Qur'an, these revelations would remain foundational and contested precedents for all later generations of Muslims engaged in similar political challenges.

Building Community

Although the Medinan period witnessed significant military struggles and frequent skirmishes, major warfare was conducted only for brief intervals over these ten years. The main focus of activity was community building, and many of the Medinan verses are directed toward fostering a moral and God-conscious community of faith. In this respect, the Medinan verses of the Qur'an expand upon the general values and principles expressed during the Meccan period. Many of these verses also aim to institutionalize these values at various levels in society. Medinan verses provide guidelines on everything from zakat distribution and congregational prayer to inheritance, marriage, and divorce. At the same time, many details about the implementation of these rules are not in the Qur'an but were given by the Prophet and later collected as hadith. A persistent theme of Medinan verses is the obligation of the Muslim community to obey the instructions of the Prophet, just as they must obey the orders of God as expressed in the Qur'an.

The *raison d'être* of the Medinan Muslim community is stated in the following passage:

> *O you who believe, be aware of God as is befitting to Him, and do not die except as Muslims.*

Hold firmly together to the bond of God and do not be disunited.
Remember God's grace upon you when you were enemies to each
other and He joined your hearts together so that, by His grace, you
became brothers when you had been on the edge of a fiery abyss, and
He saved you from it. In this way God makes clear His signs to you
so that perhaps you will be guided and so that there might arise from
you a community that invites to what is good, enjoining the right
and forbidding the wrong – those are the ones who are successful.

(Al 'Imran; 3:103–104)

The Qur'an promotes the brotherhood of the believers by acknowledging that there will be times of conflict and tension caused by group differences. It is therefore important that individuals in the community act as peace-makers, rather than exacerbating conflicts by rushing to the defense of the members of one's family or tribe. In addition, the Qur'an recognizes that nothing is more corrosive of communal harmony than to allow gossip, backbiting, and scornful treatment of others to continue unchecked. The believers are reminded that dignity and honor derive not from lineage and tribal identity but from behaving in a righteous manner:

Verily the believers are brothers, so work to reconcile your brothers,
and be conscious of God so that you will receive mercy.
O you who believe! One group of people should not belittle another
group; perhaps they are better than them. Nor should women
belittle other women; perhaps they are better than them. Do not
defame each other and do not call each other insulting nicknames;
evil is a name of iniquity after having attained faith. Whoever does
not repent of such things is among the oppressors.
O you who believe! Avoid being very suspicious; much suspicion is a
sin. Do not spy and do not backbite one another – would any of you like
to eat the dead flesh of his brother? You would hate it. So be conscious
of God; verily God is Accepting of Repentance, Compassionate.
O you people! We have created you from a male and a female and have
made you into nations and tribes so that you can know one another.
Verily the most honored of you in the sight of God is the most pious;
verily God is All-Knowing, Completely Aware.

(Hujarat; 49:10–13)

In this struggle to build a righteous community, men and women are partners in faith:

The believing men and the believing women are friends of each other.
They enjoin the right and forbid the wrong, they establish prayer
and give zakat and they obey God and His messenger.

These are the ones to whom God will show mercy; verily God is Eminent, Wise.

(Tawba; 9:71)

The spiritual equality of men and women is unequivocally affirmed in the following passage, which is said to have been revealed after a female companion of the Prophet expressed concern that the Qur'an spoke primarily to and about men. It should be noted that this passage has a lovely aural effect, with the Arabic masculine and feminine forms of the characteristics (*al-muslimina/al-muslimati, al-mu'minina/al-mu'minati,* etc.) alternating in a gentle rhythm:

Indeed the Muslim men and the Muslim women,
and the believing men and the believing women,
and the devout men and the devout women,
and the honest men and the honest women,
and the patient men and the patient women,
and the humble men and the humble women,
and the charitable men and the charitable women,
and the fasting men and the fasting women,
and the chaste men and the chaste women,
and the men who remember God frequently and the women who remember
– for them, God has prepared forgiveness and a magnificent reward.

(Ahzab; 33:35)

The Qur'an recognizes sexual desire and attraction between men and women as a reality that needs to be taken into account within the faith community. The Qur'an does not view sexuality negatively, but presents marital love as a sign of God (see above Rum; 30:21). Sexual attraction between men and women who are not married to each other, however, can lead to illicit relationships and the destruction of families and friendships. The Qur'an, therefore, gives a few basic rules for gender interaction:

Tell the believing men to lower their eyes and to protect their private parts; that will be most conducive to their purity; verily God is Completely Aware of what they do.
And tell the believing women to lower their eyes, to protect their private parts and to refrain from displaying their beauty – except what is apparent – and to draw their veils over their bosoms.
They should not display their beauty except to their husbands or their fathers or their fathers-in-law or their sons or their step-sons or their brothers or their brother's sons or their sister's sons or their

women or their slaves or their male servants who lack sexual desire
or boys who are as yet unaware of women's sexuality. They should
not walk in a way that draws attention to their hidden beauty.
And all of you – O believers – should turn in repentance to God so
you might attain success.

(Nur; 24:30–31)

'A'isha, the wife of the Prophet Muhammad, said, "God have mercy on the Emigrant women; when God revealed '– *and draw their veils over their bosoms*,' they tore their wraps to make veils out of them."[37]

These verses form the basis for notions of propriety that would be adopted by diverse peoples who embraced Islam over the centuries. Women would wear some kind of head-covering and modest dress, pious men would respect women by diverting their gazes away from their faces and bodies, and while a relaxed, intimate setting would be created in the home among family, in the public sphere, men and women would restrain their sensuality.

These notions of propriety, however, had to be embraced with conviction for them to have the desired effect. The Qur'an speaks about "hypocrites" in Medina who subverted these and other guidelines designed to create a harmonious community. One way these individuals tried to hurt the Prophet was by hurting his wives. After his long monogamous marriage ended with Khadija's death, the Prophet married a number of women, as polygamy was not uncommon among the pre-Islamic Arabs (nor among the pre-Islamic Hebrew prophets). These marriages served to bind the community closer, as diverse clans and families became related through marriage to the Prophet. Consequently, when some individuals began circulating a rumor that the Prophet's wife 'A'isha had deliberately stayed back when her caravan had moved on, in the desire to be alone with the young man who eventually found her and brought her back to the group, the whole community was upset.

When the Prophet heard the rumor, he came to 'A'isha and said, "If you are innocent, then God will declare your innocence, but if you have committed a sin, then ask for God's forgiveness and repent to Him." Although the Prophet was hurt by the rumor, he did not make this an issue of his "honor" (as later men in some Muslim cultures would) but indicated that this was a matter between his wife and God. 'A'isha's response was equally remarkable; she refered to the Qur'anic story of Joseph saying, "By God, I find no example for my case except that of Joseph's father (who said), '*Verily patience is beautiful*' (Yusuf; 12:18).'' Just after 'A'isha invoked this Qur'anic reference, God responded to her situation with another revelation:

> *Verily those who spread slander are a group from amongst you. Do not consider this evil for you (who are slandered). Rather, it is good for you, for every man from that group will get the sin he has earned, and the one who leads in spreading the slander will have a mighty punishment.*
>
> *If only when they heard (the slander) the believing men and the believing women had thought good about each other and said, "This is evident slander."*
>
> *If only they had called for four witnesses, and if (the group) had not brought forth the witnesses, then they would have been the liars, according to God.*
>
> *If it were not for the grace of God and His mercy upon you in this world and the next, you would have been subject to a mighty punishment for rushing into this.*

(Nur; 24:11–14)

As with Khawla before her, God responded to 'A'isha in her time of need with verses that would help her individually, but that would also remain foundational sources of law and morality in their status as the living words of the eternal God. The Qur'an established the rule that any accusation of sexual impropriety without four witnesses is deemed punishable slander. In later generations, jurists would work out the details regarding the application of this rule: did a specific accusation of fornication need to be made, or was a public insinuation sufficient? Did the rule apply to men as well as women accused of sexual impropriety? What if the accusation was made in writing? Further, prosecution of the offense of slander, like the prosecution of any crime, depended on a functioning and reliable judiciary, as well as the political will to support such rulings with necessary force.

Over the centuries, Muslim societies would variously succeed and fail at developing the legal and political institutions needed to enforce a just application of the norms and principles found in the Qur'an. In every generation, the eternal words of the Qur'an would remain a source of guidance and direction, as they had been when they were first revealed to the Prophet Muhammad and his community. The understanding and application of these words, however, would differ, often quite dramatically, according to the cultural and historical circumstances of the interpreting communities.

A Door to Heaven is Closed

Approximately one-third of the Qur'an was revealed during the ten years of the Medinan period. Included in this revelation are the three longest suras of the Qur'an, comprising approximately one-sixth of the written scripture. In this chapter, we have been able to highlight only a few of the major themes of the Qur'anic revelation, as well as some aspects of the cultural and historical context in which the Prophet Muhammad received these revelations. In another chapter, when we examine different methods and schools of Qur'an interpretation, we will discuss some other verses we have not mentioned, in particular, those of a legal nature.

In 632 CE, ten years after the *hijra*, the Prophet Muhammad died after a short illness. When the passionate and emotional 'Umar ibn al-Khattab heard people saying that the Prophet had died, he could not believe it, and angrily told them that it was impossible for this to happen. He said, "By God, he is not dead. He has gone to his Lord just as Moses ibn 'Imran went away and was hidden from his people for forty days, returning to them after it was said that he had died." At that point, Abu Bakr, the Prophet's close friend, entered the room of his daughter 'A'isha, in whose arms the Prophet died, and kissed the Prophet's face. Then Abu Bakr went into the mosque and said to the assembled congregation, "O people: if anyone worships Muhammad, Muhammad is dead. If anyone worships God, God is alive, immortal." Then he quoted this verse from the Qur'an:

> *Muhammad is no more than a messenger; messengers before him have passed away. If he were to die or were killed, would you turn back on your heels? Whoever turns back on his heels will not cause any harm to God, but God will reward the grateful.*
>
> (Al 'Imran; 3:144)

At this, 'Umar said, "By God, when I heard Abu Bakr recite these words I was so shocked that my legs could not bear me and I fell to the ground, knowing that the Prophet was indeed dead."

This was the first time a verse of the Qur'an had been recited without it being possible to go to the Prophet for confirmation or clarification of its meaning. And now, with the death of the Prophet, the revelations ceased.

There is a story that sometime later, Abu Bakr and 'Umar went to visit an elderly woman with whom the Prophet had been very close. Umm Ayman had been like a mother to the Prophet, having nursed him when he was young. The Prophet often used to visit her, so the two close companions of the Prophet considered it their honor and duty to do the same. It was during that visit that Umm Ayman expressed a sentiment that no doubt was shared by the whole Muslim community following the death of the Prophet:

> When (Abu Bakr and 'Umar) came to her, she started crying. They said to her, "Why are you crying? What is in store with God is better for His Messenger." She replied, "I am not crying because I am unaware that what is in store with God is better for His Messenger! I am crying because the revelation from heaven has been cut off." This moved both of them to tears and they began crying with her.[38]

Notes

1 Most notably, the documents analyzed by Nabia Abbott in her *Studies in Arabic Literary Papyri*, 3 vols. (Chicago: University of Chicago Oriental Institute Publications; vols. 75–77, 1957–1972).

2 A detailed analysis of this development and the emergence of the science of hadith is found in M. M. Azami, *Studies in Early Hadith Literature* (Indianapolis:
American Trust Publications, 1978). Fred M. Donner analyzes the theme of civil disorder (*fitna*) in his *Narratives of Islamic Origins: The Beginnings of Islamic Historical Writing* (Princeton: Darwin Press, 1998), 184–190.

3 Scott C. Lucas, *Constructive Critics, Hadith Literature, and the Articulation of Sunni Islam: The Legacy of the Generation of Ibn Sa'd, Ibn Ma'in, and Ibn Hanbal* (Leiden: Brill, 2004).

4 Malik ibn Anas, *al-Muwatta* [compilation of Yahya ibn Yahya al-Laythi], translated by 'A'isha 'Abdarahman and Ya'qub Johnson (Norwich, UK: Diwan Press, 1982), 51.

5 Some of this research can be found in Harald Motzki, ed., *Hadith: Origins and Developments* (Burlington, VT: Ashgate/Variorum, 2004).

6 A good overview of the modernists' approach to hadith is Daniel Brown's *Rethinking Tradition in Modern Islamic Thought* (Cambridge: Cambridge University Press, 1996).

7 Donner, *Narratives*, 276.

8   Donner, *Narratives*, 20–31.
9   Suyuti, 1:54–55.
10   Bukhari, *"Kitab al-Tafsir,"* 1063.
11   Issa J. Boullata, "Literary Structures," in *Encyclopedia of the Qur'an*, 5 vols., gen. ed. Jane Damen McAuliffe (Leiden: Brill, 2001–2006), 3:198. Henceforth, this work will be referenced as follows: *EQ*.
12   Ibn Hisham, 121.
13   Muslim, *"Kitab al-Salat,"* 4:105.
14   See Umar Faruq Abd-Allah, "One God, Many Names," a Nawawi Foundation paper, published online: www.nawawi.org/downloads/article2.pdf. Abd-Allah points out that just before the rise of Islam, Christian missionaries in northern Europe were redefining the pre-Christian term "god" in accordance with their theology.
15   Incidentally, this should give pause to those who, on the basis of minimal material evidence found in prehistoric cultures, draw the conclusion that goddess worship or the recognition of female deities is associated with an elevated social status for women. Indications from pre-Islamic Arabia show that such an association does not necessarily entail.
16   Abdal-Hakim Murad, "The Trinity: A Muslim Perspective," lecture given "to a group of Christians in Oxford, 1996," published on www.masud.co.uk/ISLAM/ahm/trinity.htm.
17   In translating these attributes I rely heavily upon the superb translation of Abu Hamid al-Ghazali's commentary on the attributes of God by David B. Burrell and Nazih Daher, entitled *The Ninety-Nine Beautiful Names of God: al-Maqsad al-asna fi sharh asma' Allah al-husna* (Cambridge: Islamic Texts Society, 1992).
18   The following article is an extensive study of *iltifat*: Muhammad A. S. Abdel Haleem, "Grammatical Shift for the Rhetorical Purposes: Iltifat and Related Features in the Qur'an," *Bulletin of the School of Oriental and African Studies*, LV, 3 (1992): 407–432.
19   L. Gardet, "Allah," in *Encyclopedia of Islam*, 2nd ed., ed. P. J. Bearman, Th. Bianquis, C. E. Bosworth, E. van Donzel, W. P. Heinrichs et al., 12 vols. with indexes (Leiden: Brill, 1960–2005). Henceforth, this work will be referenced by the following: *EI2*.
20   Ibn Hisham, 114.
21   Oliver Leaman, *An Introduction to Medieval Islamic Philosophy* (Cambridge: Cambridge University Press, 1985), 17.
22   Fazlur Rahman, *Major Themes of the Qur'an* (Minneapolis: Bibliotheca Islamica, 1980), 106.
23   Michael Sells, *Approaching the Qur'an: The Early Revelations* (Ashland, Oregon: White Cloud Press, 1999), 16.

24   Toshihiko Izutsu, *God and Man in the Qur'an: Semantics of the Qur'anic Weltanschauung* (Kuala Lumpur: Islamic Book Trust, 2002; reprint of 1964 Keio University publication), 254–258.
25   Rahman, *Major Themes*, 82. This position is strengthened by the fact that this chronology of the prophets is given in Meccan suras (Al-A'raf (7) and Hud (11)) before the Prophet Muhammad emigrated to Medina, where greater attention to the biblical tradition had to be given due to the presence of a significant Jewish population.
26   Ibn Hisham, 156–157.
27   This hadith does not have the strongest rating of authenticity but perhaps still gives us some insight into the situation in Mecca. Ibn Hisham, 165.
28   Shahab Ahmed, "Ibn Taymiyyah and the Satanic Verses," *Studia Islamica*, 87 (1998): 67–124.
29   Ibn Hisham, 143–144.
30   Ibn Hisham, 145.
31   Ibn Hisham, 145.
32   Ibn Hisham, 191.
33   This is one issue over which most Sunni and Shi'ite scholars disagree. The former say that available reports indicate that Abu Talib died staying true to the creed of his ancestors. The latter, eager to elevate the status of the father of their Imam, 'Ali (the son of Abu Talib), declared that Abu Talib had secretly converted to Islam before his death. The problem with such claims is that the historian has no tools to verify claims of secret activities and motives. Shi'ite scholars, according to their methodology, can accept such claims as factual if they are made by an infallible imam. Sunni scholars reject these claims of esoteric knowledge.
34   Ibn Hisham, 231.
35   For example, the Medinan Jew Mukhayriq was killed at the Battle of Uhud in which he fought, despite the fact that it was the Sabbath, in order to fulfill the commitment the Jews had made to defend Medina under the leadership of Muhammad. Ibn Hisham, 384.
36   Fred Donner, "From Believers to Muslims: Patterns of Communal Identity in Early Islam," *Al-Abhath*, 50–51 (2002–2003): 9–53.
37   Bukhari, "*Kitab al-Tafsir*," 1010.
38   Muslim, "*Kitab Fada'il al-Sahaba*," 16:9–10.

3

The Voice and the Pen

A Sacred Pedigree

On August 7, 2002, a seventeen-year-old American girl named Reem stood in front of a curtain in a humble home on the outskirts of Damascus.[1] Behind the curtain lay an elderly man, feeble of body but sharp of mind. Sheikh Abu'l-Hasan Muhyi'l-Din al-Kurdi had survived the twentieth century, a time of great social change and political upheaval in his native Syria. Most of his educated compatriots, even those religiously inclined, had considered political struggle the priority of their age. Over the decades, the focus of the struggle had changed, and these men became familiar with all the ideologies of the century: colonialism, nationalism, Marxism, capitalism, Arabism, militarism, Zionism, imperialism, secularism, and Islamism. Amidst all the turmoil and confusion, Sheikh al-Kurdi had remained focused on one goal: to fulfill his sacred duty to transmit the Qur'an to another generation. He was the twenty-eighth person in a golden chain of transmission from the Prophet Muhammad. By now, nearing the end of the eighth decade of his life, he had built the twenty-ninth generation, connecting thousands of men and women to this sacred pedigree.

Throughout her young life, Reem had loved to study the Qur'an. It was important to her parents, religious physicians who had immigrated from Syria to the United States for a life free of political oppression and economic insecurity. They enrolled their daughter in a parochial Muslim school, where she studied the standard Illinois elementary and secondary school curriculum supplemented with Islamic Studies, Arabic, and Qur'an. Reem dreamed that one day she would memorize the whole Qur'an and worked hard to accomplish that goal, studying with tutors on weekends and after school. By the age of twelve she had recited the complete Qur'an from memory, section by section, to her teachers. This was a remarkable achievement. Reciting at a moderate pace, it would take at least a full day and night – twenty-four hours – to recite the whole Qur'an. But Reem was not satisfied with her accomplishment. She wanted to know that her recitation was a perfect replication of the Prophet's words as he repeated the revelation back to the Angel Gabriel. To attain that level of certainty she needed to earn an *ijaza* (certificate) from a Qur'an scholar with a solid *isnad* (chain), so she sought out Sheikh al-Kurdi.

It would take Reem a number of years of hard work before she would have her chance to be heard by the widely sought, eminent scholar. She was attending high school in the United States, so she could only study in Damascus during her summer vacations. There she was assigned a female Reciter (*muqri'a*) who would teach her the advanced rules of *tajwid* (beautiful recitation) and make sure that her memorization of the Qur'an was flawless. Madam Hala was a middle-aged working professional who had devoted her free time to teaching the Qur'an ever since she had herself earned an *ijaza* from the Sheikh when she was a teenager.

Every day Reem met with her teacher, who guided her to a deeper and more complete mastery of the sacred book. First, although Reem knew the basics of *tajwid*, there was much more to learn. Madam Hala gave her a copy of a famous medieval poem listing the rules of *tajwid*, the *Jazariyya*. Reem was told to memorize the obscure verses, understand them, then work to apply the rules to the Qur'an. Next, although Reem had already memorized the Qur'an in sections, she had not fully retained all of it. To earn her certificate, she had to prove that she knew every verse by heart. Reem was also keen to deepen her understanding of the holy book, so she worked her way methodically through the suras, reading English translations and Arabic commentaries which she used to annotate her text of the Qur'an (*mushaf*).

For three summers, Madam Hala worked with Reem, teaching and testing her on her *tajwid*, memorization, and comprehension. Through a rigorous process of examination called "probing (*sabr*)," Reem's memorization was verified again and again. The teacher meticulously documented her progress, writing the date and outcome of each test in a special notebook. Finally, when she was confident that Reem was ready, she took her to another woman who had been appointed by the Sheikh to administer a final test to female students before they could be brought to him for certification. This woman, who happened to be Madam Hala's mother, had been certified as a "Comprehensive-Reciter" (*muqri'a* jami‘a) by the Sheikh. This meant that she had mastered not just one recitation (qira‘a) of the Qur'an, but all ten orthodox recitations. Astonishingly, she had achieved this highest level of mastery of the Qur'an while also earning a doctoral degree in mathematics and pursuing an academic career.

Dr. Daad (as Madam Hala's mother was known) pushed Reem hard on her memorization and recitation. She verified that Reem had completely mastered the text as well as the rules of tajwid, but she also counseled her to prepare spiritually and mentally for the short time she would have with the Sheikh to prove herself. In the end, success comes from God, and even an accomplished reciter could find herself faltering if she had been negligent in attending to her religious duties and spiritual state before the test.

Finally, when Reem was ready, she was taken to the house where she would be tested. When she arrived, Reem found a number of girls sitting in a plain room, awaiting their examination. Reem watched as the girls, one by one, approached a curtain, behind which sat the Sheikh. Sometimes a gap in the fabric allowed them to catch a glimpse of the elderly man seated on a day bed, alert, but obviously weak. Reem knew that the curtain served to protect the dignity of the frail scholar as much as it preserved traditional norms of modest interaction between men and women. Nevertheless, she sympathized with the girl who, upon completing her recitation, pulled open the drapes and said, "O Sheikh, I just want to see you!"[2]

Reem noticed that some of the girls, perhaps because of nervousness or awe, had recited their selections in a low voice, making it difficult to verify their mastery of the rules. Even though they all had proven themselves to their appointed teachers before submitting to this final exam, some of the girls left the house without being granted certification. When it was her turn, Reem recited in a loud, clear voice, just as she had been taught by her teachers. The Sheikh asked her to recite various passages, after which he told her to recite Sura al-Fath. Reem's teachers later told her that it was rare for the Sheikh to ask anyone to recite this sura, and that it was a sign that he believed she had been given a spiritual "opening" (fath) from God. Reem was then tested on the meanings of various Qur'anic terms and the rules of the Jaziriyya. Finally, the Sheikh said, "That is sufficient (hasbuki)," and Reem returned to the waiting area. After consulting with the Sheikh, Reem's teachers approached her with a large document; she had been awarded the ijaza.

A few days later, Reem met with her teachers, who sat with her to explain the meaning of the certificate. The document is titled, "Certificate in the Noble Qur'an in the recitation of Hafs by the Shatibi path." This means that Reem is certified in the recitation of the second-/eighth-century scholar Hafs ibn Sulayman, whose recitation is now the most popular of the ten orthodox recitations. The "Shatibi path" means that Hafs's recitation was transmitted through a particular chain of scholars until it reached the famous sixth-/twelfth-century scholar al-Qasim ibn Firruh al-Shatibi. Each "path" of recitation is distinguished by its emphasis on certain aspects of recitation, as well as points of etiquette while reciting.

Next, the certificate opens with customary prayers of praise and supplication, and then mentions a number of hadith praising those people who memorize and recite the Qur'an. Then there is a statement by Madam Hala:

> I am among those to whom God, who is exalted, has been generous with the benefaction of the glorious Qur'an through memorization and *tajwid*. I have recited a complete *khatma* (recitation of the entire Qur'an from beginning to end) with *tajwid* and mastery according to the recitation of Hafs from 'Asim and after being examined, I was witnessed by Sheikh al-Hafiz the Comprehensive-Reciter the Scholar Abu'l-Hasan Muhyi'l-Din al-Kurdi. I sought his certification (*ijaza*) and he certified me in the recitation of Hafs only.

Next the certificate gives the name of the scholar from whom Sheikh al-Kurdi was certified, and the chain continues back over twenty-seven generations until it reaches five different Companions (see chart in Figure 3.1), who took their recitation from:

> ...the Possessor of elevated rank and majesty, the locus of divine inspiration and the message, the seal of the prophets and Imam of the messengers, the commander of the noble radiant-ones, our master and our intercessor Abu'l-Qasim Muhammad ibn 'Abdullah, God's prayers and blessing be upon him, from the Imam of the select angels and the trustworthy spirit our master Gabriel, peace be upon him, from the Lord of Glory, blessed and exalted is He, sublime is His majesty, boundless are His gifts, elevated is His dignity, lofty is His praise, holy are His names, there is no God but He.

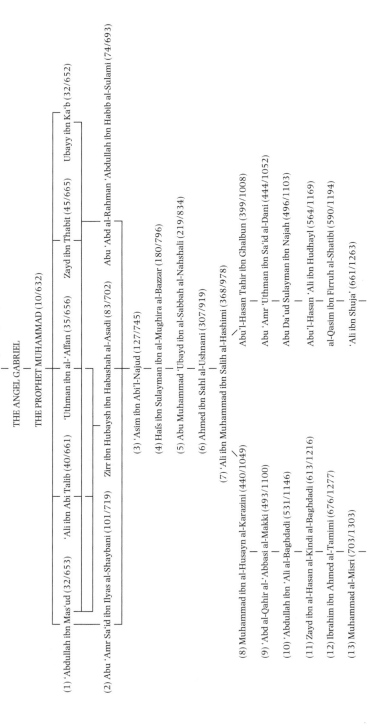

THE LORD OF MAJESTY (GOD)

THE ANGEL GABRIEL

THE PROPHET MUHAMMAD (10/632)

'Uthman ibn al-'Affan (35/656)   Zayd ibn Thabit (45/665)   Ubayy ibn Ka'b (32/652)

'Ali ibn Abi Talib (40/661)

(1) 'Abdullah ibn Mas'ud (32/653)

(2) Abu 'Amr Sa'id ibn Ilyas al-Shaybani (101/719)

Zirr ibn Hubaysh ibn Habashah al-Asadi (83/702)   Abu 'Abd al-Rahman 'Abdullah ibn Habib al-Sulami (74/693)

(3) 'Asim ibn Abi'l-Najud (127/745)

(4) Hafs ibn Sulayman ibn al-Mughira al-Bazzar (180/796)

(5) Abu Muhammad 'Ubayd ibn al-Sabbah al-Nahshali (219/834)

(6) Ahmed ibn Sahl al-Ushnani (307/919)

(7) 'Ali ibn Muhammad ibn Salih al-Hashimi (368/978)

(8) Muhammad ibn al-Husayn al-Karazini (440/1049)   Abu'l-Hasan Tahir ibn Ghalbun (399/1008)

(9) 'Abd al-Qahir al-'Abbasi al-Makki (493/1100)   Abu 'Amr 'Uthman ibn Sa'id al-Dani (444/1052)

(10) 'Abdullah ibn 'Ali al-Baghdadi (531/1146)   Abu Da'ud Sulayman ibn Najah (496/1103)

(11) Zayd ibn al-Hasan al-Kindi al-Baghdadi (613/1216)   Abu'l-Hasan 'Ali ibn Hudhayl (564/1169)

(12) Ibrahim ibn Ahmed al-Tamimi (676/1277)   al-Qasim ibn Firruh al-Shatibi (590/1194)

(13) Muhammad al-Misri (703/1303)   'Ali ibn Shuja' (661/1263)

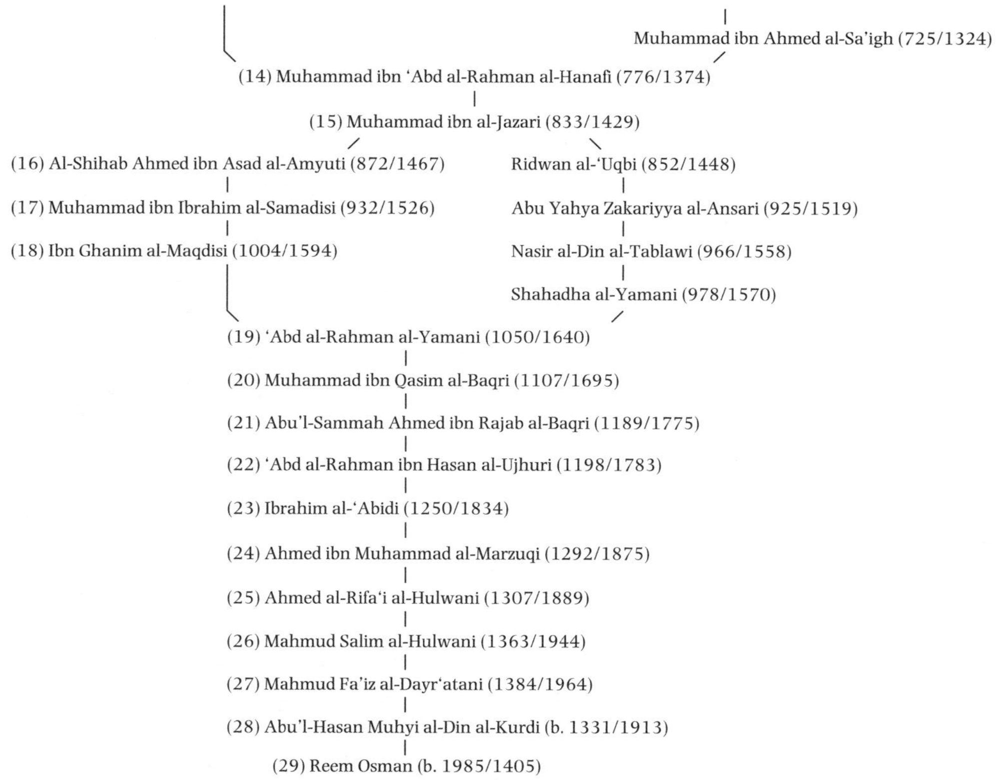

Muhammad ibn Ahmed al-Sa'igh (725/1324)

(14) Muhammad ibn 'Abd al-Rahman al-Hanafi (776/1374)

(15) Muhammad ibn al-Jazari (833/1429)

Ridwan al-'Uqbi (852/1448)

Abu Yahya Zakariyya al-Ansari (925/1519)

Nasir al-Din al-Tablawi (966/1558)

Shahadha al-Yamani (978/1570)

(16) Al-Shihab Ahmed ibn Asad al-Amyuti (872/1467)

(17) Muhammad ibn Ibrahim al-Samadisi (932/1526)

(18) Ibn Ghanim al-Maqdisi (1004/1594)

(19) 'Abd al-Rahman al-Yamani (1050/1640)

(20) Muhammad ibn Qasim al-Baqri (1107/1695)

(21) Abu'l-Sammah Ahmed ibn Rajab al-Baqri (1189/1775)

(22) 'Abd al-Rahman ibn Hasan al-Ujhuri (1198/1783)

(23) Ibrahim al-'Abidi (1250/1834)

(24) Ahmed ibn Muhammad al-Marzuqi (1292/1875)

(25) Ahmed al-Rifa'i al-Hulwani (1307/1889)

(26) Mahmud Salim al-Hulwani (1363/1944)

(27) Mahmud Fa'iz al-Dayr'atani (1384/1964)

(28) Abu'l-Hasan Muhyi al-Din al-Kurdi (b. 1331/1913)

(29) Reem Osman (b. 1985/1405)

Figure 3.1 Isnad for Reem's *ijaza*. The links in the shortest paths of the chain are numbered to show Reem as the 29th link from the Prophet Muhammad.

Finally, the certificate states that Reem has memorized the Qur'an with mastery and *tajwid*, that she was examined in this, that the Sheikh witnessed for her, and has certified her to recite and teach the Qur'an according to the recitation of Hafs. She is exhorted to never turn away without reason any student who wishes to learn Qur'an, and to say a prayer for her teacher each time she begins or finishes a *khatma*. The certificate ends with advice for Reem to stay serious about teaching and studying the Qur'an and to try to master all ten orthodox recitations. Finally, there are prayers for Reem that through the Qur'an she will be rewarded by God and will be of benefit to others. The certificate is signed by Madam Hala and Dr. Daad and is witnessed by Sheikh al-Kurdi.

The Word of God

The Qur'an continues to be recited in Arabic by Muslims because they believe it to be the "word of God." Certainly this phrase has meant different things to different groups of Muslims throughout history. All groups are in agreement, nonetheless, that the Qur'an does not contain the words of Muhammad – he neither composed the Qur'an nor is the Qur'an his attempt to put into words a perception of the Divine. The words of the Qur'an are God's words; any translation of the Qur'an is no more than an interpretation of the scripture. Consequently, *ijazas* for memorization and *tajwid* of the Qur'an, such as Sheikh al-Kurdi's, do not end with the Prophet Muhammad, but continue to the Angel Gabriel and then into the heavenly realm to "the Lord of Majesty" (*rabb al-'izza*).

It is for this reason that there are tens of thousands of Muslims living today who, like Reem, seek a sound *isnad* – a solid chain of transmission – for their recitation and memorization of the Qur'an. The *isnad* represents a spiritual pedigree that brings the transcendent God very close indeed. The Qur'an states that God is closer to a human "than his jugular vein" (5:16). In reciting the Qur'an, the very words of God are reproduced in the throats of the reciters and perceived in the ears and minds of listeners. With each articulation of a Qur'anic phrase, the believer is recreating speech of a God who is as alive today as he has been forever. This is not a performance of historical speech but a rearticulation of the eternal words of the living God.

Figure 3.2   American Dawood Yasin and his wife, an accomplished Qur'an reciter, spent a number of years in Damascus at an Islamic seminary. Here Imam Dawood instructs his daughter Hafsa in Qur'anic Arabic. (Jason Ilyas Curtis)

The oral dimension of the certification process of mastery of the Qur'an is significant. Memorization certificates make no reference to a written text of the Qur'an, but rather to the particular recitation which the student has mastered. Authentication of the recitation is determined by a teacher who has memorized the Qur'an and mastered its recitation – a Hafiz and a Muqri' – who, in turn, has had his or her recitation authenticated by another scholar in a chain of authentication reaching back to the Prophet. This is not to say that the written text of the Qur'an, the *mushaf*, is not employed in the learning process. However, the traditional certification process never certifies mastery of a book, but a recitation. Indeed, it is only a group of certified scholars who can authenticate a printed text of the Qur'an.

In his study of the oral dimension of scripture, William Graham has noted that "speech always precedes writing, cosmically and anthropologically as well as historically."[3] Certainly at the heart of the story of the Qur'an is the use first of the voice and then of the pen to ever more perfectly transmit God's words. The first verses of the Qur'an revealed to the Prophet Muhammad signal that these words must be transmitted both orally and textually:

> *Recite in the name of your Lord who created –*
> *Created humans from a clot of blood*
> *Recite, for your Lord is most Generous*
> *It is He who taught with the pen*
> *Taught them what they did not know before.*
>
> ('Alaq; 96:1–5)

Recitation precedes writing and has been the privileged means by which the Qur'an has been preserved and transmitted from the time of the Prophet Muhammad until today. This does not mean that writing has not also played a critical role in the preservation and transmission of the Qur'an, for although the Qur'an must be "recited," the "generous"

Figure 3.3 Children at a school in Dallas, Texas, sing at their year-end graduation. The children learn Arabic and memorize Qur'an as well as study the state curriculum.

Lord has also provided humanity with the ability to write down what has been revealed. Indeed, Muslims realized soon after the death of the Prophet Muhammad that writing was an important tool for ensuring the integrity of the revelation. Over time, more and more textual signifiers were employed to make the written Qur'an a book that could be independently read. This was a natural development given that the Qur'an presents itself as one of a series of books (*kutub*) revealed by God to his prophets. Nevertheless, oral teaching and transmission of the Qur'an could never be neglected. It is only through oral teaching that all aspects of *tajwid*, as well as more subtle qualities of recitation such as pitch and tempo, can be transmitted.

The Prophet and the First Collection of the Qur'an

In the earthly realm, the Prophet Muhammad is the first reciter and transmitter of the Qur'an. Previously we discussed the Prophet's subjective experience of revelation, including the different ways he encountered the Angel Gabriel. The Prophet is reported to have said that, in addition to the times when Gabriel delivered a new revelation to him, the angel also visited him to review what he had learned, and that in the final year of his life, Gabriel visited him twice to review the revelations. The message of this hadith is that the Prophet did not just convey the meaning of what was revealed to him, but the very words sent by God through Gabriel. This process of review took place specifically during the sacred month of Ramadan, a time during which the Qur'an was "sent down":

> It is the month of Ramadan during which we revealed the Qur'an
> As a guide to humanity and clarification of guidance and a criterion.
> (Baqara; 2:185)

The Qur'an refers to various aspects of its mode of revelation which facilitated its understanding and memorization by the Prophet and his Companions. First, the Qur'an was revealed in the Prophet's "own tongue," that is, in the Arabic language and in the Qurayshi dialect:

> Thus We made the Qur'an easy in your own tongue, so that with it
> you might give good news to the righteous, and warn a people given
> to contention.
> (Maryam; 19:97)

In addition, as we have already discussed, the language of the Qur'an is often rhythmic, almost poetic, making the verses easy to remember. The Qur'an should be recited in a pleasant voice and at an easy pace to take full advantage of these aural devices:

> ... and recite the Qur'an in slow, measured rhythmic tones.
>
> (Muzammil; 73:4)

Finally, the Qur'an was revealed little by little over twenty-three years, giving time and opportunity for the Companions to learn and memorize new verses before others were revealed:

> It is a Qur'an which we have divided so you can recite it to people in intervals and we have revealed it in stages.
>
> (Isra'; 17:106)

Because the Qur'an had to be recited aloud in most of the daily prayers and during nightly devotions, there were many opportunities for those who prayed with the Prophet to passively learn new verses or to reinforce verses they had already learned. Umm Hisham, a female Companion, reported that she memorized Sura Qaf only because the Prophet used to recite it every Friday in his sermon.[4]

'Abdullah ibn al-'Abbas (Ibn 'Abbas), the Prophet's younger cousin who was to become a prominent interpreter of the Qur'an, recalled one of the many opportunities he had to listen to the Prophet's recitation. One time, when he was a young boy, he slept in the small room of his aunt Maimuna, who was one of the Prophet's wives.

> I lay across the width of the cushion while God's Messenger and his wife lay across its length. God's Messenger slept until midnight or a little before or after that, then he woke up. He wiped the sleep from his face with his hands and recited the last ten verses of Sura Al 'Imran. Then he got up and went to the hanging waterskin and made ablutions – making his ablutions perfectly – then he got up and started praying. So I got up and did what he had done and stood at his side. The Messenger of God put his right hand on my head and grabbed my right ear and tweaked it. He prayed two rak'at (cycles of prayer), then two rak'at, then two rak'at, then two rak'at, then two rak'at, then two rak'at, then a single cycle of prayer (witr). Then he lay down until the Mu'adhdhin (prayer caller) came to

him and he got up, prayed two light *rak'at*, then went (into the mosque) where he led the dawn prayer.[5]

In each cycle of prayer, the Prophet would have recited aloud a passage of the Qur'an; other reports indicate that it was his practice to recite long passages in the night. In this one night then, Ibn 'Abbas had the opportunity to listen to the Prophet recite thirteen lengthy passages of the Qur'an, and then another two passages in the congregational dawn prayer.

It is apparent from this and other reports that Qur'an recitation, especially in the Meccan period, when there were few ritual or legal obligations other than abstinence from idol worship, was the hallmark of Muslim religious life. Most reports mention that when the Prophet spoke to potential converts about Islam, he recited Qur'an to them. Into the Medinan period, as Islam began to spread faster, the Prophet considered instruction in the Qur'an a priority for new converts and communities.[6]

After the Pledge of 'Aqaba, the Prophet sent some of his Companions to Medina to teach the Qur'an to the Muslims there. In this report, the Medinan Companion al-Bara' says that he learned a number of suras before the Prophet made *hijra* there:

> The first of the Companions of the Prophet who came to us were Mus'ab ibn 'Umayr and Ibn Umm Makhtum, and they started teaching us the Qur'an. Then 'Ammar, Bilal and Sa'd came as well. Afterwards 'Umar ibn al-Khattab came along with a group of twenty people; after that the Prophet came. I never saw the people of Medina so happy about anything as they were with his arrival, so that even the little boys and girls were saying, "This is the Messenger of God who has come!" He did not come to us until I was able to recite *Glorify the name of your Lord the Most High* (Sura al-'Ala) and other similar suras.[7]

During his ten years in Medina, the Prophet continued his practice of appointing certain individuals to teach the Qur'an to new Muslims. At the same time, it is likely that most of the converts during the time of the Prophet, like most Muslims in later times, did not memorize much of the Qur'an, and probably knew no more than a dozen shorter suras.[8] However, some Companions were deliberate in memorizing new verses and were particularly encouraged by the Prophet to master the recitation.

There is a report, for example, that the Prophet said to Ubayy ibn Ka'b, "God has commanded me to recite the Qur'an to you." Ubayy said, "God mentioned my name to you?!" The Prophet responded, "God has mentioned your name to me." At this, Ubayy began to shed tears of joy.[9]

In another hadith, the Prophet Muhammad is reported to have said to Abdullah ibn Mas'ud, "Recite to me." Ibn Mas'ud responded, "You want me to recite when you are the one who receives the revelation?" The Prophet said, "I like to hear it from someone other than myself." So Ibn Mas'ud began reciting from Sura al-Nisa' until he came to the verse:

> How would it be if we brought forth a witness from every community
> and we brought you forth to witness against these people.
>
> (Nisa'; 4:41)

Ibn Mas'ud said, "I saw tears in his eyes and he said to me, 'That is sufficient.'"

It should be recalled that these words, "That is sufficient," were said by Sheikh al-Kurdi to Reem to indicate that she could stop her recitation to him. Indeed, it is because of their desire to imitate the pedagogical methodology of the Prophet that it is customary for Qur'an teachers to use this phrase with their students. It is for this reason that the third-/ninth-century scholar Ahmed ibn Shu'ayb al-Nasa'i (d. 303/915) included this hadith in his book, *The Merits of the Qur'an*.[10]

The ability of many in the Prophet's community to memorize long Qur'anic passages is not surprising to scholars familiar with communication in oral societies. Most people know from common experience that even in a society like contemporary America, in which writing and textual documentation predominate, ordinary people memorize a great deal of information, including personal identification numbers, important dates and anniversaries of family members, dozens of telephone numbers and addresses, sports statistics, the names and capitals of states, American presidents, etc. In a society like seventh-century Arabia, in which writing was not well developed, it was even more common and important to memorize large amounts of information about genealogy, history, and culture. Versification greatly aids memorization, which is why much of this information in the pre-Islamic period was preserved by the Arabs in poetic form. It was therefore easy and natural for them to memorize Qur'anic verses as they were revealed over time.

Although oral communication was the primary means by which information was transmitted during the period of revelation, writing was not unknown; indeed, it played a significant supplementary role in Arabian society at that time, and frequent references to writing in the Qur'an are evidence of this fact. For example, the binding nature of moral and legal obligations is signified by them being "written" (*kutiba*). In this respect, the Qur'an uses the Arabic word *kutiba 'ala* with the same literal and normative signification as the English word *prescribe*, which comes from the Latin word "to write (*scribere*)." The Qur'an says, for example,

> *Fasting is prescribed for you (kutiba 'alaykum) just as it was prescribed for those before you so that you might become aware of God.*
>
> (Baqara; 2:183)

The notion of recording activities in detail is not foreign to the Qur'an, which refers to angelic beings who record every action of a person during his or her life. On the Day of Judgment, those persons who receive their book in their right hand will enter Paradise, while those who receive their book in the left hand will enter hell.

The Qur'an uses the term "writing" in a literal sense as well when it emphasizes, for example, the importance of putting certain types of agreements into writing:

> *O you who believe, when two parties make an agreement that involves incurring a debt for a fixed period of time, write it down. A scribe should accurately write the agreement between you. The scribe should not refuse to write as God has taught him how to do this; he should write (the document for them).*
>
> (Baqara; 2:282)

Finally, of course, the Qur'an speaks about itself as a "book" (*kitab*) or a "scripture" (i.e., a *writing*) and a major theme of the Qur'an is that this book has a place among other divine scriptures:

> *The Messenger believes in what has been revealed to him from his Lord and so do the believers. All of them believe in God, and His angels and His scriptures and His messengers –*
>
> (Baqara; 2:285)

At the same time, despite extensive references to writing in the Qur'an, it is evident that writing was neither the best nor easiest way to record and preserve communication at the rise of Islam. In the first place, writing materials were expensive and scarce. Still, this was not an insurmountable barrier. Before the invention of paper, parchment and vellum could be used to record important documents, and less elegant materials, like flat bones and pieces of wood, could also be used.

A more significant obstacle to preserving language in writing was the Arabic script itself, which, at this time, was quite rudimentary compared to its later development. In particular, there were many "homographs" in this script, that is, the same grapheme was used to signify different sounds. Although there is epigraphic evidence that,

Figure 3.4   Page of a second-/eighth-century Qur'an showing the end of Sura Shu'ara' (26) and the beginning of Sura Naml (27). (British Library Or. Ms. 2165, folio 76v–77)

even in the pre-Islamic period, dots and dashes were sometimes added to the graphemes to distinguish the different sounds, it was not until a few centuries later that it became common to do so. In addition, Arabic script was (and remains) an *abjad* (consonantal) system; it abbreviates words by omitting short vowels, doubled consonants, and inflectional endings. As Beatrice Gruendler notes, "Thus it can be read faster than alphabetic script, denoting both consonants and vowels, but it requires simultaneous linguistic reconstruction."[11] If we use Latin script to give a sense of what this means, the word "book" (*kitab*) would be written *ktb*. However, the same three-letter word could also signify "books" (*kutub*), "he wrote" (*kataba*), and "it was written" (*kutiba*).

What this means is that any writing of the Qur'an that was done during the time of the Prophet could not accurately be "read" by someone who did not already know what it said. To some extent, this writing was most effective as a mnemonic device for those who had already heard or memorized the recitation. At the same time, it should not be understood that the script could be read to mean anything. While the script limited the morphological range of the text, Arabic grammar, syntax, and composition further reduced the universe of meaningful statements that could be read into such texts if the original communication was unknown or ignored. Thus, at a minimum, this early Arabic script, although deficient, was fairly effective in documenting verbal utterances in general.

Islamic tradition holds that although the Prophet himself did not know how to write, he considered it important to document critical communications and that he dictated correspondence, contracts, and Qur'anic verses to his Companions, who acted as scribes. The *Sira* mentions a number of public documents that were written during the Prophet's life, including the *Mu'allaqat* poems hung on the Ka'ba, the Qurayshi boycott of the Muslims, the Covenant of Medina, and the Treaty of Hudaybiya. The Prophet is reported to have sent written correspondence to a number of people, including the rulers of al-Yamama, Bahrain, Oman, Alexandria, Syria, and Persia. Given this practice of transmitting or documenting important communications in writing, it is not surprising that the Prophet would ask his followers to write Qur'anic verses as they were revealed, nor is it surprising that the Companions who knew how to write would be eager to record for themselves the revelations they heard from the Prophet.

As long as the Prophet was alive, it was always possible that he would convey new revelations and, indeed, Islamic tradition holds that many verses were revealed during the final year of the Prophet's life. These verses were not always new suras, but additions to existing suras. What this means is that as long as the Prophet was alive, the composition and structure of each sura was potentially incomplete. For this reason, it would not have been a simple matter to compile the Qur'an into a book during the lifetime of the Prophet. At any time, revisions could have been made to any of the suras, altering the internal composition of the Qur'an. It was only with the death of the Prophet that each sura and the Qur'an as a whole could be considered complete. Now the challenge for the Prophet's Companions was to ensure that they were in possession of all of the suras in their final form.

Islamic tradition holds that a series of written compilations of the Qur'an took place within twenty years of the death of the Prophet. There are some differences among the reports about the details of each compilation, but most support the view that the Qur'an was collected and recorded in two stages. The initial compilation took place about a year after the death of the Prophet during the caliphate of Abu Bakr, after many Muslims had been killed in the Battle of Yamama. 'Umar ibn al-Khattab (who was to become the second caliph) told Abu Bakr that he was concerned about the number of "reciters" (qurra') who had been killed in the battle, and that certainly more would die in future battles. 'Umar advised Abu Bakr to order the Qur'an to be "collected" so that it would not disappear with the reciters. Abu Bakr hesitated to do "what the Prophet had never done," but eventually relented, and appointed Zaid ibn Thabit, one of the Prophet's most reliable scribes, to undertake the task.

If we turn back to Sheikh al-Kurdi's isnad, we see that Zaid is in the first generation of transmitters of the Qur'an. Zaid is reported to have been one of a number of Companions who memorized the whole Qur'an. Nevertheless, rather than simply writing down the recitation he and others had memorized, Zaid is said to have searched for written transcriptions of Qur'anic passages. He is reported to have said, "I gathered the Qur'an from various parchments and pieces of bone and from the chests of men." Sitting at the door of the mosque, Zaid collected from various Companions transcriptions they had made of Qur'anic passages they had heard. In keeping with the customary practice of document verification, written texts were generally accepted only if they were supported by two witnesses. Some reports indicate that these witnesses only needed to support the claim that these verses had been recited by the Prophet at some time; other reports suggest that these witnesses should have been present at the recording of the particular text being presented. Eventually, Zaid collected recitations and written texts of all the suras, and transcribed them on loose sheets of paper (*suhuf*). Abu Bakr kept these pages until he died, when they were transferred to the next caliph, 'Umar ibn al-Khattab. Before 'Umar died in 24/644, he deposited the papers with his daughter (and the Prophet's widow) Hafsa, who kept them until another project to transcribe the Qur'an was undertaken.

The second project to transcribe the Qur'an occurred during the reign of the third caliph, 'Uthman ibn 'Affan (24/644–36/656). Islamic tradition says that the impetus behind this transcription was a concern over conflicts that were emerging over the proper recitation of the Qur'an. This concern was raised by Hudhaifa ibn al-Yaman, one of the Companions in charge of the Muslim army on the frontier of Armenia and Azerbaijan, where troops from Iraq, Syria, and other regions had gathered. Hudhaifa noted that Muslims from different regions exhibited some differences in their recitation of the Qur'an, and that these differences were leading to disputes over which was the correct or superior recitation. Hudhaifa said to the caliph, "Put this community in order before they dispute over the Book like the disputes of the Jews and the Christians."[12]

In response, 'Uthman ordered Zaid and a group of other Companions to form a committee to write out a complete transcription of the Qur'an. The difference between this transcription and the earlier compilation made during the time of Abu Bakr was that this time, if any of those who memorized the text differed over the recitation, the dialect and recitation of the Quraysh would be preferred. Once the new text, called a *mushaf*, was compiled, it was read publicly in Medina, then a number of official copies were made and sent out to the various regions of the Islamic empire. Qur'an reciters were sent to teach and promulgate the official texts, and variant copies were gathered and destroyed.

According to the dominant Islamic tradition, what was lost in the standardization of the Qur'an at this early period were some of the variants (*ahruf*) in which the Qur'an was recited by the Companions. The Prophet Muhammad is reported to have allowed the Qur'an to be recited in different *ahruf* in order to facilitate its learning and recitation by different tribal groups. Unfortunately, there is no clear definition or explanation of these variants in early reports, and later scholars engage in a great deal of speculation about their meaning and significance. Many believe that the *ahruf* were variant recitations that may have included not only differences in the pronunciation of letters and modes of recitation, but also the substitution of synonymous terms in accordance with regional and tribal dialects.

Although the standardized script of the Uthmanic *mushaf* precluded some of these variants, it did not eliminate all possible differences in recitation. In addition to the limited variants that could meaningfully be read into the homographs, the consonantal script allowed for significant ambiguity with respect to the short vowels and inflections, among other things. As a result, many of the variant pronunciations, including whether certain vowels were elongated or shortened, as well as whether some verbs were read in the active or passive tense, continued to be permitted by the Uthmanic *mushaf*. These differences in recitation, as long as they could be traced to a recitation approved by the Prophet Muhammad, were accepted as authentic. Many scholars believe, therefore, that the *ahruf* were partially preserved in the different recitations that could be read into the script of the Uthmanic *mushaf*; after this time, however, variant readings were known as *qira'at*. These different modes of reciting the Qur'an yield mostly insignificant differences in meaning, although sometimes their differences allow a more nuanced understanding of certain passages. For example, the word *mlk* in the fourth verse of Sura al-Fatiha can be read with a short or long vowel in the first consonant. With a short vowel the word signifies "sovereign," and with a long vowel the word signifies "owner."

In addition to providing a degree of standardization to the readings of the Qur'an, the Uthmanic *mushaf* also fixed the order of the suras. The suras were ordered roughly according to length, beginning with the longest and ending with the shortest. The major exception is the first sura of the Qur'an, "The Opening" (Sura al-Fatiha), a short sura that is recited in every ritual prayer. All Muslim scholars agree that the internal composition of the suras was fixed by the Prophet, and some hold that the Prophet himself designated the sequence of the suras. However, most scholars believe that the final order of the suras was fixed only in the Uthmanic *mushaf*. Although there is evidence that the Prophet usually recited certain groups of suras in a particular order in his prayers, it is also true that he sometimes changed that order.

Indeed, it makes sense that the idea of "ordering" the suras only became necessary once the Qur'an was written down in one text. A written text must have a beginning and an end, a first page and a last page. An oral text is not restricted to this linear structure. This is why even after the Uthmanic text fixed the order of the suras, Muslim jurists did not require that the suras be recited in a certain order, whether in the daily prayers or over the course of a month or a year. Rather, the jurists continued to allow worshippers to recite any combination of passages they chose from any place in the Qur'an, because this was the practice of the Prophet and the Companions who learned the Qur'an from him.

In keeping with the desire to establish a standardized text of the Qur'an, Muslim authorities ordered that partial texts and complete texts exhibiting different arrangements of the suras be destroyed. Nevertheless, there are suggestions that some individuals retained their pre-Uthmanic transcriptions of the Qur'an. These Companions who had personally transcribed such documents in the presence of the Prophet treasured them as precious artifacts of his sacred legacy. Some early Muslims may have retained their pre-Uthmanic Qur'an transcriptions as private relics which they passed on to their families.[13] It is this type of document that Islamic scholar Abdullah Adhami believes may have been found in a Yemeni archeological dig in the 1990s.[14]

Some revisionist scholars have argued that reports about the compilation of the Qur'an are unreliable because they are recorded in hadith collections appearing two centuries after the death of the Prophet. In denying the reliability of these reports, some of these scholars, like John Wansbrough, developed elaborate theories that the Qur'an was composed by Muslims at a much later date, and that the *mushaf* reflects little of the original message conveyed by Muhammad.[15]

The theories advanced by Wansborough have little credibility for a number of reasons. First, he must assume the existence of a widespread conspiracy among second- and third-century Muslims to conceal the truth. That such a conspiracy could be perfectly concealed from the gaze of history and achieved among Muslims who, by the second century, were deeply divided by sectarian identities and partisan politics is untenable. Second, Wansborough and others were mistaken in asserting that reports about the compilation of the Qur'an cannot be attested before the late second century. More recently, Harald Motzki has shown that these reports can be proven to have been in circulation before the end of the first century of Islam.[16] Motzki argues further that the end of the first century is the time when such hadith were first formally taught, not when they were first narrated, and that substantively incorrect statements about the Qur'an could not have withstood public scrutiny at such an early period. Third, in recent years, more early manuscripts and epigraphic and numismatic evidence consistent with the canonical Qur'an have been discovered.[17] Finally, scholars who have conducted in-depth analyses of the various orthodox recitations and the slight graphic differences evident in early texts argue that their overwhelming consistency is proof of an early and accurate simultaneous oral and written preservation of the Qur'an. For example, Adrian Brockett concludes:

> The fidelity of oral tradition in the Near East in general is well known, and that of the Arabs in particular. Illiteracy strengthens memory. However, looked at negatively, oral tradition is characterized by variants resulting from words wrongly heard, from words confused with similar sounding words, and from whole episodes being forgotten, misplaced, or reinterpreted. Leaving aside the art of calligraphy, written tradition is characterized by variants resulting from copyists' errors, words read wrongly, revised, or left out by a careless eye, and by random passages getting lost, or being added to on the basis of other sources. Thus, if the Qur'an had been transmitted only orally for the first century, sizeable variations between texts such as are seen in the *hadith* and pre-Islamic poetry would be found, and if it had been transmitted only in writing, sizeable variations such as in the different transmission of the original document of the Constitution of Medina would be found. But neither is the case with the Qur'an. There must have been a parallel written transmission limiting variation in the oral transmission to the graphic form, side by side with a parallel oral transmission preserving the written transmission from corruption. The transmission of the Qur'an after the death of Muhammad was essentially static, rather than organic.[18]

The skeptical researcher still might ask the question, do the *qira'at* really reflect differences the Prophet knew of and approved, or are these slight variations that were voiced by individuals and allowed to stand because they could not be proven wrong? Perhaps within the first few decades of Islam different people remembered the revelation almost perfectly, but nevertheless made a few minor mistakes, and, without a standardized text, there was no way to prove the superiority of one reading over another. These differences were then rationalized with the explanation that the Qur'an had been revealed in variants that were partially preserved as different *qira'at*.

From a scientific standpoint, there is likely no way to prove or disprove this possibility. For the believing Muslim, on the other hand, the preserved Qur'an cannot contain even this kind of minor, insignificant mistake in writing and recitation because God promises:

> *We have revealed this reminder and we will certainly guard it.*
>
> (Hijr; 15:9)

Muslim scholars interpret this as a promise from God that nothing of the Qur'an that was revealed to the Prophet Muhammad could ever be lost or changed. For this reason, and because there are so many different understandings of the meaning of *ahruf*, some early and later scholars even rejected reports that there were variant readings before the Uthmanic compilation. These scholars, including most Shi'ites, accept the validity of different styles of recitation and the existence of different orthographic styles, but refuse the notion that any words which the Prophet presented as "revelation" were not preserved.[19] There were a few marginal Shi'ite leaders at various times who claimed that some Qur'anic verses upholding the primacy of 'Ali were excluded from the Uthmanic manuscript. However, the majority of Shi'ites, while basing their distinct identity on the supremacy of 'Ali, rejected these claims and upheld the accuracy of the transmission of the Qur'an.[20]

At the same time, it seems that the rejection of the possibility of variant recitations of the Qur'an has as much to do with a fixed concept of what a "book" is as with any discomfort that minor variants were lost in the Uthmanic *mushaf*. If we open our minds to the possibility that one book can encompass concurrent multiple readings (surely a possibility that postmodernists can grasp), we might appreciate that what is as remarkable as the fact that Muslims were able to standardize or "canonize" an oral and written scripture so early in the development of their religious community is the fact that they were also able to simultaneously preserve a variety of recitations. Unity did not require complete uniformity, even when it came to the sacred scripture. While the Word of God is one, the ways in which different tribes and individuals recited it were multiple. According to Muslim tradition, it was the Prophet himself who validated this diversity – a diversity that did not lead to significantly divergent meanings, but affirmed the distinct linguistic patterns of various tribes and peoples. In this respect, the preservation of different recitations of the Qur'an could itself be considered a sign of God:

> And among His signs is the creation of the heavens and the earth
> and the differences of your languages and colors; verily in that are
> signs for those who are knowledgeable.
>
> (Rum; 30:22)

The Early Generations: Regional Schools of Recitation and the Elaboration of the *Mushaf*

Sheikh al-Kurdi's *isnad* has multiple links in the first generation. The *isnad* goes back to five Companions who transmitted the Qur'an from the Prophet Muhammad; these Companions include the primary transcriber of the Qur'an, Zaid ibn Thabit, as well as the third caliph, 'Uthman ibn 'Affan, and the fourth caliph, 'Ali ibn Abi Talib.

The Qur'an played an important role in the lives of all these men, sometimes in unusual ways. Although 'Uthman's standardization of the *mushaf* was his most memorable connection to the Qur'an, history also recalls with great poignancy the fact that he was killed by political opponents as he sat reciting from the holy book.[21] Uzbekistan claims to possess blood-splattered pages of the *mushaf* he was reading.[22] For his part, 'Ali ibn Abi Talib had a tumultuous reign. First, he was opposed in his rule by 'Uthman's cousin Mu'awiya, who claimed the right to avenge the death of his relative. When Mu'awiya's troops raised sheets of the Qur'an on their lances, calling for a peaceful resolution to the conflict, 'Ali agreed. Among 'Ali's troops, however, were Qur'an reciters – *qurra'* – who considered his agreement to arbitration a capitulation to the judgment of man over the judgment of God, in whose name 'Ali had been appointed caliph. These troops deserted 'Ali and went on to kill him and oppose every other caliph who ruled for the next century.

Known as the *Khawarij* (the "secessionists"), these idealistic, uncompromising, radical, and violent groups of men terrorized Muslims living in the central lands of Islam, primarily Iraq and the Arabian Peninsula. Later scholars had no doubt that it was about these people the Prophet had warned when he said, "A group of people will appear among you whose prayer, fasting and deeds will make you think little of your own prayer, fasting and deeds. They will recite the Qur'an, but it will not get past their throats, and they will pass through the religion like an arrow passes through game. You look at the arrowhead, and you see nothing, and you look at the shaft, and you see nothing, and you look at the flights, and you see nothing. And you are in doubt about the notch."[23] Not surprisingly, many Muslims see parallels between the Khawarij and modern-day terrorists willing to kill even their fellow Muslims for political gain.

By the end of the first century of Islam, Muslim troops, traders, and preachers had roamed as far east as China and as far west as Andalusia. Although these Muslims scattered in remote areas did their part to spread Islam, the development of a dynamic Islamic civilization required urban centers with significant populations of Muslims. Medina, and to a lesser extent Mecca, remained preeminent centers of religion and learning; however, newer settlements and other cities were making significant contributions to the growth of religious, intellectual, and cultural institutions. Kufa, originally a garrison established to house Muslim troops, had, like Basra, its neighbor on the Euphrates, emerged as an important center of Islamic culture and learning. The garrison town of Fustat in Egypt was the cornerstone of Islam in Africa and the dynastic caliphate of the Umayyads ruled from Damascus.

The Arabic language and script were developed and promoted by both political authorities and scholars over the first century of Islam. The Umayyads made Arabic the official language of the administration, where its usage is attested on coins, milestones, and ornamentation from the period. In Jerusalem, the Umayyads built the Dome of the Rock, decorating it with verses of the Qur'an and other pious phrases in elegant Arabic script. Over the century, the script became increasingly standardized, a fact reflected in Qur'anic manuscripts from the period. These documents also show the beginnings of a system of markings to indicate short vowels and doubled consonants in words. This system is said to have been invented by the Iraqi scholar Abu'l-Aswad al-Du'ali (d. 69/688).

A possibly apocryphal story says that one night Abu'l-Aswad's daughter stepped outside and, looking up, exclaimed, "How beautiful the sky is!" The problem was that her statement was grammatically incorrect, for she used the wrong short vowel (indicating the nominative rather than the accusative case) at the end of one of the words. Like many parents throughout the ages, Abu'l-Aswad was appalled at his child's poor grammar, and probably blamed "changing times" for this obvious sign of cultural decay. With many Arabs living outside the

Arabian Peninsula and increasing numbers of Persians and other non-Arabic speakers entering Islam, "proper" Arabic was less easily found on the tongues of the people. While most fathers would be content to correct such mistakes with a brief lecture (ensuring that their child would never again express an aesthetic sentiment within hearing of a parent), Abu'l-Aswad went on to develop a system of textual markers to indicate the correct grammatical endings of words.[24] With these markers, the Arabic script could now represent more aspects of the recited Qur'an.

Throughout the second century of Islam, additional textual signifiers were developed to make written Arabic a more independent form of communication, no longer simply an inarticulate handmaiden of the oral language. Homographs became distinct graphemes by the addition of dots above and below the letters, and a complete system of diacritical marks was eventually developed. However, although the script and textual markers were increasingly standardized over the next few centuries, various regional differences emerged, some of which exist until today. For example, the North African script indicates the letter *qaf* with one dot over the grapheme, while other scripts use two dots. Similarly, from the early period until contemporary times, different spelling conventions have been employed in Arabic writing, just as British and American spelling differs in some cases; "color" and "colour" are written differently but signify the same word, while in early Arabic writing the *alif* grapheme and the *yeh* grapheme without dots or other marks might both signify the same long vowel.

Alongside the development of written Arabic over the first two centuries of Islam, oral transmission of the Qur'an continued. Mecca, Medina, Yemen, Damascus, Basra, and Kufa emerged as important centers of Qur'an recitation. It is through the city of Kufa that Sheikh al-Kurdi's *isnad* continues for the next few generations. Abu 'Abd al-Rahman al-Sulami (d. 74/693), born in Kufa near the end of the life of the Prophet Muhammad, became the most famous Qur'an reciter in that city. Having learned the Qur'an from the five Companions who formed the first generation of transmitters, al-Sulami went on to recite Qur'an in the Grand Mosque of Kufa for forty years. Along with Zirr ibn Hubaysh al-Asadi (d. 83/702) and Abu 'Amr al-Shaybani (d. 101/719), al-Sulami represents the second generation of transmitters in Sheikh al-Kurdi's *isnad*. After al-Sulami died, his student 'Asim ibn Abi'l-Najud (d. 127/744) took his place as head of the Qur'an reciters in Kufa. 'Asim, the third link in the *isnad*, taught many people, but his

Figure 3.5   Tenth-/sixteenth-century Qur'an with interlinear Persian translation. (British Library Add. Ms. 5551, folio 135v–136)

most prominent student was his stepson Hafs ibn Sulayman (d. 180/ 796), the fourth link in the *isnad*. Hafs had thousands of students in his long life, and his recitation from 'Asim would eventually be considered one of the main "orthodox" recitations. It is the recitation of Hafs from 'Asim that Reem earned the *ijaza* from Sheikh al-Kurdi.

One of 'Asim's students, Abu Muhammad al-Nahshali (d. 219/834 or 235/849), the fifth link in the *isnad*, moved from Kufa to Baghdad where he taught the sixth generation of scholars, including Ahmed ibn Sahl al-Ushnani (d. 307/919). By this time, Baghdad was the thriving capital of the 'Abbasid dynasty, which had overthrown the Umayyads of Damascus in 132/749. The 'Abbasids put significant resources into developing the institutions and symbols of religion to justify their revolution and seizure of the caliphate. To this end, the writing of Qur'anic manuscripts was not neglected. There was plenty of work for skilled scribes who employed set rules for various writing styles that had by now been developed.[25] The angular script used in Qur'anic manuscripts of the time is usually called "Kufic" (after the city of Kufa), although some scholars believe the term "early 'Abbasid script" is more accurate. During the second and third centuries, new features are added to make Qur'anic manuscripts more legible and distinct. The number of lines on a page was regularized, and titles of suras, where previously there had been a blank space or simple decorative element, were added. More use was made of gold and decorative elements to indicate the endings of verses or groups of verses. Massive, multi-volume *mushafs* (68 × 53 cm), probably used for ceremonial purposes, were produced during this period.

Following Sheikh al-Kurdi's *isnad*, we now arrive at the sixth link in the chain. We have seen how the transmission of the oral and written Qur'an developed in the first three centuries of Islam. During this time, many scholars were affected by struggles over political power in the larger society. Al-Nahshali, for example, lived in Baghdad during the *mihna* – a period of repression, as we shall discuss in a later chapter, when hadith scholars and judges were forced by the 'Abbasid caliph to uphold a particular doctrine on the ontological status of the Qur'an. Al-Nahshali must have had an opinion on this doctrine, but we do not have any reports indicating that he and the other Qur'an reciters and scholars were required to confess their beliefs to the caliph. What is clear is that al-Nahshali's main concern, like his teacher Hafs before him, was to ensure that he transmitted the Qur'an completely and accurately to his students. In each generation after al-Nahshali, there would emerge scholars devoted to the same sacred task, so that the chain of transmission of the Qur'an from heaven to earth would never be broken.

Standardizing the Curriculum

During the third century of Islam, the institutionalization of religion accelerated. Many factors contributed to this development, including increasing numbers of Muslims in the general population and economic stablility that supported a large and diverse group of religious professionals and scholars. Political patrons, seeking stability for their societies, as well as wanting to express personal piety and expiation for their transgressions, supported institutions of learning and worship. Religious scholars, although often wary of political power and keen to retain exclusive authority to define orthodoxy, sometimes called upon the power of the state to prevent heterodox ideas and practices from spreading.

In a Weberian sense, charismatic religious authority, which was predominant in the first two or three centuries of Islam, began to be supplemented and, in some cases, replaced by institutional authority.

This fact is reflected in all fields of Islamic religious sciences. Over time, certain perspectives won out as authoritative and the study of hadith, law, and theology became more formalized and institutionalized. By the end of the third century, particular schools of thought became dominant in all these fields and established the foundation of Sunni orthodoxy and Shi'ite identity.

Until the third century, there were no standard collections of prophetic hadith common to all students. Rather, students learned individual hadith, each of which had a personalized *isnad* leading from their teacher to the Prophet. In this context, authoritativeness rested in each righteous individual present in the chain of transmission. But even this requirement for an authentic *isnad* reflects a degree of formalization that was not present in the first two generations of Muslims. This is why many hadith are *mursal* (missing the link between the first narrator from the Prophet), because the Successors to the Companions (i.e., the second generation of Muslims) personally knew their sources and whom to trust. The development of a more formal pedagogy over time is also a reason why relatively few individuals, like al-Zuhri (d. 124/742), are very prominently represented in hadith *isnad*s in the early period, while the number of recorded transmitters grows exponentially with each generation thereafter.

By the third century, the field of hadith studies had been substantially developed, so that scholars specializing in collecting and sifting through hadith were applying relatively consistent standards to determine the authenticity of reports. Although these standards still rested to a great extent on the character of the individuals involved, objective standards, like the simple fact of whether an individual had lived in the city in which it was reported that he had heard a hadith, were now systematically applied. It was during this period that Bukhari (d. 256/870) and Muslim (d. 261/875) compiled their collections of "authentic" (*sahih*) hadith, collections that would become near canonical texts for Sunni Islam. Other collections of hadith compiled over the next century would be produced, until about a half a dozen took prominence in the Sunni curriculum. Shi'ism, emerging as a sectarian community truly distinct from Sunnism only during this century, underwent a similar process, with particular collections of Prophetic hadith and sayings of the Imams, notably the *Usul al-Kafi* by al-Kulayni (d. ca. 328/939), eventually gaining a place of privilege in teaching and learning.

It is important to note that although the reliance on authoritative or standard collections of hadith spread after this period, students were still required to acquire knowledge of these collections from individual, certified scholars. No scholar could claim the authority to teach a book unless he or she had learned it from another scholar who had an authentic *isnad* back to Bukhari or Muslim or one of the other original compilers of the hadith collections. In this way, the chain of transmission back to the Prophet Muhammad was unbroken. The application of the *isnad* system to religious texts meant that the Islamic tradition acquired the benefits of institutionalization and formalizaton without losing the spiritual and social benefits of mentoring.

In the field of Islamic jurisprudence, a similar process of standardization and winnowing of the field took place. It is said that in the second/eighth century of Islam, there were 500 schools of law.[26] What this means is that at this time the schools were, for the most part, simply the teaching circles of individual scholars. Thus, the legal methodology and specific rulings of any particular jurist comprised a school. But by the fourth/tenth century, Sunni Islam was dominated by four main schools of law: Hanafi, Maliki, Shafi'i, and Hanbali. The authority of these schools was rooted in the charismatic presence of earlier scholars after whom they were named: Abu Hanifa (d. 150/767), Malik ibn Anas (d. 179/795), al-Shafi'i (d. 204/820), and Ahmed ibn Hanbal (d. 241/855). However, it was only with the systematizing efforts of the students of these eponymous founders that the *madhhabs* became true intellectual schools with distinct methodologies, core texts, and a body of juridical opinions. It took over a century for the schools to establish a significant institutional presence, with the founding of independently endowed colleges (*madrasas*) in which the standardized curriculum of each school could be taught.

Given this tendency towards the formalization and standardization of all fields of religious science in the third/ninth century, it is not surprising that similar efforts were made in the study of Qur'anic recitation. At this time, there were as many *qira'at* of the Qur'an as there were individuals with valid chains of transmission for their recitation back to the Prophet. As in the case of hadith studies, although the personalized *isnad* system was never abandoned, a select number of paths of transmission were now held as standards. Thus, while in the early third century the Iraqi scholar Abu 'Ubayd al-Qasim ibn Sallam identified twenty-five prominent recitations in his book, a century later the seven recitations identified by Ibn Mujahid (d. 324/ 935) had emerged as dominant recitations.[27] Later, Abu'l-Hasan Tahir ibn Ghalbun (d. 399/1008), the eighth link in the Shatibi path of Sheikh al-Kurdi's *isnad*, included another recitation to the seven chosen by Ibn Mujahid.[28] Later, two more recitations were added so that ten "orthodox" *qira'at* became widely acknowledged.

It is from Ibn Ghalbun that Abu 'Amr 'Uthman ibn Sa'id al-Dani (d. 444/1052), the ninth link in the Shatibi path of Sheikh al-Kurdi's *isnad*, learned the *qira'at*. Al-Dani was born in Cordoba, Andalusia (Islamic Spain) and headed east as a young man to seek religious knowledge. He settled for a time in Egypt where he studied with Ibn Ghalbun, then returned to Andalusia, where he taught and transmitted the Qur'an. Al-Dani wrote many books on the Qur'an, its recitation and transcription, and was himself a fine calligrapher. Calligraphy was a highly desirable skill, not only because it was the only way to reproduce the *mushaf* before the age of print, but also because it was an act of worship and devotion to the word of God. It is therefore notable that large numbers of women in diverse Muslim societies are reported to have been calligraphers. For example, in one area of al-Dani's city of Cordoba, one hundred and seventy women were engaged in copying the Qur'an in Kufic script.[29]

Al-Dani lived at a time when cursive scripts, known as *naskhi*, were increasingly being used to write Qur'anic *mushafs*, making them more legible and accessible to non-specialists. The Iraqis Ibn Muqlah (d. 328/940) and then Ibn Bawwab (d. 413/1022) are credited with developing and then perfecting the six styles of writing that became the standards for later calligraphers. Not only were these cursive scripts more legible than the earlier scripts, they also allowed for the production of more compact and portable manuscripts. This, combined with the increasing availability of paper (a material cheaper than parchment), contributed to the ability of more people to own their own *mushaf*. A number of other features were added to some *mushafs* by this time, including the numbering of suras and verses, and appendices of *tajwid* rules and supplications that should be made upon completing a reading of the Qur'an. Within another hundred years or so, *mushafs* with marginal commentary became available.[30]

At the same time that practical and accessible Qur'anic manuscripts were being produced, elegant and ceremonial *mushafs* were scribed and decorated by master calligraphers for wealthy patrons. Ibn Bawwab's renowned illuminated Qur'an in the collection of the Chester Beatty

Library in Dublin is an outstanding example. The art and craft of calligraphy and bookmaking became an important aspect of Islamic culture that eventually had a significant influence on the aesthetics of the Italian Renaissance.[31]

Returning to the *isnad*, we see that one of the scholars who studied with al-Dani was the Valencian Abu Dawud Sulayman ibn Najah (d. 496/1103). He passed on his knowledge to his stepson Abu'l-Hasan 'Ali ibn Hudhail (d. 564/1169). It is from Ibn Hudhail that Abu Qasim ibn Firruh al-Shatibi (d. 590/1194), the twelfth link in Sheikh al-Kurdi's *isnad*, took his knowledge of Qur'anic recitation. Studying with Ibn Hudhail in Valencia, it is possible that al-Shatibi crossed paths with a young man just a few years his senior, Muhammad ibn Jubayr. While al-Shatibi remained in the academic field, Ibn al-Jubayr employed his writing skills in the administrative service of the Muslim ruler of Granada. Both men were brilliant, fine writers, able to acquire the highest levels of proficiency in the Arabic language and Islamic religious sciences in the flourishing Muslim institutions of their southwestern European home. At the same time, like pious Muslims everywhere, al-Shatibi and Ibn Jubayr desired to make the pilgrimage to Mecca and to see the holy sites and major cities of the central Islamic lands.

In the next section, as we follow Ibn Jubayr and al-Shatibi in their journeys, we learn something about the way in which the Qur'an was transmitted, not only through texts and recitation, but also through the ritual life of medieval Islamic society.

Qur'anic Recitation and Ritual Life

Over the centuries, the Qur'an has retained its prominence in Muslim societies not primarily because it has been studied and transmitted in schools and seminaries, but because it is at the center of ritual life. At a minimum, the Qur'an is recited in the five prayers every Muslim must perform daily and in every other ritual prayer (*salat*), including funeral and holiday (*Eid*) prayers. In many traditional Muslim societies, communities celebrate a number of other annual festivals, including the birthday of the Prophet Muhammad (the "Mawlid"), the anniversary of the Prophet's "Night Journey and Heavenly Ascent" (*Isra'* and *Mi'raj*), and the beginning of the sacred months of Rajab and Muharram. No celebration is complete without a performance of beautiful Qur'an recitation.

In contemporary Muslim societies, many of these religious festivals celebrated in premodern times and in traditional societies have been shunned by some reformist movements and marginalized by the erosion of communal religious life. One notable exception is Ramadan, a month characterized by intense devotion to the reading and recitation of the Qur'an. A contemporary popular children's song from Egypt declares, "Welcome, welcome O Ramadan; month of fasting, month of the Qur'an." During Ramadan, the ninth month of the Islamic lunar calendar, Muslims abstain from food, drink, and intimate relations each day from first light of dawn (*fajr*) to sunset (*maghrib*). The Qur'an states,

> *O you who believe, fasting is prescribed for you, as it was prescribed for those who came before you so that you might become aware of the limits set by God.*
> *(Fast for) a specific number of days; but if any of you are ill or on a journey, then (fast) some other days. Those who find it too difficult should pay redemption by feeding an indigent person. As for the one who does even more out of goodness – that is better for him, if you only knew.*
> *It is the month of Ramadan during which we revealed the Qur'an as a guide to humanity, a clarification of guidance and a criterion.*
> (Baqara; 2:183–185)

According to the Qur'an the ultimate objective of fasting is to heighten one's awareness of God, who is the creator of all goods humans enjoy, as well as the one who determines the limits they must observe in their enjoyment of these things. For those who do not cultivate this awareness, fasting is no more than a passive state of not eating, drinking, or engaging in intimacy; ideally, fasting is an active state of increasing one's awareness of the majesty and mercy of God.

The above verses state that the Qur'an was revealed during the month of Ramadan. Muslim scholars have understood this verse in different ways, some of them suggesting that Ramadan was the month when heavenly tablets (*lawh mahfudh*) containing the Qur'an were brought to the lower heavens.

The Prophet is also reported to have said that the Angel Gabriel reviewed the Qur'an with him every Ramadan and, in the last year of his life, reviewed it twice. This annual review is mirrored in the practice of communal evening prayers (*tarawih*) during which the whole of the Qur'an is recited, one portion at a time, each night of Ramadan. Although the recitation of the Qur'an in late-night prayers (*qiyam al-layl*; *tahhajud*) was an important aspect of ritual life during the life of the Prophet, this was especially true in the month of Ramadan, when, for a number of years, the Prophet performed *tarawih* prayers in the mosque with the congregation. Later, the Prophet is reported to have ceased performing them publicly, saying that if he continued, he feared that his followers would consider these prayers obligatory. Nevertheless, only a few years after the death of the Prophet, the second caliph, 'Umar ibn al-Khattab, is reported to have reinstituted communal *tarawih* prayers. 'Umar, who is credited with innovating many beneficial administrative practices in the Islamic state,[32] and who we will recall was keen to have the Qur'an compiled into a *mushaf*, is said to have feared that the ritual would be neglected if left to individuals. From a historical perspective, we observe that the additional benefit of communal *tarawih* prayers during this early period would have been to publicize the officially accepted recitation and arrangment of the Qur'an, and check deviant versions.

One aspect of recitation that became important in many Muslim societies but that we have not discussed up to now is melody. Whereas the rules of *tajwid* determine how each letter is pronounced, it does not indicate the pace at which the Qur'an should be recited, nor does it address the pitch of the voice. In fact, this aspect of Qur'an recitation is poorly documented in premodern times. The primary reason for this is that there is no indication that those who transmitted the Qur'an from the Prophet included melodic aspects of the recitation as part of their teaching. As Anne Gade notes, historical texts seem to indicate that it was only during the 'Abbasid period that Qur'an reciters began to "deploy the emerging modal system of art music (*maqam*, pl. *maqamat*)" that had developed as a theory and a practice of music by way of a synthesis of Arabic and Persian forms. Because melodic recitation of the Qur'an, known as *mujawwad*, was considered an element of human creativity and artistry introduced to the recitation, scholars insisted that fixed melodies should not be adhered to or taught. "Improvisation is thus a legal requirement."[33]

Not all Muslims felt that *mujawwad* recitation was an acceptable innovation. For example, after the sixth-/twelfth-century Andalusian scholar Abu Bakr al-Turtushi settled in Egypt, he criticized the Muslims there for adopting what he considered to be many of the practices of the non-Muslims, including reciting the Qur'an in a manner similar to

Christian chanting.[34] Such Muslims argued that the Qur'an itself says that it should be recited *tartil*, that is, with clear enunciation and a moderate pace, the word *tartil* derived from a word meaning "well-spaced teeth."[35] Because of this, the less melodic and straightforward recitation was known as *murattal*.

Given that the melodic aspect of recitation was normally not documented in premodern texts, we cannot determine the relative popularity of *mujawwad* versus *murattal* styles. What we do know is that Qur'an recitation generally was at the center of communal ritual.

The Andalusian Ibn Jubayr was especially attentive to such things as he traveled through the central Islamic lands for two years between 578/1183 and 580/1185. In the tradition of other Western Muslim travelers, Ibn Jubayr documented the people and places he found most interesting on his journey (*rihla*), and so he describes the great mosques, eloquent preachers, and diverse festivals he encounters.

Because the main purpose of his trip was religious pilgrimage, Ibn Jubayr spent almost a year in Mecca, where he witnessed many impressive celebrations. He describes, for example, how during the last days of Ramadan, a number of youth who had memorized the Qur'an were showcased in what seems to have been a type of coming-of-age ceremony. Here, Ibn Jubayr describes one of the evenings he found particularly moving, when a young man who was the son of one of the imams of the Sacred Mosque (i.e., the Ka'ba) took the pulpit:

> The Hanafi imam had made great preparations on behalf of his son for this night. He produced four candle-bearing chandeliers of varying styles, some like trees with branches laden with all kinds of fruit, fresh and dry, and some without branches. They were arranged in a row before his platform on whose summit were boards and planks covered with lamps, torches and candles, that illuminated the whole platform until it shone in the air like a great crown of light. The candles were brought forward in brass candlesticks, and then the *mihrab* with wooden balustrades was set in place, its upper part ringed with candles and itself encompassed by candlesticks that threw a halo of light around it. The pulpit, which was also covered with a cloth of many colors was placed in front of it. The massing of the people to see this lustrous spectacle was greater than at the first (night). The boy finished the recitation of the Qur'an, then moved from his *mihrab* to the pulpit, bearing himself shyly and dressed in vestments beautiful to

behold. He climbed his pulpit and gestured a greeting of peace to those present. Then he began his sermon, calmly and with gentleness, in language of transparent modesty. Considering his youth, it was more dignified and moving than [the sermon the day before]; his exhortations were more eloquent, and his pious recollections of greater benefit. The Qur'an reciters took post in front of him as they had [on other nights] and during the pauses between the readings, began to recite the Qur'an. He would keep silent until they had ended the verses they had selected and then return to his sermon. Before him on the steps of the pulpit was a group of attendants holding candlesticks in their hands, and one of them held the censer which repeatedly spread the aroma of aloe. When the preacher came to a break in a pious recollection or a moving entreaty, they raised their voices crying, "O Lord! O Lord!" three or four times, sometimes being joined in their cries by the congregation; and so it continued until he had ended his sermon.[36]

Notable in this and other descriptions of religious occasions during this period is the role of the *qurra'*. Qur'an reciters formed a special class of religious professionals, distinct from preachers (imams and khatibs) and scholars ("ulama"). At the same time, reciters worked with preachers and scholars to accentuate the message of their sermons and lectures. All of the religious professionals would have memorized the Qur'an, but the reciters excelled in beautiful recitation while the preachers and scholars were skilled in drawing upon the Qur'an to deliver a powerful sermon or lecture.

A good example of this is found in Ibn Jubayr's description of a series of lectures he attended by a number of distinguished academics in Baghdad. He describes the great eloquence and erudition of the Hanbali scholar Abu'l-Fada'il ibn 'Ali al-Jawzi. One of the things he found most remarkable was the way in which al-Jawzi worked with what can only be described as a chorus of Qur'an reciters to accentuate and complement his sermon:

On his ascending the pulpit, the reciters who numbered more than twenty, began to recite the Qur'an. Two or three of them recited a verse from the Qur'an in a moving and impassioned rhythm, and when they had done, another group of the same number recited another verse. So they went on, alternately reciting verses, from various suras, until they had ended the reading. The verses they gave were so similar that even a

brilliant mind could scarce tell the number or name the order;
yet when they had finished, this great and remarkable Imam,
passing speedily into his disquisition and pouring into the shell
of our ears the pearls of his utterance, punctuated his discourse
at each paragraph with the rhyming opening words of the
verses recited, giving them in the order of their reading without prematurity or deferment, and ending with the rhyme of
the last.[37]

Public Qur'an recitation was also a feature of daily life in most
mosques. In large mosque complexes, endowments provided salaries
for professional reciters and sometimes also supported allowances for
the poor who would regularly attend some of these recitations. In the
Umayyad mosque in Damascus, for example, Ibn al-Jubayr observed:

In the venerated mosque after the morning prayers, there daily
assembles a great congregation for the reading of one of the
seven sections of the Qur'an. This is unfailing, and it is the
same after the evening prayers for the reading of what is called
the *Kawthariyya*, when they read from Sura al-Kawthar (108)
until the end of the Book. To this assembly of the Kawthar
come all who do not well know the Qur'an by heart, and all
such participants receive a daily allowance; more than five
hundred people live from this. This is one of the virtues of
this venerated mosque, in which from morning until evening
the Qur'an is read unceasingly.[38]

Ibn Jubayr noted that Damascus, the city where eight hundred years
later the American girl Reem would master Qur'an recitation, was a city
in which the Qur'an was studied, recited, taught, and venerated. He
mentions that one of the original copies of the Qur'an sent by 'Uthman
to Syria was kept in a special cupboard in the Umayyad mosque. "This
cupboard is opened daily after the prayers, and people seek God's
blessing by touching and kissing the Book, and the crowd around it is
very great."[39]
There were so many Qur'an scholars in Damascus that it is unlikely
that Ibn Jubayr had the chance to meet Zayn ibn al-Hasan al-Baghdadi
(d. 613/1216), the eleventh link in the secondary path of Sheikh al-
Kurdi's *ijaza*. As his name implies, Zayn ibn al-Hasan originated
from Baghdad, where he took his *ijaza* from the charismatic scholar
'Abdullah ibn 'Ali, to whom crowds flocked during Ramadan to hear

his extraordinarily beautiful Qur'an recitation. Zayn ibn al-Hasan was a wonder in his own right, having earned his first *ijaza* in recitation at seven years old, and was certified in all ten orthodox recitations when he was only ten years old. Ibn al-Jazari, who a few generations later would earn an *ijaza* linking back to Zayn ibn al-Hasan, remarked that no one in history had ever achieved this mastery of the *qira'at* at such an early age. Because Zayn ibn al-Hasan lived until he was ninety-three years old, he was able to teach and transmit the Qur'an to multitudes of students for over eight decades.

As Ibn Jubayr made his pilgrimage throughout the eastern Islamic lands, there was one notable absence from his itinerary: Jerusalem. The holy city had been occupied by Christian Crusaders for almost a century, and Ibn Jubayr's chronicle reflects the bitterness he feels at this loss. When he mentions the mosque of Jerusalem, he prays, "May God restore it to the Muslims." Just ten years later, in 583/1187, the prayers of Ibn Jubayr and all the Muslims were answered when Salahuddin (Saladin) liberated Jerusalem. Salahuddin was a pious Muslim, for whom the Qur'an was a source of strength and inspiration. Historical sources also suggest that Salahuddin and Muslim generals of the time had Qur'an reciters in their ranks and had their troops carry or wear Qur'anic verses for protection.[40] Muslims from far and wide took advantage of the liberation of Jerusalem to resume pilgrimage there.

One of those who made the pilgrimage to Jerusalem was al-Qasim ibn Firruh al-Shatibi. Al-Shatibi, we recall, was Ibn Jubayr's Andalusian compatriot; both had been educated in Valencia. Like Ibn Jubayr, al-Shatibi traveled east, making the pilgrimage to Mecca. Later, al-Shatibi went to Egypt, where he was appointed the head of a major seminary there, al-Madrasa al-Fadiliyya. Al-Shatibi spent the rest of his life in Egypt, leaving only for short trips, like his visit to Jerusalem in 589/1193. We can imagine how satisfying it must have been for al-Shatibi, the great scholar of Qur'an recitation, to walk around the Dome of the Rock, reading with ease the Qur'anic verses decorating the interior and exterior surfaces. Given what we know of other medieval Muslim pilgrims,[41] it is likely that al-Shatibi also visited the Church of the Holy Sepulchre and Bethlehem, where he would have recalled Qur'anic verses praising Jesus and his mother.

It was in Egypt that al-Shatibi completed a major contribution to the study of the *qira'at*, a poem of over one thousand rhyming couplets elucidating all the variants of the seven main *qira'at*. Al-Shatibi's *Hirz al-amani wa wajh al-tahani*, known as *al-Shatibiyya*, became a popular teaching device among scholars of the *qira'at*. During the medieval period, the memorization of long and short poems such as this was considered the foundation of a good education. In traditional Islamic teaching circles, poems such as al-Juwayni's *al-Waraqat fi usul al-fiqh*[42] for Islamic jurisprudence and Laqani's *Jawharat al-Tawhid*[43] on Islamic theology are still considered useful mnemonic devices that allow students and scholars to quickly recall the major principles of these disciplines.

While al-Shatibi knew the joy of the liberation of Jerusalem, his student and son-in-law 'Ali ibn Shuja' (the thirteenth link in Sheikh al-Kurdi's *isnad*) shared the horror and despair of the Muslims who lived during the 656/1258 destruction of Baghdad by the Mongol leader Hulagu. The culmination of a ruthless campaign to conquer the eastern Islamic lands, the sack of Baghdad was a devastating material and psychological blow to the Muslims. The 'Abbasid caliphate centered in Baghdad had been the symbolic center of Islamic political and religious authority for five centuries. Now 'Abbasid rule was overthrown and the caliph murdered by the Mongols, who wanted to prove their complete dominance over those who claimed a superior civilization. Among all the acts of wanton destruction the Mongols committed, perhaps none was more painful to scholars than to see the libraries of Baghdad ravaged. Historians reported that the rivers ran black with the ink of tens of thousands of books thrown into the Tigris and Euphrates rivers. Certainly among these books, as well as the thousands of other books destroyed by the Mongols in their earlier destruction of major Muslim towns in Central Asia, Khurasan, and Iran, were Qur'anic manuscripts and books of Qur'anic sciences.

The westward expansion of the Mongols was countered just two years after the fall of Baghdad by the Egyptian Mamluks, who defeated the invading armies at Ayn Jalut in Palestine. In the meantime, Hulagu had returned to Central Asia to face opposition from his own cousin, Berke, a Muslim who was horrified by the destruction of the Islamic caliphate. Indeed, from the Muslim perspective, what was perhaps most remarkable, even miraculous, over the next few generations was how most of the Mongols ruling Muslim lands eventually embraced Islam and became patrons of the cultural and religious institutions that had seemed to be so threatened by their initial invasion and occupation. At the same time, the power of other Central Asian tribes grew, with the Saljuks and then the Ottomans moving into the central Islamic lands and countering the power of the Mongols.

By the early ninth/fifteenth century, few would have forseen that the Ottomans would become a major power in the region, much less that they would establish themselves as the longest-ruling dynasty in world history, becoming a force in Europe, Asia, and North Africa for six centuries. In 805/1402, prospects looked rather dim for the Ottomans. In that year, the Ottoman Sultan Bayezid I was defeated at the Battle of Ankara by the Mongol leader Timur (Tamerlane). Bayezid and a number of non-combatants accompanying his camp were taken prisoner.

One of the individuals captured from Bayezid's camp was the Qur'an scholar Muhammad ibn al-Jazari, the fifteenth link in Sheikh al-Kurdi's *isnad*. During the Battle of Ankara, Ibn al-Jazari may have functioned as a kind of chaplain, or perhaps was in charge of the Qur'an reciters charged to motivate and comfort the troops. Apart from this incident, most evidence indicates that Ibn al-Jazari devoted the bulk of his time to scholarship and teaching, eventually becoming one of the most celebrated scholars of the *qira'at* of the Qur'an. His biographers note that signs of Ibn al-Jazari's future greatness could be discerned even in his birth. His father, a pious Iraqi merchant, had been childless for over forty years when he made the pilgrimage to Mecca. Drinking the holy water of Zamzam, the old man prayed for a son who would become a religious scholar. Ibn al-Jazari was born the next year, 751/1350, in the sacred month of Ramadan after the *tarawih* prayers – which was surely a sign that this boy was to have a special connection with the Qur'an. Ibn al-Jazari grew up in Damascus, where he memorized the Qur'an by age thirteen. He continued to study the *qira'at*, eventually traveling to Mecca, Medina, Cairo, and Baghdad, where he studied from the great scholars of his age and collected *ijaza*s in the various recitations.

By the time Timur's soldiers had taken Ibn al-Jazari as a prisoner from Bayezid's camp, he was a senior scholar who probably had completed writing many of his books. His primary contribution to Qur'an scholarship was that he secured the orthodoxy of three add-itional recitations to al-Shatibi's seven, even composing a poem known as *al-Durra* which taught these three recitations, as a supplement to the *Shatibiyya*. Ibn al-Jazari's extensive study of the authenticity of the ten orthodox recitations of the Qur'an, *al-Nashr fi qira'at al-'ashr*, became a popular advanced textbook and is still in use in Islamic colleges today.

The ten recitations and the cities with which they were originally associated are: *Mecca*: Ibn Kathir; *Medina*: Nafi' and Abu Ja'far; *Damascus*: Ibn 'Amer; *Basra*: Abu 'Amr; *Kufa*: 'Asim, Hamza, al-Kisa'i, and Khalaf;

Yemen: Ya'qub. Each of these ten reciters has two primary transmitters through whom all *isnads* are traced; it is these transmitters whose names are normally listed when citing a recitation. Thus, for example, it is in Hafs's recitation from 'Asim that Reem was certified by Sheikh al-Kurdi; consequently, her *ijaza* is for the recitation of "Hafs." The recitation of Nafi' is known through the transmission of Warsh and Qalun, so it is possible to earn an *ijaza* in "Warsh" or "Qalun."

Ibn al-Jazari's biographical dictionary of Qur'an reciters, *Ghayat al-nihaya fi tabaqat al-qurra'*, is an important resource, including for research on the lives of the scholars mentioned in his own *isnads*. The most well-known work of Ibn al-Jazari, however, is a poem of 108 rhyming couplets that teaches the basic rules of *tajwid*. This poem, called *Manthuma al-Muqaddima fi ma yajib 'ala qari al-qur'an an ya'lamahu*, is known as *al-Jazariyya* and is the poem that Reem had to memorize and understand in order to earn her *ijaza* from Sheikh al-Kurdi.[44]

Ibn al-Jazari spent about three years under the control of Timur, until the latter died in 807/1405. During that time, it is likely that Ibn al-Jazari was able to teach, preach, and write, because Timur, although holding syncretic religious views and devoted to Mongol customs (even though he was ethnically a Turk), identified himself as a Muslim and, as such, patronized Muslim scholars and thinkers. Once freed from Hulagu's control, Ibn al-Jazari traveled and lived in many places in the central Islamic lands until his death a quarter-century later in 833/1429. Because of Ibn al-Jazari's outstanding reputation for piety and scholarship, his certification for Qur'an recitation was highly sought, and during his long life he must have certified many thousand Qur'an reciters.

At this point in our story, we could continue to follow the chain of transmission of Hafs's recitation from Ibn al-Jazari up to Sheikh al-Kurdi. It is mainly under Ottoman, but also Mamluk, sovereignty that the scholars of Sheikh al-Kurdi's *isnad* continued to transmit the Qur'an over the next four centuries. Living mostly in Egypt and Damascus, these scholars certainly experienced some hardship and political upheaval, but mostly they benefited from stable institutions and were respected carriers of the dominant cultural symbols. Political turmoil disrupted the teaching of the Qur'an for a certain time or in particular locations in the central Islamic lands, but scholars were resilient and, carrying their books in their hearts (that is, having memorized them), they were able to transmit the Qur'an anywhere they found themselves. Over the next four centuries, the Qur'an continued to be taught and transmitted in these lands, formally and informally, in mosque study circles, schools, and colleges, from teacher to student and from scholar to scholar. Muslim rulers continued to consider the support and patronage of religious institutions crucial to legitimizing their power. In this respect, the Ottoman dynasty became a major force in the Islamic world, especially after the Ottoman ruler Mehmet II conquered Constantinople in 857/1453. The organizational genius of the Ottomans was directed to the development of political, cultural, and religious institutions that provided a framework for the transmission of Islamic learning until the nineteenth century CE.

The story of the Qur'an, however, includes the history of its teaching and transmission in many lands not represented in Sheikh al-Kurdi's *isnad*: India, China, Indonesia, East and West Africa, and eastern Europe. We need to be aware that the link that we have followed – from the Prophet to Ibn al-Jazari – is only one of many such links stretching across the centuries and lands of early and medieval Islam. Over the course of these same nine centuries, tens of thousands of other chains of transmission of the Qur'an criss-crossed the Muslim world. Most of the *isnad*s were for the transmisson of a single *qira'a*: Hafs, Warsh, al-Duri, Qalun, etc. In general, only scholars learned more than one recitation of the Qur'an. Most Muslims, even most Imams who led congregational prayers, learned only one recitation, with the result that particular recitations were predominant or even exclusively taught in certain regions of the Muslim world. At the same time, it is unlikely that there were many places in the Muslim world where no religious leader had an awareness of the existence of the different *qira'at*, and certainly individual Muslim traders and pilgrims encountered the diversity of recitations as they prayed with congregations along their travels.

We cannot follow all those links and tell all the stories of the Qur'an's teaching and transmission in all these lands. But it might be useful at this point to step away from the continuous chain of Sheikh al-Kurdi's *isnad* to consider some of the broken links. After the fifteenth century CE, there are some particularly poignant stories of the inability of Muslims to continue to transmit the Qur'an. When we note, for example, that Andalusian scholars, earlier well represented in Sheikh al-Kurdi's *isnad*, no longer appear there, we feel compelled to ask, why not? Thus we now divert our attention from the unbroken chain to the severed links, and consider some of the ways Muslims tried to hold on to the Qur'an, even as it was snatched away from them.

Breaking the Tradition

In 1492 Columbus sailed the ocean blue... and Ferdinand and Isabella defeated the small Muslim state of Granada, the last Islamic political authority in Andalusia. What soon followed was the persecution of Muslims and Jews on a monumental scale. The plurality of religions that had been tolerated in southwestern Europe for centuries under most Muslim rulers and some Christians was repudiated by the Spanish monarchs, and Catholicism was enforced with brutality. Within a few years, hundreds of thousands of Jews and Muslims were forced to convert to Catholicism or to flee to the protection of the Mamluks, the Ottoman Turks, or other rulers offering sanctuary. Those who stayed behind, many of whom only feigned Christianity, were scrutinized publicly and privately for signs they were holding onto their former beliefs. The tools of the Inquisition, honed on heretical Christians even before the Reconquista, were employed with brutal precison on *Marranos* (converted Jews) and *Moriscos* (converted Muslims).

As one might expect of a people forced to abandon their religion and compelled to accept another, many Moriscos secretly retained their Islamic beliefs and practices and the Arabic language was an important vehicle for their transmission. This had been true even in those areas of Andalusia that had been conquered by the Christians long before the fall of Granada. In Castile and Aragon, many of these conquered Muslims, known as Mudejars, had been allowed to retain their faith. Because many of these Muslims were more fluent in Castilian and Aragonese than Arabic, but knew how to write Arabic because of their Qur'anic studies, they wrote the Spanish dialects in the Arabic script. Known as *aljamiado*, this written language allowed Andalusian Muslims to teach the vernacular meaning of the Qur'an.

In 1566, two generations after all Moriscos were supposed to have abandoned Islam, the Spanish Crown issued an edict completely banning the use of Arabic. Suspecting that Moriscos were using Arabic to continue to transmit their beliefs and rituals, despite the latter's forced attendance at Mass and other Christian services, the Catholic monarchs ordered that the language should no longer be written or spoken in formal or informal communication. This and other measures taken to compel true Christian faith in the Moriscos seem to have had limited success. Finally, in 1609 CE, the Spanish rulers ordered that all Moriscos be expelled from Spain. Henry Kamen, a contemporary scholar who has written a historical revision of the Spanish Inquisition, nevertheless forcefully criticizes the treatment of Spanish Muslims by the Catholic rulers: "Almost in its totality, Muslim Spain was rejected and driven into the sea: thousands for whom there had been no other home were expelled to France, Africa, and the Levant. It was the last act in the creation of an orthodox society and completed the tragedy that had been initiated in 1492."[45]

Consuelo Lopez-Morillas, a contemporary Spanish scholar who has studied *aljamiado* manuscripts, concludes that secret Muslims were keen to preserve texts of the Qur'an and its vernacular translations, despite the risk of doing so:

> Throughout the sixteenth century, up to the time of their final expulsion in 1609, the Moriscos continued to copy the Arabic Qur'an and to translate it into Aljamiado. In writing Spanish with Arabic characters they succeeded in preserving at least the outward form of the language in which God had proclaimed His message to mankind. The survival of nearly seventy Morisco Qur'an MSS into modern times bears witness not only to the abundance of copies which must have been produced – for we may assume that only a fraction escaped destruction – but to the pains which the Moriscos must have taken to ensure their preservation. Many Qur'ans, indeed, have been discovered along with other Aljamiado works in the secret caches to which their owners consigned them and in which they lay hidden for hundreds of years.[46]

Although it might have been possible for some adult Muslims to hold onto their faith in secret, a more serious problem was their inability to transmit their beliefs and practices to their children. It is precisely this transmission that the Inquisition sought to break, and an edict to hand over their children to be educated by priests was the final straw for the Moriscos. In his history of the Spanish Inquisition, Oxford scholar Cecil Roth (writing with some bitterness and alarm in the 1930s, when fascist forces in Spain were in ascendance) described what happened:

> In 1566, a member of the Supreme Council of the Inquisition was appointed President of the Chancellery of Granada, and ordered to carry out a rigorous policy of suppression. An edict which Charles V. had been pursuaded to withdraw in 1526, which aimed at all Arabic folk-ways and domestic customs as well as their religion proper, was reissued, and this time sternly

enforced. The use of the Arabic language was forbidden; Moorish garments had to be laid aside; the baths, by which they approximated cleanliness to godliness, were to be closed down, thus preparing the way for orthodox Christian lice; Christian midwives were to be present at all births, so as to ensure baptism and to preclude Islamic "superstitions"; all doors were to be left open on feast-days, Fridays, Saturdays, and during weddings, to prevent the practice of Moorish cere- monies; the use of henna for staining had to be abandoned; and so on, *ad infinitum*....A year later, orders were issued to abandon Moorish costume forthwith, and to surrender all children between the ages of three and fifteen to the priests, who would place them in schools where they might learn Christian doctrine. The result was to provoke an immediate rebellion.[47]

Ibn Khaldun (d. 808/1406), the great North African historian who is often considered the founder of sociology, emphasized the importance Muslims placed on teaching the Qur'an to children: "Instructing children in the Qur'an is a symbol of Islam. Muslims have, and (still) practice such instruction in all their cities, because it imbues the heart with a firm belief in Islam and its articles of faith which are derived from the verses of the Qur'an and certain prophetic traditions. The Qur'an has become the basis of instruction, the foundation for all habits that may be acquired later on."[48]

Over the centuries, the establishment of schools to give children instruction in the Qur'an has been a priority of Muslim societies. Edward William Lane, an Englishman who spent many years in the early and mid-nineteenth century in Egypt, described the importance of these schools in that country:

> Schools are very numerous, not only in the metropolis, but in every large town; and there is one, at least, in every consider- able village. Almost every mosque, "sebeel" (or public foun- tain), and "hod" (or drinking place for cattle) in the metropolis has a "kuttab" (or school) attached to it, in which children are instructed for a very trifling expense; the "sheykh" or "fikee" (the master of the school) receiving from the parent of each pupil half a piaster (about five farthing of our money), or something more or less, every Thursday. The master of a school attached to a mosque or other public building in Cairo also generally receives yearly a tarboosh [fez], a piece of white muslin for a turban, a piece of linen, and a pair of shoes; and

each boy receives, at the same time, a linen skull-cap, four or five cubits of cotton cloth, and perhaps half a piece (ten or twelve cubits) of linen, and a pair of shoes, and, in some cases, half a piaster or a piaster. These presents are supplied by funds bequeathed to the school, and are given in the month of Ramadan. The boys attend only during the hours of instruction, and then return to their homes. The lessons are generally written upon tablets of wood, painted white; and when one lesson is learnt, the tablet is washed and another is written. They also practice writing upon the same tablet. The schoolmaster and his pupils sit upon the ground, and each boy has his tablet in his hands, or a copy of the Qur'an, or of one of its thirty sections, on a little kind of desk of palm-sticks. All the boys, in learning to read, recite or chant their lessons aloud, at the same time rocking their heads or bodies incessantly backwards and forwards; which practice is observed by almost all persons in reciting the Qur'an; being thought to assist the memory.[49]

Lane observed that some well-to-do families had teachers come to the homes to teach their sons or daughters. He noted that girls did attend the public schools with boys, but in fewer numbers; still, "I have often seen a well-dressed girl reading the Qur'an in a boys' school."[50]

Around the time Edward Lane was wandering throughout Cairo observing the "manners and customs" of the Egyptians, some enslaved Muslims from West Africa were informing American Christians about the religious life they had left behind. Lamen Kebe, who had been a teacher, told a man named Theodore Dwight about the educational practices of his region of West Africa. Kebe describes a setting similar to that depicted by Lane: children seated on the floor writing with reeds on white boards. Kebe mentions both male and female teachers, including his aunt, who was "much more learned than himself, and eminent for her superior acquirements and for her skill in teaching." Dwight discusses Kebe's views on the different pedagogies employed for teaching the Qur'an to the non-Arabic-speaking people of his region of Africa. Like the Muslims of Spain, Kebe believed it was important to transmit both the Qur'an and its meaning in the vernacular to the children:

It is interesting to the friends of education in America, to hear of improvements introduced in the schools of other countries. Lamen Kebe has a high opinion of a certain process practiced in some of the institutions of his native land, which he calls doubling; while of those in which it is not practiced, he speaks

Figure 3.6 Mauritanian youth with wooden tablets upon which they write Qur'anic verses they are learning. (Peter Sanders)

with comparative contempt. In schools of the latter and common class, the Qur'an is taught in Arabic alone, which not being the vulgar language of any of the negroes, is totally unintelligible. In those in which the important process of doubling is adopted, the meaning of the Arabic words is explained as well as translated.[51]

It is ironic that Kebe, a man so devoted to education, was kidnapped by enslavers while he was on a trip to buy paper for his pupils.

Kebe was not the only Qur'an-literate African brought as a slave to America. A number of such men are documented as having written complete copies of the Qur'an from memory while in America.[52] It is possible that some of these men had written the Qur'an from memory at least once before when they were in Africa. The Fulani of Mali, among others, required students to write out a complete text of the Qur'an from memory before they would be certified as a Hafiz.[53] In such societies, each Hafiz possessed his or her own handwritten *mushaf*. At the same time, Kebe and Lane's reports from early nineteenth-century Africa confirm that before the modern period, most children did not need or use a *mushaf* to memorize the Qur'an. Rather, children learned the Qur'an by listening to a passage recited by their teacher, writing the passage on a tablet, then memorizing what they had heard and written. In most places, oral examination was sufficient to obtain certification as a Hafiz. In such communities, there might be few *mushafs*, despite the presence of many individuals who had memorized the Qur'an.[54] In any case, the ability of enslaved African Muslims to write complete Qur'ans from memory is a testament to the success of their pedagogy.

Slave owners were mostly alarmed at African Muslim literacy, but abolitionists and missionaries were convinced that literate Africans, once converted to Christianity, could use their skills to spread the faith. We cannot be confident of the motives of the enslaved men in cooperating with missionaries, at least until they were in a situation to express themselves freely. For example, in 1828, the manumitted Ibrahim ibn 'Abd al-Rahman was sent back to Africa by abolitionists to preach the gospel. Ibrahim had displayed his ability to transmit Christian teachings by writing copies of "The Lord's Prayer" in Arabic for his patrons. It turns out, however, that what Ibrahim had written was Sura al-Fatiha, followed by a customary blessing for the Prophet Muhammad, and that he reverted back to Islam upon his arrival in Africa.[55]

Despite the touching stories of success that some African Muslims had holding on to their beliefs under terrible circumstances in America, they, like the Spanish Moriscos, were brutally prevented from passing their beliefs on to their children. Even when slaves were allowed to raise their own children, they were forbidden from teaching them about Islam, and they certainly could not transmit the Qur'an, orally or textually, to the next generation. As a result, the chain of the transmission of the Qur'an among perhaps thousands of African Muslims was ended with their enslavement in America.

Transmission of the Qur'an in the Modern Age

By the early nineteenth century CE, the Qur'an remained in Spain only where it had been hidden and now forgotten behind walls and false ceilings. Fully aware of this fact, Muslims throughout Africa and Asia had no doubt that European colonialism was a grave threat to their values, their culture, and their religion. The French, British, Dutch, and Italians were the main colonizers of Muslim lands, and their presence was opposed, appeased, and repelled to different degrees by indigenous people and their rulers.

In the field of education especially, a "culture war" ensued, with traditional Muslim institutions coming under attack by the colonial powers. In another chapter, we shall discuss the ways in which traditional forms of Qur'an interpretation and the authority of scripture itself were dismissed as superstition by "enlightenment" ideology. For now, it is sufficient to point out that memorization of the Qur'an was often dismissed as "rote learning" and characterized as an unthinking absorption of tradition. Indeed, there are many today who hold the same opinion.

The prejudices of European colonizers, missionaries, and secular bureaucrats cannot be taken at face value. Certainly there were ineffective and authoritarian teachers of the Qur'an in Muslim societies, as there have been in every society. However, the intellectual depth and creativity displayed by so many Muslim scholars throughout history – scholars whose education was founded on Qur'anic memorization – are proof that traditional Islamic pedagogy was by no means a necessary impediment to intellectual growth and creativity.

In the early part of the twenty-first century, Helen Boyle, a professor of education, studied children's schools in three Muslim countries: Morocco, Nigeria, and Yemen. Boyle was particularly interested in the difference between traditional and modernized schools in these countries. Although we cannot assume that contemporary "traditional" Qur'anic schools reflect a perfect continuity with schools of past centuries, their structure and culture are much closer to the former than are modernized schools. In her study, Boyle faulted some traditional schools for resorting more often to corporal punishment and sometimes harsh discipline, yet she also evaluated the traditional schools to generally have a more child-centered pedagogy and greater student retention. Traditional schools have a good deal of individualized instruction, allow students significant time for independent study and preparation before testing, utilize peer tutoring, and help students progress by having them master material before moving on to the next text.[56]

Most importantly, Boyle notes that the Qur'anic memorization that is at the heart of the curriculum of traditional schools establishes a grounded and holistic education:

> Qur'anic memorization is valuable because it is a process whereby children come to embody the Qur'an (or parts thereof). Embodiment as a theory advances the notion that bodiliness is an inescapable part of the creation of culture by

suggesting that the mind and body are intricately linked and as such both are implicated in the processes of mental and physical activities that constitute cultural production.... Qur'anic memorization has been portrayed as a process of mindless rote learning and indocrination into Islam. My research suggests that viewing it in this way reduces its significance in the lives of Muslims by implying that the process of learning *ends* with the process of memorization. Embodiment theory facilitates a description of the ongoing learning process that *begins* with Qur'anic memorization. Memorization, then, is an investment in a lifetime of potential learning, one that will provide guidance and direction to the student beyond the school years. The Qur'an is living as an oral text through the mental and physiological capabilities of the students' bodies, to translate what has been engraved in their minds to their lips, where it comes forth living, to be shared as recitation or in prayer and to be reflected upon over a lifetime, as a source of understanding, inspiration, and learning.[57]

Boyle further compares the children to buildings engraved with beautiful and complex Qur'anic calligraphy:

Calligraphic writing can be very difficult to read because it is complex and its letters are bunched up and intertwined. However, its beauty, swirling patterns, and graceful shapes can be appreciated at any age, by the literate or illiterate. When one learns to read, one can decipher words from the intricate letters and read the verses so beautifully engraved on the walls and contours of one's surroundings. As one learns more complex concepts and grows in perspective and understanding of the world and the self, one can comprehend meaning and deeper meaning embedded in the plaster curls, the stone curves, and the alabaster lines that form the beautiful calligraphic piece.

The little *kuttab* students are like these buildings, which hold a verse or two or ten or twenty on the walls of their minds, over which they can let their minds' eyes wander as they grow. They can appreciate the beauty of words – the rhythm, the rhymed, the intonation (much as American children might be able to recite and enjoy nursery rhymes and poems or songs whose meanings are not actually clear to them). As the words of the Qur'an are engraved on the mind of the child, they can be retrieved, uncovered, and rediscovered. The meaning of the words unfolds itself over time, providing insights on how to live. Central to this entire process is engraving. Memorization is the basis for recollection: it is the process of engraving the sacred verses onto the physiology of the person from childhood.[58]

Looked at from this perspective, we can understand why colonized Muslims felt that their way of life and value system were under attack when their traditional schools were closed or severely limited in scope. At the same time, it should be noted that Boyle studied Qur'an schools mostly in countries where Arabic is the mother tongue of the students. It is apparent that in non-Arab Muslim societies, Qur'anic memorization must be supplemented by translation and interpretation in the vernacular for it to be "embodied" by the students in any meaningful way. Lamen Kebe's disdain for West African teachers who did not teach the meaning of the Qur'an and Islamic texts alongside memorization demonstrates his awareness of the limitations of such an education.

The story of the Qur'an in modernity is, to a large extent, the story of the separation of the teaching of the Qur'an from its traditional context. In many cases, this separation was deliberate; in other cases, it could be considered an unintended consequence of the introduction of new technology. However, the idea that any new technology could be put at the service of religion without a consideration of the *value* it would add to the status quo is naïve. Individuals and societies put resources into the development and acquisition of new technologies because they believe that these innovations will increase a good – like economy, accessibility or social cohesion. New technologies are never introduced unintentionally, although there may be unforeseen consequences of their utilization in a society.

In general, Muslims who had significant contact with European societies and educational systems enthusiastically embraced new technologies as a way to catch up with a Europe that was simultaneously oppressing them with superior military power as well as enticing them with beautifully crafted, albeit often poorly implemented, constitutional representative governments. Liberty, equality, and, perhaps most importantly, national identity could be fostered by the use of a printing press. By printing brochures, newspapers, and leaflets and sending them throughout the country, the reformers could develop an audience far greater than the preacher of even the largest mosque in Cairo or Damascus. Because a printed Qur'an could be produced more cheaply than transcribed texts, more people could afford to have their own copy, purportedly furthering the egalitarian goals of Islam and the reformist agenda.

On the other hand, some political authorities saw the printing press as a means to break or bypass the power of traditional scholars. One such ruler was Muhammad Ali Pasha (d. 1265/1849), the military general who treacherously murdered the Mamluk rulers in Cairo, then declared himself independent of the Ottoman sultan who had appointed him viceroy of Egypt. Over the objections of the scholars, Muhammad Ali ordered the first Egyptian printing of the Qur'an in 1833 CE. There is no doubt that one of Muhammad Ali's aims was to transfer to the state some of the scholars' authority by printing official copies of the Qur'an for the general public and smaller selections of the Qur'an for schoolchildren.

The initial opposition of some scholars to the printing of the Qur'an was not unreasonable.[59] In the first place, specialists who produced copies of the Qur'an had an important place in many Muslim societies. These scribes were themselves *huffaz* for whom writing the Qur'an was not just a job, but an act of worship. Scribes treated the *mushafs* they prepared with great care, making sure they were in a state of ritual purity when they touched the text. They uttered supplications and prayers at certain points in the production process. A printing machine expressed no awe or reverence as it pressed the name of God into the paper. A machine could not form the intention to worship as it was printing copies of the Qur'an. If the printing press replaced thousands of men and women writing the Qur'an, it would eliminate a large sector of sacred devotion in a society.

Despite the validity of such concerns, the scholars could not hold back the tide of technological innovation for long, and eventually they turned their efforts towards ensuring that printed *mushafs* were accurate. State and private printing houses in Cairo, Istanbul, Beirut, and Damascus were producing scholar-approved *mushafs* by the late nineteenth century. Wherever modern technology had been introduced, handwritten *mushafs* now became valuable for their crafts-manship and rarity, not because they were necessary.

One consequence of printing the *mushaf* that perhaps the scholars had not foreseen was that some of the *qira'at* which had been domin-ant in certain regions of the world were now marginalized. This is because the early *mushafs* were printed only in the recitation of Hafs. In Egypt and Sudan, where the recitation of Abu 'Amr had been popular, the use of officially printed *mushafs* in government-controlled educational and religious institutions meant that the recitation of Hafs now became dominant. Currently, this is the most popular recitation in the Muslim world, although the recitation of Warsh is predominant in most of North Africa.

With printed *mushafs* available and public education increasing literacy in the general population, more and more ordinary Muslims were now able to read the Qur'an for themselves. This was the second time in history that a technological innovation made the *mushaf* more accessible to a larger segment of Muslim society; the first time was about eight centuries earlier with the ability to transcribe the Qur'an on paper rather than parchment or vellum.

With respect to orthography, we recall that a thousand years earlier, the introduction of dotted letters and vowel markers made it possible to represent the spoken Qur'an in the written text. However, the sound of the recited Qur'an was not fully represented in the traditional script. Although symbols representing some of the rules of *tajwid* were intro-duced in the *mushaf* earlier, many of the rules could only be learned orally from a qualified scholar. But in the early 1990s, a significant innovation in the printed *mushaf* quickly spread across the Muslim world. This was the invention of a system of rendering the letters of the *mushaf* in different colors to signify the sounds required by *tajwid*. Various shades of red, for example, signify the different degrees to which vowels should be lengthened (known as *madd*). This system was developed by a Syrian engineer who was studying *tajwid* with a scholar in Damascus.[60] The *Tajweed Qur'an* has been given official approval by the scholars of al-Azhar in Cairo, and is quickly being adopted for use in Muslim societies. The *Tajweed Qur'an* is so accessible and easy to use compared with medieval texts that explain the rules of *tajwid*, like the books of al-Dani, al-Shatibi, and Ibn al-Jazari, that one expects it to be the former, rather than the latter, that will increasingly be used as the primary textual means of learning *tajwid*. This is especially true since easy-to-use and effective computer and video programs have been developed to teach this system. Although Qur'an scholars are still needed to verify the accuracy of printed and electronic representa-tions of the Qur'an, engineers and computer programmers who have developed these technologies are the scribes of contemporary Islam.

Innovations in printing and orthography have had a tremendous impact on the accessibility and use of the Qur'an in modern Muslim societies. Innovations in sound recording have probably had an even greater impact. In the early twentieth century, recordings of Qur'an reciters were played on the radio, and over the century, with each new development in sound recording and broadcasting, Qur'an recitation became ever more available to the ordinary Muslim. Albums, cassettes, CDs, and podcasts of recitations and video-taped and web-based classes in the rules of recitation have allowed Muslims to learn *tajwid* and memorize the Qur'an without having a personal relationship with a scholar. These technologies are used not only by independent learners but also in many modern Islamic schools, adult study circles, and other institutions and organizations, each of which is developing its own culture of teaching the Qur'an. In many other cases, however, for the first time in the history of the Qur'an, individual Muslims can memorize and learn to recite the Qur'an quite competently, without having to rely on the presence of a teacher. The social and cultural ramifications of this separation of Qur'anic learning from religious institutions and authorities are on-going. Certainly the impact of being able to independently learn the Qur'an is seen even more strongly in the field of interpretation and application of Qur'anic norms than in the field of recitation and memorization, as we shall discuss in another chapter.

At the same time, there are limits to self-learning. Most Muslims still feel that true mastery of the Qur'an can only be judged by a qualified scholar who listens to the student's recitation, just as Gabriel listened to the Prophet Muhammad reciting the revelation back to him. It is for this reason that Reem sought out Sheikh al-Kurdi for certification; even though she had already learned *tajwid* and memorized the Qur'an, it took her a few more years of study with a certified teacher to perfect her recitation to the degree that she could be awarded the *ijaza*.

Of course, not every Muslim is interested in or capable of learning the rules of *tajwid* and memorizing the Qur'an. Most Muslims have what might be described as a more passive relationship with the Qur'an in that they appreciate listening to skillful and beautiful recitation. This has been true throughout history, for we recall stories from the medieval period of reciters who attracted large crowds due to their moving recitation. In the modern period, in the early days of recording and broadcast technology, Egyptian reciters seem to have dominated the Muslim world. This was probably due to the fact that after the fall of the Ottoman caliphate in 1923, al-Azhar University in Cairo assumed increasing prominence as the center of Sunni orthodoxy. Those who came from other countries to study at al-Azhar returned home with an attachment to the ideas and practices of Egyptian scholars. New recording and broadcasting technologies meant that

Egyptian reciters could be heard anywhere, and Sheikh 'Abd al-Basit 'Abd al-Samid, Sheikh al-Husari, and Sheikh Minshawi, among others, became "famous" in many Muslim societies.

The Egyptians recorded both *murattal* and *mujawwad* recitations, although it was the latter, with their highly artistic and melodic recitations, that attracted ardent fans. Some Egyptian reciters deliberately studied classical *maqamat* to enhance their recitation; for others, the melodic patterns had been internalized naturally having grown up in a society in which music was widely played. There were also critics of the *mujawwad* recitations; many considered them too "musical" and argued that they served the interests of artistry more than religion. In fact, during the early years of sound recording, some Egyptian musicians expressed an interest in combining Qur'an recitation with music to create a powerful aesthetic effect. The scholars of Azhar rejected this proposal as an unacceptable use of the Qur'an, and there has been a consensus among Muslims scholars since then that this is the only valid legal opinion (*fatwa*) on this issue.

Egyptian reciters, although popular in many Muslim societies, have had particularly devoted followers in Indonesia. In her research of Qur'anic recitation in that country, Anne Gade was told that short-wave radio broadcasts of Egyptian reciters were taped and played over and over again by aspiring Indonesian reciters. One reciter joked that "the voices of the Indonesian reciters who listened to the radio in this period had even picked up the sound of the distortion from the short-wave broadcasts." Reciters from remote areas reproduced from memory melodies, ornamentation, and particular improvisations of specific performers.[61]

In the last few decades, Saudi Arabia has superseded Egypt as the major center of influence in Sunni Islam, due to the enormous resources the government and private foundations have put into producing Islamic materials. The King Fahd Complex for the Printing of the Qur'an has distributed over two hundred million *mushafs* since 1985, publishes translations of the Qur'an in dozens of languages, and has begun printing *mushafs* in all orthodox recitations. Saudi reciters have become more popular in the last few decades for a number of reasons, most importantly because with the introduction of commercial air travel, more and more Muslims have the opportunity to go on pilgrimage to Mecca and Medina. With prayers at the Ka'ba and the Prophet's mosque being led by Saudi imams, pilgrims associate the Qur'an recitation of Sheikh Shuraim, Sheikh Sudais, and others with their moving spiritual experiences in those sacred places. Further, since the introduction of live broadcasts of prayers at the Ka'ba and the Prophet's mosque via satellite, Saudi imams have become household names in many Muslim societies. Their sober *murattal* recitations are increasingly considered by many Muslims to be more orthodox than the *mujawwad* recitations of the older Egyptian reciters.

At the same time, as it does with so many other aspects of contemporary life, the Internet allows Muslims to escape geographical parochialism (if not religious and cultural parochialism) and sample and enjoy Qur'an recitations from all over the world. This makes it possible for some Muslims to become, as it were, connoisseurs of Qur'an recitation, and many Muslims have a list of "favorite" reciters. At the beginning of the twenty-first century dozens of Internet websites offering free listening and downloads of reciters. One site was loaded with at least five hundred reciters, with all the orthodox recitations represented.[62] This also means that proficient Qur'an reciters can now find worldwide audiences, and their websites (complete with scanned copies of *hifz* and *tajwid ijaza*s) and recorded recitations allow them to enter the world of "famous" people in the globalized culture. Not every reciter, however, wants this kind of attention; indeed, some shun it.

Most women reciters avoid public recognition. We might consider this a consequence of social norms that unfairly exclude women from public life in many Muslim societies. However, many of these women consider themselves the guardians of authentic Islamic piety that discourages anyone – man or woman – from seeking attention and praise for performing what should be, after all, an act of worship. Significantly, it is almost impossible to find a recording of a female reciter on the Internet, or in another publicly available form. Some women, like Reem's teachers, will make recordings for their students, but they believe they can best serve the Qur'an and preserve a pure and righteous intention in their work by avoiding recognition. More importantly, in many Muslim societies, there is a belief it is "improper" for men to listen to a woman reciting Qur'an. This feeling stems from the conviction that it takes little for men to be attracted to women; even the Qur'an, if recited by a woman with a beautiful voice, might be enough to cause improper infatuation in some men. Interestingly, Indonesian Muslims seem to have no such fear. In this largest of Muslim countries, female reciters are as common as men; their recordings are publicly available and their recitations are broadcast on radio and television. Hajja Maria Ulfah of Indonesia has emerged as the most famous female reciter in the world.

The consequences of the accessibility and portability of such recitations are many. Technology has made it possible for individuals to access the Qur'an without having to be in direct contact with a scholar or a religious institution. Recordings of the best reciters are heard by isolated individuals going about their daily business: a New York taxi driver plays cassettes in his car, an Indian housewife listens on her iPod as she exercises on a treadmill, a business traveler listens on headphones on Gulf Airlines, a Malaysian teenager listens from a webcast streaming through his home computer. Qur'anic recitations bring peace, tranquility, beauty, and meaning into their lives. And for some of them, perhaps, the disembodied recitation allows them to feel a relatively direct connection with the original source of the words – with the headphones on, it is almost as though an angel were whispering the words in their ears.

Finally, modern technology has created new public and shared forums for Qur'an recitation. That a modern Muslim family can sit together in their living room and listen and watch prayers broadcast live from Mecca has a significance not only for religious life, but also for family and community life.

Conclusion

Over the centuries, Muslims have displayed a remarkable commitment to preserving and transmitting the Qur'an as it was revealed to the Prophet Muhammad. To this end, Muslims have used every available means of preservation and communication: parchment, paper and ink, slate and chalk, printing presses, audio cassettes, and the Internet. The Qur'an has been taught and studied in secret and in the open, in humble homes, grand mosques, neighborhood kindergartens, and seminaries. But in the end, it is only because in each generation there have been many sincere Muslims who dedicated themselves to the difficult challenge of memorizing the Qur'an and mastering its recitation that this sacred text continues to be fully preserved, accurately transmitted, and celebrated in Muslim societies. It is appropriate, therefore, to end this chapter by returning to Reem's story.

After Reem earned her *ijaza* from Sheikh al-Kurdi, she felt a sense of accomplishment, but also a sense of loss, as now she would no longer enjoy the intense periods of study with her teachers whom she so loved and admired. She also felt the weight of her obligation to continue this noble tradition by making herself available to those who wished to study with her. When Reem returned to the United States, she enrolled in college and married a young Muslim man whose character mirrors her own: pious, humble, and keenly intelligent. He is also the grandson of a scholar who is thought to have the shortest *isnad* for Qur'anic memorization and recitation of any living person. Reem hopes to be able to earn another *ijaza* from this scholar, to bring her recitation even closer to that of the Prophet Muhammad and the heavenly realm.

In the meantime, Reem has accepted many students dedicated to mastering *tajwid* and Qur'anic memorization. These students include, like Reem, other children of immigrants to America, but they also include American converts to Islam. Among these converts are African American Muslims, many of whom call themselves "reverts" in reference both to the theological belief that all people are born *muslim*, i.e., they are born with an innate belief in the Creator, and to the historical fact that many of them must have had at least one ancestor who was a Muslim. An increasing number of Latina/os in the United States and throughout the Americas are also becoming aware of their Andalusian Islamic cultural heritage, and are embracing Islam.

Thus, in places and among people where the chains of transmission of the Qur'an had been broken – among African Muslims enslaved in the Americas and among the descendants of Andalusian Muslims – it is being repaired. In fact, among those who can now connect themselves as a twenty-ninth link in the chain of transmission of the Qur'an through Sheikh al-Kurdi all the way back to the Prophet Muhammad, the Angel Gabriel, and the Lord of Majesty are African Americans and Latino Americans, as well as many others across the world. There are countless other transmissions through thousands of certified scholars in Indonesia, India, Nigeria, Egypt, and other countries.

Islamic eschatology holds that some day, every chain of transmission will cease; all links, except the original link, will disappear, for the Qur'an says,

> *Everything on (the earth) will perish; but the face of your Lord, full of majesty and dignity will abide.*
>
> (Rahman; 55:26–27)

But for now, the transmission continues.

Notes

1 Given the volatility of the political situation in Syria, I have chosen to protect the identities of the women involved in this story by referring to them only by their first names. The information I have is from interviews I conducted with Reem during 2005–2006 and from an examination of her documents. I have also interviewed a number of other individuals who went through the same process and who have provided additional and corroborating information.

2 When I heard this anecdote, I was struck by how it mirrors the Qur'anic description of Moses asking to see God (A'raf 7:143). It is possible that, having studied the Qur'an so extensively, the young woman's intense emotions were naturally expressed through this discourse she had internalized.

3 William A. Graham, *Beyond the Written Word: Oral Aspects of Scripture in the History of Religion* (Cambridge: Cambridge University Press, 1987), 65.

4 Interestingly, Umm Hisham prefaces her report with the statement that her family used to share a stove with the Prophet's family for a few years; the implication is that she heard the Prophet's recitation from the mosque while she was outside using the stove on Fridays (since the Prophet and his family lived in small rooms attached to the mosque). Muslim, *"Kitab al-Jumu'a,"* 6:161.

5 Bukhari, *"Kitab al-Tafsir,"* 946.

6 M. M. Azami, *The History of the Qur'anic Text: From Revelation to Compilation: A Comparative Study with the Old and New Testaments* (Leicester: UK Islamic Academy, 2003), 59–60.

7 Bukhari, *"Kitab al-Tafsir,"* 1069–1070.

8 Abu Hamid al-Ghazali says, "The Messenger of God, may God bless him and give him peace, died leaving behind twenty thousand companions, only six of whom memorized the Qur'an in its entirety, and in the case of two of these there is a disagreement. Most of the Companions used to memorize one sura or two. Anyone who would memorize (Sura) al-Baqara and (Sura) al-An'am was considerd one of their scholars." Muhammad Abul Quasem, *The Recitation and Interpretation of the Qur'an: al-Ghazali's Theory* (London: Kegan Paul International, 1982), 79.

9 Muslim, *"Kitab Fada'il al-Sahaba,"* 16:20.

10 Ahmed ibn Shu'ayb al-Nasa'i, *Fada'il al-Qur'an*, ed. Faruq Hamadah (Casablanca: Dar al-Thaqafa, 1980), 109–110.

11 Beatrice Gruendler, "Arabic Script," *EQ* 1:140.

12 Bukhari, *"Kitab Fada'il al-Qur'an,"* 1086.

13   Abu 'Ubayda al-Qasim ibn Sallam, *Fada'il al-Qur'an*, ed. Wahbi Sulayman Ghawaji (Beirut: Dar al-Kutub al-'Ilmiyya, 1991); Abu 'Amr 'Uthman ibn Sa'id al-Dani, *Al-Muqni' fi rasm masahif al-amsar* (with *Kitab al-Naqt*), ed. Hasan Sirri (Alexandria, Egypt: al-Tawzi' marakaz al-Iskandariyya li'l-kitab, 2005).

14   This opinion was conveyed to me orally by Abdullah Adhami, author of the book *Ithaf al-Munawwarat bi Tabyin Ijazat al-Qari'at* (New York: Sakeenah Books, forthcoming).

15   John Wansbrough, *Quranic Studies: Sources and Methods of Scriptural Interpretation*, foreword, translations, and expanded notes by Andrew Rippin (Amherst, NY: Prometheus Books, 2004).

16   Harald Motzki, "The Collection of the Qur'an: A Reconsideration of Western Views in Light of Recent Methodological Developments," *Der Islam* (2001): 1–34.

17   *Masahif San'a* (Kuwait: Dar al-Athar al-Islamiyya, 1985); Estelle Whelan, "Forgotten Witness: Evidence for the Early Codification of the Qur'an," *Journal of the American Oriental Society*, 118, 1 (January–March 1998): 1–15, and "Writing the Word of God: Some Early Qur'an Manuscripts and their Milieux, Part I," *Ars Orientalis*, 20 (1990): 113–114.

18   Adrian Brockett, "The Value of the Hafs and Warsh Transmissions for the Textual History of the Qur'an," in *Approaches to the History of the Interpretation of the Qur'an*, ed. Andrew Rippin (Oxford: Clarendon Press, 1988), 44.

19   Hossein Modarressi, "Early Debates on the Integrity of the Qur'an: A Brief Survey," *Studia Islamica*, 77 (1993): 5–39.

20   Muhammad Ismail Marcinkowski, "Some Reflections on Alleged Twelver Shi'ite Attitudes towards the Integrity of the Qur'an," *The Muslim World*, 91, 1/2 (Spring 2001): 137–154.

21   Tabari, *History*, vol. 15, translated by R. Stephen Humphreys as *The Crisis of the Early Caliphate* (1990), 205–206.

22   See the UNESCO website for photos and details: www.unesco.org.

23   *Muwatta*, 103.

24   'Abd al-Rahman ibn Muhammad ibn al-Anbari, *Nuzhat al-alibba fi tabaqat al-udaba'*, ed. Attia Amer (Stockholm: Almqvist & Wiksell, 1963), 16–23.

25   François Déroche, "Manuscripts of the Qur'an," *EQ* 3:259.

26   George Makdisi, *The Rise of Colleges: Institutions of Learning in Islam and the West* (Edinburgh: Edinburgh University Press, 1981), 2.

27   Efim Rezvan, "Orthography," *EQ* 3:604–608.

28   Tahir ibn 'Abd al-Mun'im ibn Ghalbun, *Tadhkirah fi'l-qira'at*, ed. 'Abd al-Fattah Buhayri Ibrahim (Cairo: al-Zahra' li'l-'ilam al-'arabi, 1990).

29   Salah al-Din al-Munajjid, "Women's Roles in the Art of Arabic Calligraphy," in *The Book in the Islamic World: The Written Word and Communication in the Middle East*, ed. George N. Atiyah (Albany: State University of New York Press, 1995), 145–146.

30 Déroche, 263.

31 Rosamond E. Mack, *Bazaar to Piazza: Islamic Trade and Italian Art, 1300–1600* (Berkeley: University of California Press, 2002).

32 Muhammad ibn Abi Bakr ibn Qayyim al-Jawziyya, *The Legal Methods in Islamic Administration*, translation of *al-Turuq al-hukmiyya fi'l-siyasa al-shar' iyya* by Ala'eddin Kharofa (Kuala Lumpur: International Law Book Services, 2000), 15–19.

33 Anna M. Gade, *Perfection Makes Practice: Learning, Emotion and the Recited Qur'an in Indonesia* (Honolulu: University of Hawai'i Press, 2004), 181.

34 Jonathan P. Berkey, *The Formation of Islam: Religion and Society in the Near East, 600–1800* (Cambridge: Cambridge University Press, 2003), 197–198.

35 Kristina Nelson, *The Art of Reciting the Qur'an* (Cairo: American University in Cairo Press, 2001), 83.

36 Muhammad ibn Ahmed ibn Jubayr, *Risalat Ibn Jubayr fi Misr wa Bilad al-'Arab wa'l-'Iraq wa'l-Sham wa Saqliyya 'asr hurub al-Salibiyya*, ed. Husayn Nassar (Cairo: Maktabat Misr, 1992); I have used the translation (with a few small changes) of R. J. C. Broadhurst in his book *The Travels of Ibn Jubayr: Being the chronicle of a mediaeval Spanish Moor concerning his journey to the Egypt of Saladin, the holy cities of Arabia, Baghdad the City of the Caliphs, the Latin Kingdom of Jerusalem, and the Norman Kingdom of Sicily* (London: Goodword Books, 2001; first printed in London, 1952), 153–154.

37 Ibn Jubayr, 229–230.

38 Ibn Jubayr, 282–283.

39 Ibn Jubayr, 279.

40 Carole Hillenbrand, *The Crusades: Islamic Perspectives* (New York: Routledge, 2000), 122, 238, 305, etc.

41 See, for example, the pilgrim journal of 'Ali ibn Abi Bakr al-Harawi (d. 611/1215), *A Lonely Wayfarer's Guide to Pilgrimage*, translation by Josef W. Meri of *Kitab al-Isharat ila ma'rifat al-ziyarat* (Princeton: Darwin Press, 2004).

42 Imam al-Haramayn 'Abd al-Malik ibn Yusuf al-Juwayni, *Kitab al-Waraqat*, in the text of Jalal al-Din Muhammad ibn Ahmed al-Mahalli's *Sharh al-waraqat fi 'ilm usul al-fiqh* (Cairo: Muhammad 'Ali Subayh, 1965).

43 Ibrahim ibn Ibrahim al-Laqani (d. 1041/1631), *Jawharat al-Tawhid* (Cairo, 1967); this book was being taught in 2006 by the "Sunni-Path," a neo-traditionalist American Muslim online academy (www.sunnipath.com).

44 The *Jazariyya* is widely available in popular and academic publications. Many of Sheikh al-Kurdi's students use the book *Mulhaq al-mufid fi 'ilm al-tajwid*, a commentary on the *Jazariyya* by one of his certified reciters,

a woman scholar named al-Hajja Hayat 'Ali al-Husayni. The book is a personal publication, made in 1997. A widely available scholarly commentary on the *Jazariyyah* was made by one of the links in Sheikh al-Kurdi's *isnad*, Abu Yahya Zakariyya ibn Muhammad al-Ansari (d. 925/1519), under the title *al-Daqa'iq al-muhkamah fi sharh al-muqaddimah al-Jazariyya fi 'ilm al-tajwid* (Damascus, 1980).

45 Henry Kamen, *The Spanish Inquisition: A Historical Revision* (New Haven: Yale University Press, 1997), 228–229.

46 Consuelo Lopez-Morillas, *The Qur'an in Sixteenth-Century Spain: Six Morisco Versions of Sura 79* (London: Tamesis Books, 1982), 14.

47 Cecil Roth, *The Spanish Inquisition* (New York: Norton, 1964), 154.

48 'Abd al-Rahman Muhammad ibn Muhammad ibn Khaldun, *The Muqaddimah: An Introduction to History*, translation by Franz Rosenthal of *Al-Muqaddima*, abridged and ed. N. J. Dawood (Princeton: Princeton University Press, 1967), 421.

49 Edward William Lane, *An Account of the Manners and Customs of the Modern Egyptians*, "The Definitive 1860 Edition," reprinted from the fifth edition of 1860, introduced by Jason Thompson (Cairo: American University in Cairo Press, 2003), 60–61.

50 Lane, 63.

51 Allan D. Austin, *African Muslims in Antebellum America: Transatlantic Stories and Spiritual Struggles* (New York: Routledge, 1997), 121.

52 Austin, 24, 55. Among those who were reported to have written the complete text of the Qur'an from memory were Charles Larten and Job Ben Solomon.

53 The process is described by Abdel Kader Haidara, curator of the Mamma Haidara Memorial Library in Timbuktu, Mali in a lecture given at the Library of Congress, Washington, DC on September 3, 2003. www.loc.gov/today/cyberlc/feature_wdesc.php?rec=3399.

54 Priscilla P. Soucek,"Material Culture," *EQ* 3:308.

55 Austin, 64–83.

56 Helen N. Boyle, *Quranic Schools: Agents of Preservation and Change* (New York and London: RoutledgeFalmer, 2004), 70–73.

57 Boyle, 97–98.

58 Boyle, 91–92.

59 Paul Lunde, "Arabic and the Art of Printing," *Saudi Aramco World* (March/April 1981): 20–35.

60 The *Tajweed Qur'an* is published by Dar Al Maarifah; information on its development and associated products is available at: easyquran. com/.

61 Gade, 189.

62 www.islamweb.net/ver2/engblue/audio.php?page=rewaya.

4

Blessed Words: The Qur'an and Culture

The Qur'an as the Word of God

An obvious, but not to be overlooked, fact is that Muslims across the world read and recite the Qur'an in Arabic; that this is true now, as it has been from the beginning of Islam, is not a historical necessity. In the early twenty-first century, only a minority (fewer than 20 percent) of Muslims are Arab; the rest are indigenous speakers of other languages: Persian, Urdu, Bangla, Malay, Wolof, Amharic, Turkish, Berber, Hausa, English, etc. The cultural diversity of the Muslim world is not a new development. Indeed, it is likely that within two centuries of the rise of Islam, the majority of Muslims were non-Arabic speakers.[1] As we have emphasized earlier, a significant loss in translation is the sound of the Arabic Qur'an. To translate the Qur'an to another language is to lose the powerful aural effect of the rhymes, assonance, and other harmonious and poetic aspects of the Arabic words. In addition, it is clearly impossible to reproduce the *tajwid* of the recited Qur'an in a translation. However, languages other than Arabic have their own beauty and efficacy and, over the centuries, Muslims have employed their mother tongues to deliver sermons, compose religious poetry, to narrate stories of prophets and righteous imams, explicate and interpret the Qur'an, and explore Islamic law and ethics. That Muslims across the world continue to employ Arabic to read and recite the Qur'an is a fact that merits some explanation.

Most importantly, the Qur'an declares itself in a number of places to be "an Arabic Qur'an," e.g.,

> *Verily We revealed it as an Arabic Qur'an.*
>
> (Yusuf; 12:2)

Muslims understand these verses to indicate an inexorable connection between the language and substance of the revelation. Hence, any translation of the Qur'an cannot be considered "Qur'an."

That God sent the Qur'an through Gabriel to the Prophet Muhammad is something his Companions knew and believed. These men and women lived the miracle of the prophetic experience; they did not need to frame this experience in philosophical language. When Abu Bakr heard that the Prophet Muhammad said that he had been taken to Jerusalem and then into the Divine Presence in the "Night Journey," he declared, "If he says so then it is true. And what is so surprising in that? He tells me that news comes to him from heaven to earth in an hour of a day or night and I believe him, and that is more extraordinary than that which stupifies you!"[2]

For later generations of Muslims, however, the ontological status of the sacred book became an issue of increasing concern. By the end of the first century, Muslims were raising questions about the meaning of phrases such as "the word of God" and "God's speech." Did these expressions mean that God spoke in the manner of human beings? If this was not the case, how could Moses, for example, have heard God when he "spoke" to him (7:143)? At the same time, the Qur'an describes the revelation as being brought by the "trustworthy spirit" (understood to be Gabriel) to the "heart" of the Prophet. What, then, was the mechanism by which Muhammad received the revelation? Did he "hear" it or did he just "understand" it? The Qur'anic description that it is to be found on a "guarded tablet" (85:22) led to further ambiguities. For some theologians, this phrase gave occasion to propose a kind of liminal stage of revelation, when the eternal and unchanging speech of God was captured in concrete form. It was from this heavenly transcription that Gabriel took the Qur'an that he brought to the Prophet Muhammad. In the end, the question remained, even if the Prophet perfectly conveyed the words of the Qur'an, as all Muslims agreed, to what extent did the sound of the words replicate the actual speech of God?

For some theologians, the notion that God could or would produce sounds capable of being heard by humans suggested that God shared some aspects of his creation. In their estimation, this understanding approached anthropomorphism and violated the Qur'anic statement, *There is none like him* (42:11). To preserve the utter "otherness" of God from his creation, these theologians concluded that it was necessary to describe the Qur'an as the *created* word of God. A group of these theologians, who became knows as the "Mu'tazilites," promoted this doctrine in bitter opposition to other Muslim scholars, particularly the hadith scholars, who were highly skeptical of the philosophical discourse being used to frame the issue and the potential for degrading the unique authority of the Qur'an by making it part of creation.

By the early third century, the ontological status of the Qur'an had become a highly contentious and politicized issue when the 'Abbasid caliph Al-Ma'mun used it to test the loyalty of prominent scholars and judges. Researchers have suggested a number of possible motivations for Al-Ma'mun's establishment of this "test" (mihna). Among other possibilities, there is substantial evidence to suggest that Al-Ma'mun was eager to claim not just political but also religious authority for himself. Many of his predecessors had ceded much religious authority to scholars, who sometimes used that authority to criticize the policies of the rulers. On a personal level, Al-Ma'mun, like the English King Henry VIII many centuries later, found himself prevented from divorcing his wife by a religiously based law he did not have the authority to override.

Whatever Al-Ma'mun's motives may have been, the letter he sent out to judges and scholars explaining his position is a clear explication of the Mu'tazilite position:

> Among those things which the Commander of the Faithful [i.e., the caliph] has made plain to himself by reflection, and has studied intently by his thinking so that the great danger attending it has become obvious, as well as the seriousness of the corruption and harm which will rebound on religion, are the statements which the Muslims are passing round among themselves about the Qur'an, which God has established as an exemplar for them and an enduring legacy to them of the Messenger of God and His chosen One, Muhammad. The confusion of opinion about the Qur'an in the minds of many people is such that it has seemed good to them and attractive to their intellects that it is not created. They thereby lay themselves open to the risk of rejecting God's creative power, by which He is distinguished from His creation and remains apart in His splendor in the bringing into existence of all things by means of His wisdom and their being originated by His power, and in His priority in time over them by reason of His primordial existence, whose beginning cannot be attained and whose extent cannot be comprehended. Everything apart from

Him is a created object from His creation and a new thing which He has brought into existence. Even though the Qur'an itself speaks about God's creative power, sets forth its proof and decisively confutes all difference of opinion about it, these people talk just like the Christians when they claim that Jesus the son of Mary was not created, because he was the word of God.[3]

The reference to Christian trinitarian doctrine shows that one of the Mu'tazilites' major concerns was to articulate a theology of the Qur'an that maintained the perfect unicity (*tawhid*) of God. Indeed, many researchers suggest that the Mu'tazilites resorted to philosophical discourse to describe the relationship of God to the Qur'an precisely to counter critiques of Islam by Christian and other non-Muslim apologists.

Whatever the origin of the controversy, the political dimension of the imposition of a dogma unpopular with the majority of religious scholars was of paramount importance for those living under the 'Abbasid ruler during al-Ma'mun's reign and for centuries afterward. Thus, the great Iraqi historian al-Tabari (d. 310/923), despite his dislike for some Badhdadi Hanbalites who, in fact, harassed him for his views, presents a positive description of their eponym's refusal to concede to the demands of the state. Ahmed ibn Hanbal was a prominent hadith scholar and charismatic religious leader in Baghdad. It was no doubt Ahmed's widespread influence among the people of the capital city that made him a target for tests of political loyalty. Ahmed, like other scholars who were summoned to publicly support the Mu'tazilite doctrine, was threatened with imprisonment and corporal punishment if he refused. While many others capitulated under the intense pressure, a few did not; among them was Ahmed ibn Hanbal.

The conversations that reportedly took place between Ahmed and his inquisitor, Ishaq ibn Ibrahim, reveal a great deal about Ahmed's view of the proper way for the believer to approach the ontology of the Divine:

Ishaq ibn Ibrahim asked Ahmed, "What is your view concerning the Qur'an?"
Ahmed replied, "It is the word of God."
Ishaq asked, "Is it created?"
Ahmed replied, "It is the word of God, I cannot add any more to these words."

[Ibrahim continued to question Ahmed about some things
then said:] "What do the words, *'a hearing and a seeing one'*
mean?"
Ahmed replied, "God is even as He has described Himself."
Ishaq said, "But what does it mean?"
Ahmed replied, "I do not know. He is just as He has described
Himself."[4]

Ahmed's response is interesting not so much for what he says as for
what he does not say, or perhaps more accurately, *how* he will not say
what is being demanded of him. At the most basic level, Ahmed refuses
to allow the interrogator to frame the question. For Ahmed, it is not
acceptable for humans with their limited understanding to impose
categories and concepts upon God. Only God has the authority to
describe himself and it is only through his revelation that we have
certain knowledge of his nature.

The reach of the *mihna* was neither deep nor wide, for only judges
and scholars of hadith were tested. Nevertheless, the dramatic events
had a profound effect on the scholarly community and significant
ramifications for the division of political and religious authority during
this formative period of Islamic history. The 'Abbasids learned that
their violent attempts to control religious scholars did not further their
legitimacy as defenders of the faith. They ended the *mihna*, and,
although the 'Abbasid caliphs and their administrators did not
completely back away from trying to control religious authority, they
became less directly involved. Instead of interpreting law and theology
themselves, political authorities encouraged and supported the development of more formal educational institutions and standards to
stabilize the growing community of religious specialists. In turn, this
meant that the *mihna* had the long-term effect of strengthening the
social profile of the scholarly class, who henceforth tried to assert their
independence from political rulers to judge on matters of religious law
and belief, while simultaneously calling upon the power of the state
from time to time to enforce the orthodoxy they delineated.

By the end of the third century, most Muslim scholars rejected
non-engagement in theological discourse *à la* Ahmed ibn Hanbal as a
viable option, despite their admiration for his courageous refusal to
submit to political pressure. Once questions and doubts had been raised
about the nature of God, the ontological status of the Qur'an, and the
epistemological relationship of reason to revelation, these questions

had to be answered. As with the study of law, a few intellectual schools formed around the systematizing efforts of particular scholars, who emerged as leaders in the struggle to define orthodoxy. Sunni Islam came to be dominated by the Ash'arites and the Maturidis: the schools of the Iraqi scholar Abu'l-Hasan al-Ash'ari (d. 323/935) and the Central Asian scholar Abu Mansur al-Maturidi (d. 333/944), respectively.

In order to preserve the unique ontological status of revelation, both schools rejected the Mu'tazilite doctrine that the Qur'an was created and upheld the view that God's speech is one of his uncreated attributes. At the same time, these theologians were keen to avoid the implication the Mu'tazilites had feared, that the Qur'an is somehow an incarnation of God's word.

At the popular level, orthodox Sunni theology was articulated in the relatively short "creed" ('aqida) of the Egyptian scholar Abu Ja'far al-Tahawi (d. 321/935), a contemporary of al-Ash'ari and al-Maturidi. Among the hundred or so articles of the creed is the following addressing the nature of the Qur'an:

> The Qur'an is the word of God. It came from Him as speech without it being possible to say how. He sent it down on His Messenger as revelation. The believers accept it as absolute truth. They are certain that it is, in truth, the word of God. It is not created as is the speech of human beings, and anyone who hears it and claims that it is human speech has become an unbeliever.[5]

On the academic level, the Ash'aris and the Maturidis developed a sophisticated analysis of language and meaning, distinguishing between the recited words of the Qur'an (the signifiers) and their perceived meaning (the signified). The following passage from a major fifth-century Ash'arite treatise, "The Guide (al-Irshad)" of Imam al-Haramayn al-Juwayni (d. 478/1085), demonstrates how this distinction is used to show that the created sounds of Qur'an recitation, articulated by a human reciter, are not God's eternal speech, but rather signify God's eternal speech:

> The recitation, according to the orthodox, consists of the sounds of the readers and their intonation, which are acquisitions of theirs, commanded of them in the state required by certain acts of ritual obeisance or recommended at many other

times.... Recitation is something that is agreeable on the part
of one reader and disagreeable when done by another. It can
be defective or regular and exact. The eternal attribute, however, transcends all of the things to which we allude here. No
person of true discrimination would ever think that the sounds
that make his throat hoarse or engorge abnormally his jugular
veins, and which, in accord with proclivity or desires, may be
pronounced incorrectly or correctly, loudly or furtively, are the
actual words of the Exalted God. This is our creed with respect
to the recitation. In regard to what is recited in the process of
recitation, a part of the recitation is grasped and understood
and that is the eternal speech which the expressions signify but
which are not it. Moreover, what is recited is not incarnate in
the reciter nor does it subsist in him. The situation of the
recitation and what is recited is like an invocation and what
is invoked. The invocation belongs to the statements of those
who invoke, and the Lord who is invoked, hallowed and
glorified, is not the invocation, nor the hallowing nor the
glorifying.... The words of the Exalted God are written in
copies of the Qur'an, preserved in the breast, but they do not
inhere in the copy nor subsist in the heart. The writing, by
which it is expressed, either through the movements of the
person who writes or through inscribed letters and imprinted
lines, is altogether temporally contingent. What the lines
signify is the eternal speech.[6]

This subtle understanding of the written and recited Qur'an as the
signification of the speech of God was not acceptable to all schools
of thought. The Hanbalites generally held onto their eponym's refusal
to describe the Qur'an in any terms other than it described itself. In
turn, Ash'arite and Maturidi scholars continued to characterize the
Hanbalite position as vulgar and anthropomorphic.

In the end, although discussions of the ontological status of the
Qur'an were obscure to the vast majority of Muslims, the issue became
an aspect of dogma upon which all theological schools took a position.
For centuries, ordinary Muslims repeated statements about the uncreated word of God as they recited dogmatic creeds taught to them in
schools and mosques. Such creeds were dropped from the curriculum
in many modern Muslim educational systems, which aimed to avoid
sectarian controversies. However, the issue never disappeared completely in modern Muslim discourse and indeed, it resurfaced with
some vengeance in the latter part of the twentieth century. Since

that time, neo-traditionalist Ash'arites and Maturidis have tried to reclaim authority from Hanbalite theologians who had gained the upper hand through the widespread distribution of their views by means of publications and lectures originating in Saudi Arabia.

The Qur'an and Sacred Architecture

Theological controversies aside, Muslims are united in the belief that the Qur'an is the word of the Divine. In whatever sense they have understood this phrase, Muslims have been in agreement that the Qur'an has a unique ontological status. It is for this reason that Muslim societies are infused with the sound and script of the Qur'an. Oral and written tradition support and complement each other to allow God's word to reach the heart of every believer.

In pre-Islamic Arabia, the master poems, the *Mu'allaqat*, were recited in the market of 'Ukaz and hung on the Ka'ba. After the rise of Islam, God's words were recited day and night in the sanctuary of Mecca, and the Ka'ba was draped in cloth embroidered with Qur'anic verses.[7] Across the centuries, as Semitic, European, Asian, and African peoples embraced Islam, their soundscapes and landscapes too were transformed with the words of the Qur'an. Qur'anic recitation fills the air of Muslim societies as schoolchildren repeat verses after their teachers, loudspeakers broadcast morning and evening prayers from the mosques, groups gather to recite Qur'an upon the death anniversary of relatives, and shopkeepers play recitations of famous *Qaris* ("Reciters") for their customers.

On the visual plane, Qur'anic verses rendered by hand in elegant calligraphy and masterful engraving decorate mosques and homes; elsewhere, verses printed on mass-produced calendars and kitschy wall-clocks are displayed. Everywhere, the protective, blessed, and talismanic presence of the Word of God is experienced.[8]

By the time Islam established a presence in Europe and Asia, most major religious traditions already present on these two continents (excluding Judaism) invoked the sacred with images, although many of these traditions, including Christianity and Buddhism, had passed through significant periods of aniconism or iconoclasm.[9] Islam's rejection of figurative religious art can be traced to the Prophet Muhammad's destruction of the idols housed in the Ka'ba. When Mecca surrendered to the Prophet in 8/630, the inhabitants of the city agreed to embrace Islam and Muhammad as their spiritual and political leader.

On the basis of this authority, Muhammad cleansed the Ka'ba of the idols, just as his ancestor Abraham had destroyed the idols of his people. Abraham had prayed that his descendants would never again resort to idol worship (14:35; 21:55–67); despite his prayer, the Quraysh had allowed the Ka'ba to become a house of idols. Perhaps this furthered their economic goals, for allowing merchants a space in the Ka'ba for their idols may have helped Mecca become an important center of commerce. We might find in Muhammad's destruction of the idols echoes of Jesus' forceful action in clearing the temple of the moneychangers.

Because the Ka'ba occupies a unique position in Islamic spirituality and worship as the place of pilgrimage and the direction of prayer, it is the Prophet's mosque at Medina that provides the basic model for all other mosques. Thus, all later mosques have an open, roughly rectangular prayer hall with some indication of the direction of the Ka'ba (the *qibla*) in the wall. Very early in Islamic history, mosques adopted a variety of architectural features to facilitate the functions performed there, as well as to honor and dignify the place of prayer. Among these features is the *mihrab*, a niche in the wall indicating the *qibla*, often the site of elaborate decoration. The minaret, a tower from which the *mu'adhdhin* makes the call to prayer (the *adhan*), quickly became another feature of most mosque architecture and a platform for decorative expression.[10]

Wherever Muslims settled in the world, they incorporated elements of local sacred architecture into their mosques. In central Muslim lands, the Byzantine dome was quickly adopted, no doubt because it was especially effective in engendering a feeling of transcendent expansion (what the mystics call *bast*) in worshippers, particularly in those places where the climate demands a well-covered roof for at least part of the year. The square minarets of Syrian, African, and Andalusian Islam may have been inspired by church bell-towers. In much of China, the influence of Buddhist temple architecture is seen in the elevation of the mosque prayer hall, giving worshippers a sense of ascending towards the sacred. In short, early Muslims embraced many of the elements of indigenous sacred architecture wherever they went, while at the same time retaining the basic structure of the Prophet's mosque in Medina and shunning figurative and iconic representations of the Divine. In their place, Muslims put the word of God – Qur'anic calligraphy.[11]

Because there is no indication that Qur'anic verses were hung in the Prophet's mosque in Medina, some early Muslims were reluctant to use the Qur'an in this way. In addition to wanting to scrupulously follow the Sunna of the Prophet, some Muslims felt that it was improper to use Qur'anic verses for decorative purposes in ways that hindered their readability.[12] The majority of Muslims throughout history, however, have wholeheartedly embraced Qur'anic calligraphy as a means to both sanctify space and to give visual instruction to the faithful, just as icons, friezes, murals, and statues have been used for such purposes in other traditions. In fact, the Umayyad caliph al-Walid ibn Marwan patronized a major expansion of the Prophet's Mosque at Medina that included Qur'anic verses rendered in mosaic as early as 90/709; perhaps even the entire Qur'anic text was inscribed within the sanctuary.[13]

Muslim architects and their patrons generally select sacred words that bear some relationship to the function of buildings or architectural features on which they are to be placed.[14] One example is the exquisitely beautiful verse from the "Chapter of Light" that can often be found encircling the clerestory at the base of a dome or framing the *mihrab* of a mosque:

> *God is the light of the heavens and the earth! The parable of His light is as if there were a niche enclosing a lantern. The lantern is enclosed within glass; the glass shines like a brilliant star lit from a blessed olive tree that is neither of the east nor of the west; the oil is luminous even though no fire touches it. Light upon light! God guides those whom He wills to His light, and God sets forth parables for all people. God is knowledgeable of all things.*
>
> (Nur; 24:35)

Elsewhere are verses that refer specifically to the mosque, in particular:

> *O Children of Adam! Wear your beautiful apparel at every mosque and eat and drink, but not to excess, for God does not love those who are excessive.*
>
> (A'raf; 7:31)

> *Verily the mosques belong to God, so do not call on anyone besides God.*
>
> (Jinn; 72:18)

> *The mosques of God will be visited and maintained by such as believe in God and the last day, establish prayer and pay charity and fear nothing except God; so that they may be among the truly guided.*
>
> (Tawba; 9:18)

Calligraphers often employ contrasting colors and bright highlights to ensure that Qur'anic verses on architectural structures are readable. In some cases, the script is so elaborate that it might appear illegible to some observers. However, as one scholar notes, because many Muslims have memorized significant portions of the Qur'an or at least have listened to it recited dozens, if not hundreds, of times, they need only "to decipher a word or two in order to identify the verse being quoted."[15] This is further support for the position that it is primarily the *recited* Qur'an that is the foundation of Muslim spirituality and culture.

We recall that the first *mushaf*, collected a few years after the death of the Prophet Muhammad, could not be read as an independent text but was used to support and complement the oral text. A skeletal script that did not even distinguish even among all consonants, this first *mushaf* primarily ensured that nothing new could be added to the text; secondarily, for individuals, the early *mushaf* could work as a mnemonic device, supporting memorization. Elaborate Qur'anic calligraphy in architecture serves a similar mnemonic purpose, whereby as soon as a thread of text is deciphered, a possible verse is brought to mind and then checked against the remaining script. Thus, it is common to see Muslim visitors to an important Islamic site grouped in

Figure 4.1 Qur'anic calligraphy on the exterior of the Dome of the Rock in Jerusalem. (© Chris Bradley/Axiom/Getty Images)

front of a calligraphic panel, each trying to identify a word or a phrase; finally, one person makes out a few words and others from the group recall the verse and they complete it together. This collective reading-recitation strengthens feelings of religious community and a shared connectedness with their Islamic cultural heritage and spiritual tradition.

The earliest extant examples of monumental Qur'anic calligraphy in Islamic sacred architecture are found within and without the Dome of the Rock, construction of which began just over a half a century after the death of the Prophet Muhammad. This magnificent domed structure, until now the most prominent feature on the Jerusalem landscape, is not a mosque but a monument built around a rock outcropping where Muslims believe that the Prophet Muhammad ascended to heaven to receive instructions at the throne of God. The octagonal structure has two concentric arcades which are decorated with supplications and passages from the Qur'an rendered in mosaic tiles. Among the Qur'anic passages reproduced are the following:

> *O People of the Book, do not go to extremes in your religion. Do not say anything about God except what is true. Verily the Messiah, Jesus the Son of Mary is the Messenger of God, and God's word that He cast into Mary, and a spirit from Him. So believe in God and in His messengers and do not say "Three"; it is better for you to desist. Rather, God is one god. He is too exalted to have a son, and everything in the heavens and on earth belongs to Him. It is enough to have God as the disposer of affairs.*
> *The Messiah does not scorn being a servant of God, nor do the favored angels. Those who scorn servitude to Him and are arrogant will be gathered back to Him all together.*
> (Nisa'; 4:171–172)

> *Such is Jesus the son of Mary; it is a statement of truth about which they dispute.*
> *It is not befitting of God that He should take a son, He is exalted above that.*
> *When he decides a matter He only says "Be" and it is.*
> *Verily God is my Lord and your Lord so worship Him;*
> *this is the straight path.*
> (Maryam; 19:34–36)

There are many theories about why the Umayyad caliph 'Abd al-Malik ibn Marwan (reigned 65–86/685–705) commissioned the construction of this temple.[16] Some believe that his main goal was to neutralize any legitimacy that had accrued to his political rival, the counter-caliph 'Abdullah ibn al-Zubayr, due to the latter's control over the Sacred Mosques of Mecca and Medina at that time. Although this theory has some merit, the Qur'anic verses chosen to adorn the temple clearly indicate that engagement with Christianity was the main purpose of the building. At the time of the building of the Dome of the Rock, Jerusalem was a city of important Christian monuments; particularly significant was the Church of the Holy Sepulcher, built in the fourth century CE. Some observers have therefore suggested that the Dome of the Rock was built in a competitive spirit to demonstrate that the majesty of Islam was no less than that of Christianity. This is one explanation offered by the fourth-/tenth-century historian al-Muqaddasi.

We should be careful, however, in assuming that al-Muqaddasi's perspective, articulated some centuries after the building of the Dome of the Rock, represents the sentiments of first-/seventh-century Muslims. We need to recall that the Muslim rulers of Jerusalem did not suppress Christianity, nor did they damage any Christian monuments. This tolerant policy towards Christianity (and Judaism, for it is the Muslim conqueror of Jerusalem, 'Umar ibn al-Khattab, who lifted the Byzantine ban on Jews entering Jerusalem) was based on verses of the Qur'an and examples from the Prophet's Sunna. It can be argued further that the Qur'an does more than offer guidelines for a legal policy of tolerance and that its attitude towards other faith communities in general and Christianity in particular is, in many ways, inclusive. As we have discussed earlier, this does not mean that the Qur'an does not explicitly present itself as a correction to distortions and errors accrued to the religious doctrines of earlier communities that were given divine revelation. But at the same time, a reformation of doctrine can only be undertaken within the bounds of the same community. The verses chosen for the Dome of the Rock, therefore, attest to a time when Muslims seem to have been articulating a more distinct identity with respect to the People of the Book, while at the same time still trying to reach out across a doctrinal divide that possibly could be bridged. Al-Muqaddasi's view that the Dome of the Rock was built in a spirit of religious competition, therefore, may be somewhat anachronistic and overstated. But once the Dome of the Rock had been built, later Muslims could not avoid being influenced by their historical, social, and political context in their attempts to impart meaning to the Qur'anic verses found therein.

Naturally, patronage of religious monuments did not end with the building of the Dome of the Rock. Over the centuries, Muslim rulers and wealthy individuals have continued to patronize the building of mosques, religious retreats (*ribat*), Islamic seminaries (*madrasas*), and mausoleums. In many cases, even buildings with eclectic and syncretic cultural influences draw upon the blessing and imagery of the Qur'an in some way. It is suggested, for example, that the Taj Mahal, built by the Moghul emperor Shah Jahan (ruled 1628–1658 CE), is an allegorical representation of the throne of God above the Garden of Paradise on the Day of Judgment.[17] This Qur'anic eschatology is reinforced by verses inscribed on the building, such as the following:

> *O you soul at peace!*
> *Return to your Lord, contented, in His good-pleasure.*
> *Enter among my servants;*
> *Enter my Garden!*
>
> (Fajr; 89:27–30)

The fourteenth-century CE Alhambra Palace in Granada is another exceptional example of magnificent Islamic architecture that integrates the Qur'an's approach to both earthly and heavenly matters with great success. On the one hand, the palace is rich with gardens filled with fragrant plants and fruit trees growing around clear pools and flowing water that recall the Qur'anic descriptions of Paradise.[18] On the other hand, the walls of Alhambra are filled with a sobering reminder that is repeated over and over: "There is no victor except for God (*la ghalib illa Allah*)." This phrase is taken from the Qur'anic statement (12:21) "God is the Victory" (*Allah al-Ghalib*), and is a reminder to rulers, even in the midst of their worldly splendor and power, that it is God who ultimately controls all affairs.

The Elevation of the Qur'an

Where they are inscribed on buildings or hung on walls, Qur'anic verses are generally elevated, in keeping with the superiority of God's Word over the words of humans. The idea that ontological superiority is implied by physical elevation, while dishonor can be signified by literally lowering a thing or placing it under one's feet, may be universal. This accords with an anthropocentric perspective, for as a

Figure 4.2 "Victory belongs to God" carved into the wall of Alhambra. (© M. Freeman/PhotoLink/Getty Images)

human develops in strength and maturity, he or she rises from the floor to become tall and erect. It is also the experience of sages of many traditions that sacred insight can best be found on the mountaintops. The Qur'an was first revealed to Muhammad in a cave on a mountain, Moses spoke to God on Mount Sinai, the transfiguration of Jesus took place on a mountain, Syrian Christian saints of late antiquity stood on tall pillars for years seeking God's presence, and Buddhists climb the steps of temples like the temple in Borobodur, Java, where the highest level symbolizes freedom from worldly desires. It is the collective experience of humanity that once one leaves the familiar markings of one's own landscape, looking upwards at the stars, the moon, and the sun is the most effective way to be guided. The Qur'an explicitly associates the critical role of heavenly bodies in helping humans to regulate and direct their affairs[19] with God's sovereignty over all of creation:

> God is the One who elevated the heavens without any pillars that
> you can see, and He established Himself on the throne. He subjected
> to His authority the sun and the moon; each one runs an appointed
> course. He regulates all affairs and gives exquisite detail to the signs
> so that you will be certain about meeting your Lord.

> (Ra'd; 13:2)

Apart from its symbolic implications, it is obvious that physically elevating precious objects can protect them from being trampled upon, knocked over, and dirtied. The symbolic and pragmatic work together to inspire feelings of awe and respect in the worshipper as he or she approaches a Christian or Hindu altar, a Buddhist stupa, or a statue of Apollo mounted on a pedestal. It is understandable, therefore, that Muslims are keen to ensure that physical copies of the Qur'anic *mushaf* – the record of God's exact words revealed to humanity – should be treated with respect.[20] In most Muslim cultures, this means that the Qur'an is never placed on the floor, is usually stored on a high shelf, and even when stacked with other books (for example, when a scholar or student is doing research), the Qur'an is usually repositioned on top of the pile. As a Muslim reaches up for the Qur'an, he or she is reminded that "the word of God is superior" (*al-'ulya*, literally, "the highest"; Tawba; 9:40).

A remarkable demonstration of the importance many Muslims give to this gesture of respect towards the Qur'an can be found at the start of the twenty-first century among Muslim prisoners held at the American detention camp at Guantánamo Bay, Cuba. The prisoners were allowed only a handful of items in their "cages." Among these items was not only a Qur'an but also a hygienic face mask that prisoners hooked onto the wires of their cages to suspend the sacred book off the ground. Later, it was revealed that despite these accommodations, some guards and intelligence officers had deliberately mistreated the Qur'an to provoke or punish some prisoners. Some men reported that it was this mistreatment of the Qur'an, rather than the physical and emotional humiliation they endured, that was truly unbearable.[21] One released prisoner told reporters, "I could bear all the obscene abuse and all the beatings but I was agonized to see one US soldier stomp on the Holy Qur'an, while another soldier in Kandahar threw it into the toilet."[22]

Some non-Muslim observers were surprised at the depth of hurt and anger these reports elicited among Muslims across the world. Journalists and analysts sought parallels from other traditions and cultures. Depending on their denomination, Christians stated that they would feel similar outrage if they experienced like mistreatment of the Bible, the consecrated Eucharist, or an icon of Jesus or Mary. Certainly, it is not unusual for an individual to be able to bear personal abuse better than abuse of objects to which he or she attributes deep religious or even patriotic significance. In his book *Flag: An American Biography*,

Marc Leepson reports that the violent riots in Chicago during the Democratic National Convention in 1968 were precipitated by the deliberate desecration of Americans' beloved national symbol. "Police officials said that disrespect for the flag was the primary reason that they took physical action against the antiwar demonstrators. The 'profanity and spitting' by the demonstrators 'did not have the same effect on the police that incidents involving the flag did,' a Chicago police official later testified. 'Abuse or misuse of the flag deeply affected the police.' "[23] To avoid potential desecration of the Qur'an, the Prophet forbade the transport of the *mushaf* into enemy territory and Muslim scholars in premodern times forbade the sale or gift of the *mushaf* to non-Muslims.[24]

Among Muslims, the elevation of the Qur'an should inspire a feeling of reverence, humility, and submission (the literal meaning of *islam*). Many Muslims express this deep feeling of love for the word of God by wrapping their Qur'an in fine fabric or kissing it after taking it off the shelf. Modernized Muslims might be uncomfortable with such gestures, considering such reverence for the text of the Qur'an "superstitious" and potentially distracting from the awareness of the absolute transcendence of God. Such exaggerated fear of a slippery slope towards idolatry has perhaps left some of these Muslims with a rather dry approach to faith. Traditional Muslim societies seem to allow more room for emotional expressions of faith, and a close connection between the body and the spirit. Certainly there can be excesses in this direction as well; however, one cannot help but feel that the traditional approach yields a richer spiritual culture in which the sacred words of God infuse one's surroundings and, as we shall discuss below, have a deep visceral effect on the individual.

Ritual Purity and Purifying Rituals

One rule that almost all Muslims rigorously observe to express reverence for the Qur'anic *mushaf* is to refrain from touching it unless they are in a state of ritual purity. This ruling is established in the Qur'an itself, in one of its many self-referential passages:

> *Indeed this is a noble Qur'an,*
> *In a protected book.*
> *None shall touch it except for those who are purified.*
> (Waqi'a; 56:77–79)

Qur'anic verses can signify many different levels of meaning simultaneously; thus, a metaphorical interpretation of this verse would yield the understanding that only those with pure hearts can access the inner meaning of the Qur'an. Parallel to this interpretation is the apparent (*zahir* – often called "literal") meaning of the verse, that no one should touch the *mushaf* unless in a state of ritual purity.

Purity, for the Muslim, is both a physical and spiritual state.[25] Although the goal of Islamic spirituality is to become free of the limitations of "self" (*nafs* – also, "soul" or "spirit"), because humans live in their physical forms on the earth and normally locate their sense of self in their bodies, Islam works with the body to ennoble the spirit. The obligatory rituals of *salat*, fasting, and pilgrimage all engage the body and spirit together to uplift and dignify the believer. Although these rituals can be rigorous, they are not intended to punish the body or cause harm to the individual. Islam does not view the body itself as a source of sin or evil; bodily desires can be harnessed for good or for evil. Islamic rituals, therefore, are intended to help believers achieve consciousness about the way in which they use their bodies. When fasting, a Muslim cannot eat, drink, experience sexual intimacy, or engage in

Figure 4.3 Throughout the month of Ramadan, Muslims gather with family and community members each evening to break the fast before gathering for special prayers.

arguments. Having to refrain from these actions for a time, the believer later approaches eating, drinking, and intimate and social relationships with greater intentionality, thus taking responsibility for her greatest distinction among all of creation – the ability to impart meaning to her actions.

Ritual purification is one way a Muslim prepares him or herself to undertake acts of worship such as prayer, pilgrimage, and reading Qur'an.[26] Taking this extra step of purification before commencing acts of worship helps the believer attain focus and begin the rituals in a reverential state. The Qur'an (5:6) and Sunna of the Prophet give specific instructions for the way in which believers should perform ablution. That spiritual purification is the ultimate goal is evident from the ruling that if water is not available for washing, then clean sand should be used in a symbolic cleansing. The great Muslim scholar of the seventh/twelfth century, Abu Hamid al-Ghazali, advised:

> When attending to ritual purity in the things that envelop you in progressively closer layers – your room, then your clothes, then your skin – do not neglect your inner being, which lies at the heart of all these. Endeavor to purify it with repentance and remorse for your excesses, and a determined resolution not to commit them in future. Cleanse your inner being in this way, for that is the place to be examined by the One you worship.[27]

That an act of physical purification can help the seeker along the path of spiritual purification is a lesson contained in the conversion story of 'Umar ibn al-Khattab. Initially one of the staunchest enemies of Islam among the Meccans, 'Umar was enraged when he discovered that his sister Fatima had become a Muslim. After a violent argument with her, 'Umar asked to see the parchment from which she was reading a passage of the Qur'an. Fatima replied, "My brother, you are impure in your polytheism and only the purified may touch it." After 'Umar rose and washed himself, his sister gave him the page on which was written Sura Ta Ha (20). Reading the words, 'Umar declared, "How fine and noble is this speech!" Then 'Umar went to the Prophet Muhammad and declared his conversion to Islam.[28]

One notable aspect of this story is that Fatima exercised her judgment in what is often reduced by many Muslims to a simple Islamic legal issue, viz., whether it is permissible to touch the *mushaf* – or a portion of it – without having performed ritual purification. In strict legal terms, it is impossible for a non-Muslim to complete ritual purification, since a condition of this act of worship, like all other acts of worship (*'ibadat*), is that one forms the explicit intention (*niyya*) to perform this act in obedience to God in accordance with the instructions of the Prophet Muhammad. If no other relevant factors are taken into account, the logical conclusion is that no non-Muslim should be permitted to handle the *mushaf*. However, sound Islamic legal reasoning entails consideration of many factors involved in a case – including assessment of the harms and benefits (*al-darr wa'l-nafa'*), the common good (*al-maslaha al-'amma*), and the broad goals of the Law (*al-maqasid*). Thus, throughout the centuries, Muslim scholars, like this early Muslim woman Fatima, exercised their judgment in determining when and how it might be permissible to give or sell a *mushaf* to a non-Muslim. At the same time, it is probably accurate to say that the strictly legal requirement of purity for touching the *mushaf* is less of an issue to most Muslims than the previously discussed concern that the *mushaf* will be treated in a disrespectful fashion. It is this same concern that led many scholars to discourage or forbid young children from handling the *mushaf*, since their inability to truly understand the sacrality of the text could lead them to handle it inappropriately.[29]

Scholars are divided over whether it is permissible for a menstruating woman to touch the *mushaf*. Because a menstruating woman does not perform *salat* until her period has finished, most scholars have reasoned that she should also refrain from handlng the *mushaf* during that time. However, the earliest author of a book dedicated to the treatment of the *mushaf* disagreed with this position. 'Abdullah al-Sijistani (d. 316/928) cites an authentic hadith in which the Prophet Muhammad is reported to have said to his wife 'A'isha who was reluctant to hand him an item in the mosque because she was menstruating, "The menstruation is not in your hand." This is proof, al-Sijistani offers, that the body of the woman is not impure during menstruation, therefore she can handle the *mushaf*. Still, many Muslim women who wish to read the Qur'an during their period will avoid touching the *mushaf* and instead read passages of the Qur'an from books of commentary or, in technological societies, from electronic devices like computers. Not surprisingly, some modernists who underplay or even belittle the notion of "blessing" (*baraka*) inhering in any object acknowledge few if any restrictions on the handling of a *mushaf* by menstruating women. Muslims who follow the traditional schools of law, and who generally also have more affinity with traditional notions of the sacrality of the *mushaf*, tend to uphold the prohibition.[30]

The story of the conversion of 'Umar, like many other Islamic conversion narratives, demonstrates the awesome power of even a small portion of the Qur'an to open hearts to faith. In Christian narratives, it is, naturally, the voice of Jesus, "God's Word" (in Christianity and Islam, although the phrase is understood differently in the mainstream of the two traditions), that transforms Saul from being the most violent opponent of Christianity into the most forceful proponent of the faith. Similarly, in Islam, it is a direct encounter with God's word in the Qur'an that can effect a total transformation of the spirit which also resonates in the body:

> *Is not the one whose breast God has opened to Islam*
> *thus on (a path of) enlightenment from his Lord? Woe to those*
> *whose hearts are hardened against remembering God, they are*
> *clearly misguided.*
> *God has revealed the finest speech – a book coherent, reiterant. It*
> *makes the flesh of those who fear their Lord tremble, then their flesh*
> *and their hearts are softened to the remembrance of God. That is*
> *God's guidance. He guides whom he pleases, and one whom God*
> *leaves astray will have no guide.*
>
> (Zumar; 39:22–23)

This Qur'anic teaching, that its words affect the very flesh and viscera of one who is drawn to faith, is developed into a more explicit statement about the healing power of this guidance in the following verse:

> *O humanity! There has come to you an exhortation from your Lord;*
> *it is a cure for what is in your breasts and a guidance and mercy to*
> *the believers.*
>
> (Yunus; 10:57)

Again, it is possible to read such a verse as signifying the power of the Qur'an to work its healing power on multiple levels. In this respect, the Qur'an reflects a premodern notion that in postmodernity again seems to be regaining credibility: that physical, mental, and spiritual (or emotional) health are interconnected aspects of human well-being. It is not surprising, therefore, that Muslims consider the Qur'an to be the most efficacious healer of any disorder for which a person might seek treatment.

The Qur'an often refers to the "heart" as the locus of spiritual health. A heart open to God is "soft"; a heart that is closed to God's guidance is "hard" and "diseased." As a heart becomes more and more diseased, sickness becomes the norm and it takes greater exertion on the part of the individual to regain spiritual health.

Although falling into habitual sin is the most common consequence of a diseased heart, many Muslims believe that spiritual illness can make some individuals vulnerable to losing control over their own will – leading to insanity or possession by jinn. Belief in the ability of unseen creatures like jinn to possess humans was probably widespread in premodern Muslim cultures. Many contemporary Muslims feel more comfortable with medicalized explanations of mental illness for the same behaviors. Although the Qur'an does not address the issue of possession, it does recognize the existence of jinn who are characterized as creatures who, like humans, are endowed with free will. The jinn, who are made "from fire," while humans are made "from clay" (Qur'an 15:26–27; 55:14–15), have powers of movement and transformation far beyond those of humans, who can be easily deceived by them because of this fact. The very last verse of the Qur'an invokes the protection of God from the harm of "jinn and humans." The Sunna indicates that this final chapter of the Qur'an, as well as the one preceding it, collectively known as "The Two Protections" (al-Mu'awwidhatan), should be regularly recited for protection from all harm, including harm from unseen forces.

Premodern and contemporary Islamic texts and popular literature seem to be in consensus that the "Verse of the Throne," a beloved and widely memorized verse attesting to God's dominion and majesty, is especially efficacious in protecting from all kinds of harm, particularly forces invisible to most humans:

> *Allah! There is no god but He, the Living, the Eternal, the Self-Subsistent. Neither age nor sleep overcome Him. To Him belongs all that is in the heavens and all on that is upon the earth. Who can intercede with Him except by his permission? He knows what they have in their hands and what is behind them.*
>
> *Yet they shall not grasp any of his knowledge except what He wills. His throne extends to the heavens and the earth, and He never wearies in guarding them. He is the Most High, the Most Grand.*
>
> (Baqara; 2:255)

The range of popular treatments for jinn possession is vast, eclectic, and mostly undocumented. Even in the "high culture" of institutionally trained religious scholars, exorcism seems to have remained mostly outside the formal curriculum, but instead has been taught as the need arises to individuals judged to be spiritually strong and sober.[31] This oral tradition teaches that because jinn are made from a different substance than humans, they have the ability to possess spiritually weak individuals and exert control over them.[32] Possession is confirmed when the spiritual healer recites Qur'an – if the recitation produces a calming effect, then possession is discounted; if the recitation creates agitation, then possession is a possibility. Sometimes the person suspected of possession will speak with a different voice or in a different language; this is understood to be the voice of the jinn. The spiritual healer will demand that the jinn leave the body of the possessed and, if the jinn refuses, the healer will force him out. Because the jinn have powers beyond those of humans, a healer can force the jinn out the body of the possessed only with the power of God's Word. This is done by continuing to recite Qur'an, especially particular verses that are known to be effective for this purpose, or by giving the possessed water over which Qur'an has been recited. In an interesting symbolic inversion, this holy water is said to "burn" the jinn.

For those suffering from physical illness, water from the blessed spring of Zamzam in Mecca is considered to be highly beneficial. Verses from the Qur'an might also be recited over this water to increase the efficacy of its healing power, although plain water can be used if Zamzam water is not available. Although not always sanctioned by religious scholars, Muslims engage in a range of popular practices to further infuse water with the blessed words of the Qur'an. One common practice is to pour water into a bowl inside of which Qur'anic verses are inscribed; the water is then drunk by the person seeking healing. Taking the concept further, some people will write verses of the Qur'an with an edible dye, like saffron, then dissolve the verses in water which they will then drink. What we observe, then, is that across Muslim societies, belief in the healing power of the Qur'an can be concretized with a number of diverse practices. In traditional societies, it is relatively common for Qur'anic verses and prayers to be written on small pieces of paper and worn in a neck pouch; even a whole *mushaf* can be written in tiny script and worn around the neck. From the premodern period, there are examples of children and soldier's clothing written with Qur'anic verses.[33] In modern societies, gold and silver pendants are inscribed with Qur'anic verses and pinned to the clothes of babies and worn on necklaces.

Such practices are a concern for some imams and scholars, who see in them the risk of ascribing healing power to water, paper, and pendants rather than to God. For others, such practices are a logical extension of the belief that the Qur'an, as the eternal Word of God, occupies a status different from any created thing. Of course, the water and ink used in a healing ceremony are created, but the words that infuse the water are reflections of the eternal attribute of God's speech. Some might see in the division among Muslims over this issue reflections of debates between Catholics and Protestants over the validity of the use of relics and the efficacy of ritual sacraments. Although there are differences in the nature of the debates, there are evident similarities, and certainly in both cases the disagreement has sometimes led to divisive intolerance. Among Muslims, followers of the nineteenth-century CE Arabian reformer Muhammad ibn 'Abd al-Wahhab (the "Wahhabis") have harshly condemned and even launched accusations of idolatry against those who use amulets for protection. Proponents of such practices have rebutted these accusations with theological proofs, as well as with scathing assessments of the intellectual shallowness of their opponents, whom they characterize as brutishly intolerant.[34]

Other spiritual practices for healing are uncontroversial. The Prophet Muhammad is reported to have taught his followers a number of supplications for healing, as well as directed them to recite particular sections of the Qur'an over the body of an ill person. The Prophet's wife 'A'isha reported that whenever he became ill, he would recite the *Mu'awwidhatan* into his cupped hands then blow into them and pass his hands over his body. With some poignancy, 'A'isha relates how during the Prophet's final illness, she dearly wanted him to recover, so "I used to recite over him and rub his hand over his body, hoping for its blessings."[35]

The Prophetic Sunna attests then to the practice of reciting Qur'an for oneself or for others to promote physical healing. It is not even required that the sick person be a Muslim for the recitation to be effective. There is an authentic hadith that a Companion of the Prophet healed the chief of an Arab tribe from a snakebite by reciting Sura al-Fatiha over him and that the Prophet later confirmed that Fatiha is a healing prayer (*ruqiya*). Due to this hadith, recitation of Fatiha is generally the foundation for any healing prayer ritual.[36]

The Qur'an in the Life Cycle of a Muslim

Not everyone will recover from illness and eventually everyone will die; the Qur'an states:

Every soul shall taste death; then you will return to Us.

('Ankabut; 29:57)

The Qur'an says that those who experience a great loss (*musiba*) should say:

To God we belong and to Him we return.

(Baqara; 2:156)

This phrase (*inna lillahi wa inna ilayhi raji'un*) is repeated by Muslims when they hear about a death. In this situation, as in many others, a few words of the Qur'an have entered the culture of Muslim societies to become a common phrase that is uttered by individuals who do not even know that it is Qur'anic in origin.

Figure 4.4   British graffiti artist Mohammed Ali puts finishing touches on the words "To God we belong and to Him we shall return." In 2007, the artist made the wall mural with West African immigrants living in the Bronx, NY who had recently lost many family members in a tragic fire. (Atif Ateeq)

For those mourning the deceased, the Qur'an emphasizes the futility of wondering "what if?" A believer accepts that the time of death is decreed by God:

> *O you who believe! Do not be like those who disbelieve – who say of their brethren when they traveled through the land or engaged in fighting, "If only they had stayed with us, they would not have died or been killed." It is God who brings to life and causes to die, and God sees everything you do.*
> *If you are slain in the path of God or if you die, certainly forgiveness from God and his mercy are better than anything you might acquire.*
>
> (Al 'Imran; 3:156–157)

Muslims, therefore, console one who is mourning with exhortations to remain steadfast in their belief that they could not have prevented the death of their loved one. This belief that God determines the time of death does not prevent Muslims from assigning a material cause to death, for the Qur'an is also clear that humans have free will and created capacities for action within the domain of the absolute sovereignty of God. Thus, it is perfectly acceptable, and necessary, to investigate the material causes of death and to assign blame if found.

It is a communal obligation of the Muslim community to hold a congregational funeral prayer over the body of the deceased before burial. This ritual prayer is short, consisting mostly of supplications (*du'a*); from the Qur'an, only the Fatiha is recited silently by each member of the congregation. The centrality of the Fatiha in the funeral prayer likely gave rise to the widespread practice of reciting this sura when hearing that someone has died or when passing a grave. In many Muslim societies, reminders or requests to passers-by to recite the Fatiha are placed near the grave or, in contemporary societies, in newspapers.

The Qur'an does not give much detail about the subjective experience of death other than to say that angels remove the soul from the body (6:61); in contrast, the Qur'an gives great attention to the Day of Judgment and the consequences of that day: reward in Paradise or punishment in Hell. This is in keeping with the Qur'an's main objective, which is to motivate individuals to choose a righteous life. Hadith literature, on the other hand, contains instructions from the Prophet on how to minister to a dying person, how to treat the body of the dead, as well as extensive descriptions of what is experienced in the grave.

Again, this is in keeping with the role of the Prophetic Sunna in providing details about how to live the righteous life that the Qur'an demands.

The Prophet Muhammad instructed that a person in the throes of death should be encouraged to repeat the *shahada* – the declaration of faith: "I witness that there is no god but God and I witness that Muhammad is the Messenger of God." Those attending to the dying person are encouraged to recite Sura Ya Sin because of its focus on God's mercy, forgiveness, and ability to resurrect the dead. The sura ends with the following verses:

> *(The disbeliever) creates his own similes for Us, but he forgets his own creation.*
> *He says, "Who can give life to bones when they have turned to dust?"*
> *Say: They will be brought to life by the One who created them the first time, and He knows everything about creation –*
> *The One who brings fire out of the green tree and behold you kindle your hearth with it.*
> *Is not the One who created the heavens and the earth capable of creating something like it?*
> *Indeed, He is the All-Knowing Master Creator.*
> *When He intends a thing, He need only give the command "Be," then it is.*
> *So glory to Him in whose hand is the dominion of all things and to Him you will return.*
>
> (Ya Sin; 36:78–83)

The Damascene scholar Ibn Qayyim al-Jawziyya (d. 751/1326) in his *Book of the Soul* says that Sura Ya Sin benefits the dying soul, for it conveys the good news (*tastabshir*) that God loves to meet him or her. Ibn Qayyim calls Sura Ya Sin "the heart of the Qur'an" and says that it "is an amazing privilege in that it is recited to the dying person." Indeed, this sura has a remarkable place in the culture of mourning in Muslim societies; not only is it recited to the dying person, but it is recited in death anniversary commemorations and grave visits across the Muslim world. In many Muslim societies, families gather forty days after the death of a loved one and recite Sura Ya Sin, as well as other prayers, for the benefit of the deceased. The sura is printed separately in small booklets that can be found in great numbers in mausoleums, where its verses are recited by individuals and groups visiting the graves.[37]

The perception of which benefits accrue to whom during these grave visits varies across Muslim societies and schools of thought. This is because there are different understandings about the state of the dead in their graves, in particular, the state of righteous people. The Qur'an is very clear that those who have committed evil in their lives will wish at their deaths for another chance to do good. However, once death has come, there is a barrier (*barzakh*) that prevents them from action and they must wait in their graves for the Day of Judgment, when God will raise all people and judge their deeds:

> *When one of them approaches death he says, "O Lord, let me go back so that I might perform righteous deeds in what I left behind." No – these are just words that he utters. Behind them is a barrier until the day they are resurrected.*
>
> (Mu'minun; 23:99–100)

Because of this verse, some Muslims believe that all those who die exist in *barzakh* – a realm inaccessible to the living – and that they are no longer able to interact in any way with the living. From this perspective, the relationship between the living and the dead is strictly one-sided; the living can and should pray for their dead co-religionists, but the latter cannot respond in any way.

Other Muslims believe that the righteous dead can hear the living and can pray for them, just as the living can pray for the dead. Indeed, the Qur'an states that at least those who were killed "in the path of God" are not really "dead" but exist in a special state:

> *Do not say about those who are killed in the path of God, "they are dead,"*
> *rather, they are alive, but you cannot feel it.*
>
> (Baqara; 2:154)

Some scholars have interpreted this verse as referring only to martyrs; others extend the scope of this verse to include highly righteous individuals, citing among other proof the following verse:

> *Whoever obeys God and the Messenger, they will be with those upon whom God has bestowed His grace: the Prophets, the Sincere, the Martyrs and the Righteous. What a beautiful fellowship they have!*
>
> (Nisa'; 4:69)

As a consequence of this belief, some Muslims visit the graves of righteous people to ask them to supplicate to God for them. To many Muslims, this is a clear violation of the Islamic principle prohibiting *shirk* – ascribing power to any being other than the one God. Advocates of intercession (*wasila*), however, argue that this is no more *shirk* than asking a living person to supplicate God on one's behalf; in both cases, the act neither exempts one from supplicating for oneself, nor implies that such a person has any power to compel God to respond positively to the supplication. The main distinction between the two groups, then, revolves around the issue of whether the righteous dead are capable of responding to requests for prayers from the living. Proofs for both positions can be found, depending how one interprets various verses of the Qur'an and reports of the Sunna of the Prophet Muhammad.

The issue of intercession is not an obscure academic topic for Muslims; rather, it is an issue that deeply affects the rhythm and structure of religious life and culture. This is because the practice of *ziyara* – "visiting" the graves of the righteous – spurred the need for structures to protect the grave, and no doubt influenced by local pre-Islamic cultures, many people felt that it was only proper to honor a "saint" with a substantial monument. Thus, despite the fact that the Prophet had given specific instructions upon his deathbed to refrain from building such monuments, in the centuries after his death, mausoleums and shrines of all sizes were erected in great numbers across the Muslim world.

When such sites, such as the grave of the Prophet's Companion Abu Ayyub al-Ansari in Istanbul, are maintained under official patronage, it is possible to enforce a certain decorum and solemnity among the visitors. In other places, as might be expected, opportunists of all sorts lurk, ready to take advantage of desperate and emotionally vulnerable people. Many contemporary Muslims, following the lead of early modern Muslim reformers, are opposed to the doctrine of intercession not only because they consider it theologically incorrect, but also, like European Protestant Reformers, because they are repulsed by popular pilgrimage culture. The Damascene Hanbali scholar Ibn Taymiyya (d. 728/1328) seems to have been ahead of his time in his vigorous and public denunciations of this practice. It was not until some centuries later that opposition to *ziyara* spread more widely among Muslims of various ideological leanings, including modernists who advocated a less clerical, more "rational"

Islam, as well as those influenced by Muhammad ibn 'Abd al-Wahhab (d. 1206/1791).

Interestingly, no doubt because of their affiliation with Reformed Christianity, European Protestant observers were not unsympathetic to this aspect of the activities of those who became known as "Wahhabis." The Danish explorer Carsten Niebuhr, for example, in his *Travels in Arabia*, made the following observation:

> Among the Mussulmen (Muslims) it is customary to inter those who have obtained the reputation virtuous, or saints, in a private sepulcher, more or less ornamented, where their protection is invoked for the supplicant; and God is supposed to befriend their intercession. If the reputation of any particular saint becomes fashionable, the devotion increases, the chapel is enlarged, with administrators, servants, and so forth, chosen generally from among the individuals of his family, by means of which the relations of the saint acquire a situation more or less opulent.... Already had the well-informed Mussulmen begun to despise these superstitions secretly, though they seemed to respect them in the eyes of the people. But 'Abd al-Wahhab declared boldly that this species of worship rendered to the saints was a grievous sin in the eyes of the divinity because it was giving Him companions. In consequence of this his sectaries have destroyed the sepulchers, chapels and temples elevated in their honor.[38]

According to some reformers, even engraved tombstones are deemed to be in violation of the simple practice of the early Muslims (the *"salaf"* – hence the name "Salafi" for those who turn to the early generation of Muslims for legal precedents). For the poor, the issue is moot in any case – they can no more afford an engraved tombstone than they can afford to build the Taj Mahal. Indeed, for many modern Muslims, in addition to their desire to follow what they believe to be the Prophetic Sunna of burial in a simple unmarked grave, it is the desire to demonstrate Islam's egalitarian nature that leads them to embrace the practice of erecting no more than a simple stone. In premodern Islamic societies, however, those who could afford to erect at least a modest tombstone often did so. In some places, it was common to inscribe the stone with the spiritually powerful "Verse of the Throne." Other verses, like those incorporated into this touching inscription

from the sixth-/twelfth-century Arabian Peninsula, attest to the fleet-
ing nature of earthly life and the majesty of God:

> In the name of God, the Beneficent, the Merciful.
> Everyone that is on (the earth) will pass away, except for the face
> of your Lord, the Possessor of Majesty and Dignity [Rahman; 55:26–27].
> This is the grave of Khadija daughter of Qasim b. Ahmed b. Qasim
> b. Ja'd b. Abu Qasim b. 'Ali b. 'Ad b. 'Abd al-'Aziz the Qurayshite,
> the Perfumer, who died on Monday in Dhu'l-Hijja in the year 552 [AH].
> May God have mercy upon her.
> God's kindness fell upon her all the time,
> on the pretty face of the deceased.[39]
> If all women died like this, they would be superior to men.[40]

Language, Naming, and Common Expressions

Because Muslims believe that the Arabic words of the Qur'an are God's
words, and because Islamic law requires recitation from the Qur'an in
daily acts of worship, the Arabic language has always been important
to Muslim identity and the construction of religious authority. Before
the end of the first century of Islam, Muslim scholars had decided that
the increasing numbers of non-Arab converts – mostly Persians – had
to learn enough Arabic as soon as possible after their conversion to say
their prayers in Arabic. During the same time, the Umayyads arabized
the chancellery and placed the Islamic testament of faith, the *shahada*,
in Arabic script on their coins.

While Arabic played an important role in the formation of early
Islamic culture, the Qur'an in turn had a profound effect on the
development of Arabic as a literary language. In the first century of
Islam, the Arabic increasingly employed in the Muslim administration
was not simply a written version of the spoken language of the Arabs but
a literary expression that was continually refined and shaped by
the language of the Qur'an itself. Wadad al-Qadi has shown how the
epistles of 'Abd al-Hamid ibn Yahya, the Chancellor for the Umayyad
caliph Marwan ibn Muhammad (d. 132/750), are infused with
Qur'anic phrases and influences.[41] Significantly, 'Abd al-Hamid was
not an Arab, yet he had a great impact on the shape and development
of literary Arabic during this critical early period.

The shift of the Islamic capital to Baghdad in the mid second/eighth
century under 'Abbasid rule did not decrease the importance of Arabic,

despite the fact that Iraq was primarily a Persian-speaking land at that time. Indeed, Persian Muslims like Sibawayh (d. 177/793) were among the most prominent grammarians of the Arabic language. The early contributions of Persians such as 'Abd al-Hamid and Sibawayh to the formation of classical literary Arabic give non-Arab Muslims a sense of entitlement to this language. This language is as much their heritage and birthright as Muslims as it is for Arabs.

Until today, at least a rudimentary instruction in the Arabic language is considered an essential foundation for Islamic religious education. In the religious context, "Qur'anic Arabic" rather than local Arabic dialects or Modern Standard Arabic is taught. In pre-modern times, Arabic was the *lingua franca* of educated Muslims, and today remains the preferred language of communication for religiously educated Muslims.

The primacy of Arabic in Islamic education affected local languages wherever Islam spread. After the emergence of Islamic rule in Iraq, for example, Persians switched to writing in a modified Arabic script and over time, much of Arabic vocabulary was adopted into the language, despite the fact that Persian is an Indo-European language whereas Arabic is a Semitic language. A similar pattern emerged in other lands as Islam was embraced by political rulers, with Turkish, Urdu, and Malayan Jawi among the languages written in Arabic, or Arabic-derived Persian scripts, and employing significant amounts of Arabic-derived vocabulary.

In the eighteenth and nineteenth centuries CE, as part of an effort to "divide and conquer" colonized people, European powers sometimes encouraged non-Arab Muslims to reject the Arabic language and script as foreign to their indigenous culture. In the wake of the European intrusion, secular nationalists in places like Egypt and Syria encouraged the adoption of local dialects and languages in an attempt to break with a form of Arabic so closely associated with a religious worldview. Ataturk, the founder of Turkish nationalism, ordered that the Turkish language should be written in Latin, rather than Arabic, script. This change left Turks who did not receive special religious instruction outside the public school system unable to read the Qur'an, and cut them off from six centuries of Ottoman Turkish history as expressed through written texts and documentation. Not surprisingly, in Turkey and elsewhere throughout the twentieth century, the role of classical Arabic in Muslim societies remained a contentious political issue.

One area of linguistic expression that strongly reflects political and cultural affinities and values is personal naming. During the revelatory period, the Prophet Muhammad changed the names of some converts so they would be in conformity with Islamic values and beliefs. The Prophet changed one man's name from 'Abd al-Shams ("Servant of the Sun") to 'Abdullah ("Worshipper of God"). Enforcing the Qur'anic prohibition of calling people humiliating names (Hujarat; 49:11), the Prophet also changed the name of a woman from "Ugly" (*Qabiha*) to "Beautiful" (*Jamila*).[42] Historical texts show a tendency for non-Arab converts to bestow upon their children names that would identify them as Muslims;[43] many of these names are derived from the Qur'an and include most prominently the names of prophets, such as Yusuf (Joseph), Ibrahim (Abraham), Nuh (Noah), and names incorporating the attributes of God, such as 'Abd al-Rahman (Servant of the Most Merciful), 'Abd al-Quddus (Servant of the Holy), 'Abd al-Khaliq (Servant of the Creator), etc. Feminine forms of these names, for example, Amatullah (Maidservant of God) and Amat al-Nur (Maidservant of the Light), are used, but are much less common than the male forms. Qur'anic names for heaven or places in heaven are often used as female names, for example, Jenna, Kawthar, and Tasnim.

The extent to which Muslims ornament their conversation with Qur'anic phrases and expressions is, to a great extent, dependent upon the degree to which their societies have been secularized. There are still some American and European Christians and Jews who unselfconsciously use phrases like "God willing" or "God forbid," but secularization has crowded much of this kind of language out of shared public discourse. This is not the case in most Muslim societies, and the observations of the nineteenth-century Englishman E. W. Lane still hold for many places:

> There are often met with, in Egyptian society, persons who will introduce an apposite quotation from the Qur'an or the Traditions of the Prophet in common conversation, whatever be the topic; and an interruption of this kind is not considered, as it would be in general society in our own country, either hypocritical or annoying; but rather occasions expressions, if not feelings, of admiration, and often diverts the hearers from a trivial subject to matters of a more serious nature.[44]

The effect of the Qur'an on linguistic expression in Muslim societies is vast and merits a separate monograph, but we cannot leave this subject without mentioning some Qur'anic phrases used by Arab and non-Arab Muslims as common expressions. These expressions include *in sha Allah* ("if God wills"), *ma sha Allah* ("what God has willed"), *alhamdu lillah* ("Praise is for God"), and *bismillah* ("in the name of God"). These four expressions are so frequently articulated in Muslim societies, even by secular individuals and non-Muslims living among Muslims, that they alone testify to the profound way the Qur'an has shaped and affected Muslim cultures throughout the world.

Notes

1   Richard W. Bulliet, *Conversion to Islam in the Medieval Period: An Essay in Quantitative History* (Cambridge, MA: Harvard University Press, 1979).
2   Ibn Hisham, 183.
3   Tabari, *History*, vol. 32, translated by C. E. Bosworth as *The Reunification of the Abbasid Capital* (1986), 206–207.
4   Tabari, *History*, 32:212–213.
5   Abu Ja'far Ahmed ibn Muhammad al-Tahawi's *al-'Aqida al-Taha-wiyya* is found in a number of commentaries, including: *Sharh al-Tahawiyya fi'l-aqida al-salafiyya* by 'Ali ibn 'Ali ibn Abi'l-'Izz (Cairo: Zakariyya 'Ali Yusuf, 196–?). I have used the translation of the text by Iqbal Ahmad Azami on the website: www.masud.co.uk/ISLAM/misc/tahawi.htm.
6   Imam al-Haramayn al-Juwayni, *A Guide to Conclusive Proofs for the Principles of Belief*, translation by Paul E. Walker of *Kitab al-irshad 'ila qawati'l-'adilla fi usul al-i'tiqad* (Reading, UK: Garnet Publishing, 2000), 72–73.
7   The cloth covering the Ka'ba, called the *kiswa*, has varied in color and design over the centuries, according to the tastes and interests of the rulers of Mecca. In the sixth/twelfth century, the Andalusian traveler Ibn Jubayr described the *kiswa* thus: "The outside of the Ka'ba, on all its four sides, is clothed in coverings of green silk with cotton warps; and on their upper part is a band of red silk on which is written the verse, 'Verily the first House founded for mankind was that at Bakkah [Mecca]' [Qur'an 3:96]. The name of the Imam al-Nasir li Dinillah, in depth three cubits, encircles it all. On these coverings there has been shaped remarkable designs resembling handsome pulpits, and inscriptions entertaining the name of God Most High and calling blessings on Nasir, the aforementioned 'Abbasid (Caliph) who had ordered its installment. With all this,

there was no clash of colour. The number of covers on all four sides is thirty-four, there being eighteen on the two long sides, and sixteen on the two short sides." Ibn Jubayr, 79.

8 Grabar says that the "rejection of mimetic representation in anything official or formal" in the first century had a wider impact on the aesthetics of Muslim society: writing on objects became one of the dominant modes of decoration. By the ninth and tenth century, it was fashionable in Baghdad to adorn all sorts of "objects of daily use," including bottles, kerchiefs, and turbans, with poems and pithy phrases. Oleg Grabar, *The Mediation of Ornament* (Princeton: Princeton Unversity Press, 1992), 63.

9 For various positions taken over these issues during the European Reformation, see Diarmaid MacCulloch, *The Reformation: A History* (New York: Penguin, 2004), 145–155, 267.

10 Jonathan M. Bloom, *Minaret: Symbol of Islam*, Oxford Studies in Islamic Art VII (Oxford: Oxford University Press, 1989).

11 Reformed Protestants would arrive at a similar solution, stripping their churches of images and replacing them with "often exuberantly floridly framed biblical texts, plus big boards bearing the three texts which all Protestants should know by heart: Nicene or Apostles' Creed, Ten Commandments and Lord's Prayer." MacCulloch, 559.

12 Abu Zakariyya Yahya ibn Sharaf al-Nawawi, *al-Tibyan fi adab hamalat al-Qur'an*, translated by Musa Furber as *Etiquette with the Quran* (Burr Ridge, IL: Starlatch Press, 2003), 103–104.

13 Priscilla P. Soucek, "Material Culture," *EQ* 3:300.

14 Oleg Grabar with contributions from Mohammad al-Asad, Abeer Audeh, and Said Nuseibeh, "Art and Architecture in the Qur'an," *EQ* 1:169.

15 Robert Hoyland and Venetia Porter, "Epigraphy," *EQ* 2:27.

16 See Julian Raby and Jeremy Johns, eds., *Bayt al-Maqdis*, 2 vols. (New York: Oxford University Press, 1992–1999); Oleg Grabar, *The Shape of the Holy: Early Islamic Jerusalem* (Princeton: Princeton University Press, 1996).

17 Sheila S. Blair and Jonathan M. Bloom, *The Art and Architecture of Islam: 1250–1800* (New Haven, CT: Yale University Press, 1994), 280; Amina Okada and M. C. Joshi, *Taj Mahal* (New York: Abbeville Press, 1993).

18 There are a number of good studies on the relationship between the Qur'anic description of Paradise and Islamic art and architecture; these include: Sheila S. Blair and Jonathan M. Bloom, eds., *Images of Paradise in Islamic Art* (Hanover, NH: Hood Museum of Art, 1991); Elizabeth B. Moynihan, *Paradise as a Garden in Persia and Mughal India*

(New York: G. Braziller, 1979); John Brookes, *Gardens of Paradise: The History and Design of the Great Islamic Gardens* (London: Weidenfeld and Nicolson, 1987); D. Fairchild Ruggles, *Gardens, Landscape and Vision in the Palaces of Islamic Spain* (University Park: Pennsylvania State University Press, 2000).

19 At the same time, the Qur'an (41:37) warns against confusing these powerful signs of God that serve as material guides for our daily affairs for powers in themselves.

20 According to the third-/ninth-century scholar al-Sijistani, the Prophet ordered that no piece of writing that contained the name of God should be placed on the floor. See Abu Bakr ibn Abi Daud 'Abdullah al-Sijistani, *Kitab al-Masahif*, ed. Muhammad ibn 'Abduh (Cairo, 2002), 448.

21 Evan Thomas, "How a Fire Broke Out: The Story of a Sensitive *Newsweek* Report about Alleged Abuses at Guantánamo Bay and a Surge of Deadly Unrest in the Islamic World," *Newsweek*, May 23, 2005.

22 Wisam Abd al-Rahman Ahmad interview on Aljazeera.net posted July 7, 2004, english.aljazeera.net/NR/exeres/68168BCC-608B-4593-91A4-637656C20625.htm.

23 Marc Leepson, *Flag: An American Biography* (New York: St. Martin's Press, 2005), 231.

24 Al-Sijistani, 411–418; Al-Nawawi, 113; Lane, 281–282.

25 For an example of the deep layers of meaning that can be discerned in ritual purification by the mystics, see Martin Lings, *A Sufi Saint of the Twentieth Century: Shaikh Ahmad Al-'Alawi – His Spiritual Heritage and Legacy*, 2nd ed. (London: George Allen and Unwin, 1971), 176–184.

26 These acts do not require the performance of a new ablution as a condition for valid performance, but require that the worshipper is in a state of ritual purity (i.e., from an ablution performed earlier) during performance. Ritual purity is lost, among other things, by attending to the toilet, by having sexual relations, and by menstruating. Once these acts/states are completed, ritual purification restores purity.

27 Abu Hamid Muhammad al-Ghazali, *Inner Dimensions of Islamic Worship*, selections from *Ihya 'ulum al-din* translated by Muhtar Holland (Leicester, UK: The Islamic Foundation, 1983), 44.

28 Ibn Hisham, 156–157.

29 Al-Nawawi, 113.

30 Nevertheless, Sayyid Sabiq, who offers the modernist or "Salafi" view in his book *Fiqh al-Sunna* upholds the prohibition, although he mentions the view of the Zahiri scholar Ibn Hazm that there is no such prohibition. Al-Sayyid Sabiq, *Fiqh al-Sunna*, 3 vols. (Beirut:

Dar al-Kitab al-'Arabi, n.d.), 1:67–68. The neo-traditionalist scholar Nuh Keller, in his annotation to the classical Shafi'i *fiqh* text, *'Umdat al-Salik*, calls this "a deviant opinion contrary to all four schools of jurisprudence and impermissible to teach." Nuh Ha Mim Keller in *Reliance of the Traveller: A Classical Manual of Islamic Sacred Law*, his translation of and commentary on Ahmad ibn Naqib al-Misri's *'Umdat al-Salik*, rev. ed. (Evanston, IL: Sunna Books, 1994), 74.

31 In his book *Prophetic Medicine*, Ibn Qayyim al-Jawziyya (d. 751/1350) discusses possession, magic, and the evil eye in limited detail. See Muhammad ibn Abi Bakr ibn Qayyim al-Jawziyya, *al-Tibb al-Nabawi*, ed. 'Abd al-Ghani 'Abd al-Khaliq (Beirut: Dar al-Kutub al-'Ilmiyya, 1957). Some Muslim modernists, uncomfortable with "superstitious" beliefs like the existence of jinn (although still able to maintain a belief in God), tried to rationalize the issue, as we shall discuss in the next chapter. The popularity of books about jinn in the late twentieth century indicates that many literate Muslims (since only the literate can read these books) do not have the same difficulty embracing both science and a belief in the unseen. 'Umar Sulayman Ashqar, *'Alam al-jinn wa'l-shayatin*, translated by Jamaal al-Din M. Zarabozo as *The World of Jinn and Devils* (Denver, CO: al-Basheer Publications and Translations, 1998).

32 This information is from the author's own observation of current practice in a number of Arab, African, and Turkish Muslim communities.

33 These are practices the author has observed in contemporary Muslim communities across the world. Lane observed the same practices in early nineteenth-century Egypt. Lane, 247–256.

34 The traditionalist Sufi position is strongly defended by Muhammad Hisham Kabbani in his *Encyclopedia of Islamic Doctrine*, 7 vols. (Mountain View, CA: As-Sunna Foundation of American Publications, 1998).

35 Bukhari, "*Kitab al-Tibb*," 1231.

36 Ibn Qayyim, 137.

37 Sura Ya Sin is also among the Qur'anic passages recited in the evening. See Howard M. Federspiel, *Popular Indonesian Literature of the Qur'an* (Ithaca, NY: Cornell Modern Indonesia Project, 1994), 97–98.

38 F. E. Peters, *Mecca: A Literary History of the Muslim Holy Land* (Princeton: Princeton University Press, 1994), 289–299.

39 The mention of the deceased woman's "face" as the locus of God's blessing following the Qur'anic statement that only God's "face" will never perish is poignant and significant. The phrasing perhaps suggests that the holy woman becomes a kind of mirror for God's blessings.

40   From the website of the Smithsonian Museum of Natural History, www.mnh.si.edu/epigraphy/e_islamic/fig52_naskh01.htm. I am unable to access the original stone, therefore I cannot attest to the complete accuracy of the translation of lines 8 and 9 of the translation provided, although I made changes to some of the other lines where I could better read the inscription.

41   Wadad al-Qadi, "The Impact of the Qur'an on the Epistolography of 'Abd al-Hamid," in *Approaches to the Qur'an*, eds. G. R. Hawting and Abdul-Kader A. Shareef (London: Routledge, 1993), 285–313.

42   In some traditional cultures, children are given names with negative connotations to ward off the evil eye or to trick invisible spirits who might steal bright and beautiful children to raise as their own.

43   Bulliet, 18–19.

44   Lane, 280.

5

What God Really Means: Interpreting the Qur'an

Exegesis before Hermeneutics

As we have seen earlier, when 'Umar ibn al-Khattab was informed of the death of the Prophet Muhammad, he refused to believe the news. Like many others faced with the sudden death of a loved one, 'Umar at first simply denied that it could be true. Abu Bakr rejected 'Umar's impassioned assertion that the Prophet could not have died, and convinced 'Umar of the Prophet's death by showing him his body, and by reciting the Qur'anic verse: *Muhammad is no more than a messenger; messengers before him have passed away. If he were to die or were killed, would you turn back on your heels?*

By applying the appropriate Qur'anic verse to the relevant material evidence, Abu Bakr was able to determine the truth: indeed, the Prophet was dead. This was Qur'anic exegesis in action, and it was the first time that the Qur'an had to be interpreted and applied without the possibility of resorting to the infallible guidance of the Prophet. From this point forward, the Qur'an was to be the last word on any matter Muslims faced, but determining what the Qur'an meant would not always be easy.

One of the most important issues the community had to address was the question of authority: who was authorized to say what the Qur'an meant? The Qur'an did not explicitly address a succession plan for leadership of the Islamic community after the death of the Prophet. Not surprisingly, there was no unanimity among the Prophet's followers about who was most qualified to exercise political leadership, nor about the extent to which political leadership and religious authority were intertwined.

The community of Medina, which claimed sovereignty over the Muslims of the Arabian Peninsula after the death of Muhammad, was unanimous on one issue of leadership: it rejected any further claims of prophethood. They understood the Qur'an to be clear on this matter when it said:

> Muhammad is not the father of any of your men, but the Messenger of God and the seal of the prophets; and God is, about everything, All-Knowing.

(Ahzab; 33:40)

Because there were no more prophets, the leader of the Muslims after Muhammad simply became known as the *khalifa*, "caliph," that is, "successor (to the Prophet)." When Musaylima, a tribal leader in the eastern Arabian Peninsula, challenged the caliphate of Medina by calling himself a new "prophet" after the death of Muhammad, he was deemed "The Liar" and was fought as a renegade.[1]

As we have seen, the early caliphs played an important role in the development of a unified written text of the Qur'an. Some of them were, in addition, memorizers of the Qur'an who passed on their knowledge to later generations, as is claimed in *hifz* and *tajwid* certificates, such as the *ijaza* of Sheikh al-Kurdi. As close Companions of the Prophet and his successors, each of the caliphs had a good sense of the meaning and context of the Qur'anic revelation. At the same time, none of them is shown in historical reports to have claimed a unique right to interpret the Qur'an. Rather, the caliphs are shown seeking out other Companions who might have had knowledge of occasions of revelation, or the meanings of obscure words in the Qur'an.

Among those said to have been particularly knowledgeable of Qur'anic vocabulary and usage was 'Abdullah ibn al-'Abbas, a first cousin and close Companion to the Prophet Muhammad. Ibn al-'Abbas is portrayed in early sources as perhaps the first true scholar of the Qur'an; he used to hold regular classes in Mecca, where he devoted certain days to particular topics relevant to understanding the context of the Qur'an. Ibn al-'Abbas's teachings were transmitted by his students and are widely found in later works of *tafsir* (Qur'an commentary) and law.

To understand the development of Qur'an interpretation in the centuries after the death of the Prophet Muhammad, it is important to recognize that the act of exegesis does not require an explicit hermeneutics. That is to say, all sorts of people have interpreted and do interpret the Qur'an without an explicit or consistent methodology. Historically, the early generations of Muslims did not begin by saying: let us first develop a proper system of hermeneutics, then we can proceed to interpret the Qur'an. Rather, interpretations were offered, some were challenged, and this necessitated the development of a more formal methodology. The interpretations that "won out" at any particular time, however, were not necessarily the most coherent or obvious. Political power, personal charisma, economic crises, social upheaval, and emotional appeals, among other factors, contributed to the popularity of some interpretations and some interpreters over others.

In the tumultuous first decades of Islam, there were many Muslims who had strong opinions about the meaning and message of the Qur'an. Although different interpretations were often complementary, others conflicted. As early as the reign of 'Uthman, for example, some prominent Companions voiced opposition to the policies and practices of the state on the basis of their understanding of the Qur'an. Abu Dharr, one of the prominent Companions who left Medina to preach in Syria, believed that Muslims should continue to live the ascetic lifestyle of the Prophet. He argued that not only individuals, but even states should not accumulate wealth. He based his position on the Qur'anic verse:

> ... As for those who hoard gold and silver and do not spend it in the
> path of God, announce to them a grievous punishment.
>
> (Tawba; 9:34)

Abu Dharr was therefore disturbed by his observation that Muslim leaders in Syria were living in what he considered luxurious conditions, as well as accumulating significant wealth in the treasury. Abu Dharr criticized the Syrian governor Mu'awiya for his private and public policies in this regard.

Mu'awiya, who, after all, was not a newcomer to Islam, but had also been a Companion of the Prophet, challenged Abu Dharr's application of this verse to his government policy, answering, "This verse is not for us, but for the People of the Book." Indeed, Abu Dharr had quoted only the last part of the verse which in total reads:

> O you who believe, indeed there are many among the priests and rabbis
> who consume the wealth of the people unjustly and serve as barriers to
> the path of God. As for those who hoard gold and silver and do not
> spend it in the path of God, announce to them a grievous punishment.

Abu Dharr responded to Mu'awiya by saying, "(The verse) is both for us and for them."[2]

178 What God Really Means: Interpreting the Qur'an

Here we see two of the main issues in Qur'an interpretation: First, to what extent is the meaning of any words of the Qur'an limited by the rest of the verse or passage (or, perhaps, even the whole of the Qur'an) in which they are found? Second, what is the scope of application of any Qur'anic pronouncement?

In this case, Abu Dharr had selectively cited only that part of the verse that proved his point. Mu'awiya, who knew the Qur'an well, brought the greater context to Abu Dharr's attention in order to limit the application of its words. Mu'awiya contended that the verse was applicable only to the specific categories of people mentioned – priests and rabbis. Abu Dharr did not accept Mu'awiya's interpretation, and held that the condemnation of hoarding was the main message of the verse, and a moral principle that was universally applicable.

The political dimension of this disagreement is also instructive of the practical dynamics of competing exegesis. Abu Dharr had no political office, but as an ascetic and charismatic preacher had significant moral authority among Muslims in Syria. He therefore hoped to bring about a change in Mu'awiya's policy by preaching to publicly gathered crowds. For his part, Mu'awiya resented the challenge to his authority to set policies according to his best judgment, and, in these early years of the development of a regional government in Syria, did not welcome this deliberate disturbance of public order. Mu'awiya appealed to the caliph 'Uthman, who, finding Abu Dharr unwilling to tone down his rhetoric, banished him to live the remainder of his life in a remote village.

Although the political authorities were able to remove Abu Dharr from the public sphere, they were unable to remove his interpretation from normative discourse. Stories about Abu Dharr's opposition to Mu'awiya's policies, and his opinions about the meaning of this and other Qur'anic verses, were collected and circulated, no doubt gaining more popularity over the first century of Islam as opposition to the Umayyad dynasty (of which Mu'awiya would be the first sovereign) increased. Although few, if any, rulers – including the 'Abbasids, who would eventually overthrow the Umayyads – would adopt Abu Dharr's opinions about the redistribution of wealth, his views would continue to be mentioned alongside other interpretations in Qur'an commentaries. Consequently, at various points in history, such as during the early twentieth century when socialism was proposed as one of the ideological bases for modern Arab nation-states, Abu Dharr's opinion could easily be found and offered as a legitimate Islamic principle for radical economic restructuring.

Historical accounts show that in the rough and tumble struggle for political authority and stability in the first Islamic century, the Qur'an was regularly cited as a motivation or justification for various, often conflicting, behaviors. A formal hermeneutics would later emerge to bring some order to this exegesis on the ground, but at this time, all parties were simply eager to show that the Qur'an supported them, and that they supported the Qur'an – sometimes, as in a later conflict between 'Ali and Mu'awiya – in a fully literal fashion.

Soon after the caliph 'Uthman had been assassinated by malcontents from Egypt, 'Ali was recognized as the next caliph by a group of Medinans. Other Companions were upset that 'Ali had not done more to protect 'Uthman while he had been under siege, and that he did not immediately prosecute 'Uthman's killers after his death. Mu'awiya, a close relative of 'Uthman, claimed that it was his duty to see the assassins brought to justice, and refused to recognize 'Ali's authority as the new caliph until this was done. For his part, 'Ali indicated that his first priority was to quell political unrest, and therefore insisted that Mu'awiya take the oath of allegiance before other actions were taken. A power-struggle ensued, and 'Ali and Mu'awiya eventually met on the battlefield.

There is no doubt that historical accounts of this conflict, collected more than a century after the events they purport to describe, are tendentious and problematic.[3] We need to remind the reader of our earlier discussion of the historiographical challenges we face in assessing the validity of these narratives. At the same time, without implying that the stories do not have any historical content, we might suggest that they are especially helpful for showing us the values held by early Muslims, as well as the way Qur'anic language and themes influenced their discourse.

The first generation of Muslims were raised in a culture in which tales of exciting battles, heroic warriors, and ignominious foes were told in the market-place and around campfires; they could not help but portray their own struggles in similar terms. At the same time, such stories set standards for behavior and created expectations about the proper comportment of noble men and the values they should uphold. Shakespeare's famous line that "All the world's a stage, and all the men and women merely players" implies that culture, as much as biology, is destiny. The warriors of pre-Islamic Arabia exhibited honor and courage in particular culturally acceptable ways. For example, a man would invoke his lineage (*nasab*) as a source of pride that would give him the confidence to fight. After Islam, some of these cultural patterns continued, while others were replaced by new values and ideals arising out of the Qur'an and the Sunna of the Prophet Muhammad. The historical actors described in the struggle between 'Ali and Mu'awiya are shown, for example, engaging the sacred text as a justification and a source of strength. There is no doubt that some bias against Mu'awiya appears in the narratives, but these stories are instructive even for that purpose – to show how certain individuals are shown to be justified or illegitimate because of the way they engage the Qur'an. Thus, we see 'Ali weaving Qur'anic verses easily and naturally into his speeches, while some other figures use the Qur'an rhetorically, cynically, and, in the case of Mu'awiya's troops, in what could be read either as a powerfully symbolic and heartfelt or vulgar and manipulative fashion.

For example, in a message sent to one of his commanders, 'Ali wrote:

> Hasten to save your companions. When you reach them, you are in charge, but do not begin fighting the enemy – unless they attack you first – before meeting them, appealing to them, and having been heard by them. *Do not allow their hatred to provoke you* [5:2] into fighting them before you have appealed to them and given them every chance, again and again, to change their views.[4]

Here, 'Ali integrates Qur'anic phrasing into his own speech in an appropriate and relevant fashion. Just as importantly, 'Ali's message reflects the Qur'anic ethic of seeking reconciliation and using force as a last resort.

Unable to bring Mu'awiya's supporters under his authority, 'Ali eventually met them on the battlefield. However, just before the hostilities began, Mu'awiya's troops raised sheets of Qur'anic text (*masahif*) upon their lances and said, "This is the Book of God between us and you." 'Ali's troops, who included many devoted Reciters of the Qur'an (*qurra'*), lay down their weapons and supported a call for arbitration. By this point, 'Ali had become convinced that he had to assert his authority as caliph, and that his opponents' appeals for arbitration were only a ruse to divide his troops. Nevertheless, unable to persuade his naïve and idealistic followers of his views, 'Ali agreed to arbitration.

Later, these same Reciters changed their minds and decided that by agreeing to arbitration, they had gone against the "judgment of God," referencing the Qur'anic statement:

Judgment belongs to none but God.

(An'am 6:57; Yusuf 12: 40, 67)

'Ali argued that it was too late to change their minds; they had made an agreement, and despite his reservations, they must stick to it. The Reciters now claimed that 'Ali, because he accepted the arbitration, had gone against the judgment of God, and must repent or become a disbeliever. 'Ali argued that arbitration in itself was a valid means of resolving conflicts, even when the conflict was against rebels refusing to submit to the authority of the state. In response, the Reciters mutinied and, having abandoned 'Ali, became known as the *Khawarij*, the "Secessionists." The Khawarij proceeded to go on a rampage, killing any Muslim who disagreed with their views on the grounds that such people had become "disbelievers."

As long as he was able to communicate with the Khawarij, 'Ali continued to try to reason with them and reconcile them to his decision. For example, here, 'Ali tries to explain the role of human authority in interpreting and implementing the Qur'an:

> The Khawarij said, "Tell us, do you think it is 'just' to give men authority in matters of blood?" 'Ali replied, "We have not given men authority; we have made the Qur'an the authority. But this Qur'an is merely a scripture placed between two covers. It does not speak; it is merely men who speak through it."[5]

'Ali further tried to show the Khawarij that they were violating the clear Qur'anic prohibitions against murder and violence in their pursuit of a political goal:

> Explain why you consider it lawful to fight against us and split off from the community. The people did not choose two men [as arbitrators] so that you should put your swords on your shoulders, slaughter people, cut off their heads and shed their blood, *indeed that is clear depravity* [22:11; 39:15]. By God, even if you killed a chicken like that, its slaughter would be a serious matter with God – so what about a (human) life whose murder God has prohibited!

The Khawarij, like any cultish group, had to avoid dialogue with those holding opposing views if they were to preserve their extremist and marginal views. Thus, in response to 'Ali's pleas, one of the leaders of the Khawarij called out, "Do not speak to them or argue with them. Prepare to meet the Lord; hasten, hasten to Paradise!"[6]

Rhetorical and selective use of the Qur'an and a violent and rigid mindset are shown to have been characteristics of the Khawarij. Superficially devoted to the Qur'an, in fact, the Khawarij veered far from its message. In contrast, the beloved cousin of the Prophet and one of his first followers, 'Ali ibn Abi Talib, who was eventually assassinated by one of the Khawarij, showed a deep understanding of the Qur'an and its principles. In his final testament to his family, 'Ali continued to convincingly integrate Qur'anic phrases (rendered in italics) and paraphrasical references, as well as Qur'anic values and principles, into his discourse:

> *In the name of God, the Merciful, the Compassionate*
> This is the testament of 'Ali ibn Abi Talib. He testifies that *there is no god but God without any partner* and that Muhammad is his servant and messenger *whom He sent with right guidance and the religion of truth to make it triumphant over every other, even though the polytheists abhor it. My prayer and my worship, my life and my death belong to God, the Lord of the worlds, Who has no partner. Thus I was commanded and I am among those who are Muslims.*
>
> I commend to you, Hasan, and all of my offspring and family, the fear of God, your Lord. *Die only as Muslims and hold fast together to the rope of God; do not separate.* I heard Abu'l-Qasim [the Prophet Muhammad] say, "The restoration of unity is better than all your prayer and fasting." Pay attention to your relatives and unite them, so that God will make your reckoning easy. Fear God, fear God with respect to the orphans. Do not underfeed them nor neglect them while they are in your care. Fear God, fear God with respect to your neighbors, for they are the commendation of your Prophet, who never ceased to commend them, so that we thought he would include them as canonical heirs.
>
> . . .
>
> (*Do not fear the blame of anyone*) over God; *He is the Sufficient Protector* for you against anyone who has designs upon you and oppresses you. *Speak good to the people* as God has commanded you and do not abandon *the commanding of good and the prohibiting of evil*, or the worst ones among you will obtain power; then you will call for help, but no answer will be given to you. You must pursue mutual harmony and generosity,

avoiding mutual opposition, separation, and splintering. *Help one another in piety and fear of God but not in sin and enmity to Him. Fear God for His retribution is mighty.*

May God preserve you as members of a family and your Prophet as one of you. I entrust you to God and I bid you farewell, and the mercy of God be upon you.[7]

From the time Mu'awiya's troops raised pages of the Qur'an on their lances to the start of the first Gulf War in 1991, when Saddam Hussein put the Qur'anic phrase *Allahu akbar*, "God is Greater," on the Iraqi flag, up to the international terrorist movements of our time, there have been Muslims who have used the Qur'an to encourage, justify, and challenge highly specific political agendas, some violent and intolerant. At the same time, there have been more Muslims who have been inspired by the Qur'an to pay charity, be generous, establish peace treaties, and work for a just and accountable political order. In Muslim societies in which religious identity is strong, the language of the Qur'an is the dominant normative discourse, and some will use the Qur'an in a manipulative fashion, while others will sincerely try to be guided by its message. It is impossible to prevent the Qur'an from being "used" to justify bad behavior. Shakespeare wrote that "the devil can cite scripture for his purpose," and this is as true of the Qur'an as it is of the Bible, which has been used at various times to justify everything from the enslavement of Africans to the subjugation of women and the forcible expulsion of indigenous peoples from their lands.

Ridding societies of religious discourse will not prevent injustices from being committed in the name of secular values either. Nationalist and secular regimes and their founding texts are not immune from manipulation for unjust purposes. For most of its history, the explicitly egalitarian spirit of the US Constitution was interpreted away by restricting the application of the word "men" to white males. Throughout the twentieth century, secular "modernizing" regimes in the Middle East elevated the importance of Turkish, Persian, and Arab national identities and their founding myths to justify severe discrimination against ethnic minorities.

One need not be a scholar to recognize many instances of the deliberate manipulation of scripture to acquire power (although sadly, we are all too often deceived). But in most cases, motives are less clear, our sincerity elusive, even to ourselves. It is this quest for a true openness to the guidance of scripture that has been the primary concern of Qur'anic hermeneutists: how does the sincere believer – the man or woman who does not seek to manipulate the Qur'an, but wants to be guided by it – find a way to understand its true meaning?

The Epistemological Challenge

The greatest challenge for those who sincerely seek to be guided by the Qur'an is to be able to listen to God's words without imposing one's own fears and desires upon the revelation. In the end, the issue is epistemological: how can a Muslim be certain that she has grasped the true meaning of the Qur'an, and has not forced herself upon the text?

The Qur'an clearly condemns those who speak about God without "knowledge" (*'ilm*):

> *Say: my Lord has only forbidden shameful deeds, done in public or in private, sins and coveting something without right, to associate with God what He has not revealed, and to say about God things about which you have no knowledge.*
>
> (A'raf; 7:33)

Those who preach or teach their own notions about God, rather than having the humility to sincerely seek revelation, will be punished for misleading others:

> *They will bear their full burdens on the Day of Judgment, as well as some of the burden of those whom they misled with something other than knowledge; what a terrible burden they will bear!*
>
> (Nahl; 16:25)

The fundamental question that needs to be asked in this regard is whether there is any interpretive source (human, textual or otherwise) external to the Qur'an that matches its epistemological certainty. Muslims believe that the Qur'an is a flawlessly reliable source of truth because it is the accurately preserved record of the words of the Living God. There is consensus among Muslims, therefore, that the best interpretation of the Qur'an is the Qur'an itself. Nevertheless, as 'Ali pointed out to the Khawarij, the reality is that it is people who interpret the Qur'an. Even sacred language is not transparent, and it is human interpreters who will decide the meaning of the words of the Qur'an and the relationship of some passages to others.

The barriers to sound comprehension of the Qur'an are many, but generally fall into two categories: intellectual and spiritual. In the following pages, we will focus primarily on the intellectual challenges and the exegetical tools employed by scholars. In the final chapter of our book, we will look deeper into the spiritual challenges faced by individuals and communities as they strive to understand and implement the Qur'an in their lives.

In the first place, the Qur'an must be understood intellectually. This means that it is necessary to study its words, their implications and significations in their original Arabic articulations and to understand Qur'anic grammar and rhetoric. Knowing these things, however, only means that one has comprehended the literal meaning of the words of the Qur'an.

If one wants to understand the normative implications of these verses, much more work needs to be done. To derive norms from the Qur'an – moral injunctions, legal rulings, and ethical imperatives – it is necessary to consider the way different parts of the Qur'an relate to one another. This means that the following questions, among others, need to be asked: Does the Qur'an address the same issue in more than one place? If so, are the meanings of these verses compatible, or is there an apparent contradiction? What is the relationship between general statements and particular rulings – does one bind or supersede the other? Is there any information that is outside of the Qur'an that can be used to clarify or restrict its meanings?

Additional questions are raised about the context in which the verses were revealed. How do we relate the Prophet's Sunna to the Qur'an? What about other sacred scriptures that are mentioned in the Qur'an – can they be used to clarify Qur'anic narratives? What if there is an apparent contradiction between a Qur'anic statement and science? What precisely is the role of human reason? If the apparent meaning of the Qur'an contradicts our sense of reason, can we suggest metaphorical interpretations?

Qur'an exegesis, known as *ta'wil* (to give the "original" meaning) or *tafsir* (to explain), is a vast field of Islamic studies. From the time of the Companions until today, Muslim scholars have attempted to understand the meaning and implications of the Qur'an, and have taught, lectured, and written on the subject. Exegesis comprises many sub-genres, including studies of Qur'anic vocabulary, rhetoric, grammar,

Figure 5.1   A graduate student at the University of Chicago has access to thousands of volumes of Qur'anic commentary from fourteen centuries of Muslim scholarship. (Ahmed Hashim)

occasions of revelation, stories of the prophets, legal content, scientific indications, and hidden meanings.

Qur'an commentaries include not only a variety of sub-genres but a significant diversity of approaches as well. The range of methods and critical tools used by generations of Qur'an commentators lecturing and writing over the centuries belies the stereotype that Muslims are somehow bound to a literal approach to scripture. Classical (that is, premodern) commentaries exhibit a range of approaches and include, for example, al-Zamakhshari's *The Unveiler of the Truths of Revelation and of the Essences of Utterances Concerning the Aspects of Exegesis*,[8] a masterful study of the language of the Qur'an in which the author, a sixth-/twelfth-century Mu'tazilite, applies that theological school's understanding of the "justice and unity" of God to interpret the text. For example, al-Zamakhshari (d. 538/1144) glosses "God's face" as his "essence" (or "self") and interprets phrases like "God's hands" as metonymical.[9] Mystics, like the third-/ninth-century scholar Tustari, searched for the "hidden" (*batin*) meanings of Qur'anic verses in their exegesis. In later centuries, al-Sulami (d. 412/1021), al-Qushayri (d. 465/1072), Ibn al-'Arabi (d. 638/1240), and Ibn 'Ajiba (d. 1224/1809) were among the most influential practitioners of mystical exegesis. The comprehensive commentary of al-Tabari (d. ca. 310/923), *The Sum of Clarity Concerning the Interpretations of the Verses of the Qur'an*,[10] in which the author collects opinions and interpretations from numerous sources, remains an indispensable scholarly source. A later massive *tafsir*, by al-Razi (d. 606/1209), *The Extensive Tafsir*,[11] includes much of al-Tabari's material, but also integrates perspectives from philosophy, science, astrology, and other significant disciplines of his time. Indeed, most substantial *tafsirs* engage the important issues of their time, including political and social issues. One of the most influential classical *tafsirs*, known as *Tafsir al-Jalalayn*, collected the commentaries of two scholars named "Jalal," Jalal al-Din al-Mahalli (d. 864/1459) and Jalal al-Din al-Suyuti (d. 911/1505). Although these scholars offered little new material in their exegesis, their clear and lucid writing and concise discussions made much of classical *tafsir* accessible to a wider readership.

Looking first at the early years of Qur'anic exegesis, we see that a primary concern was the language of the Qur'an itself. This language presented some challenges to comprehension because, as we discussed earlier, the Arabs contemporary with the Prophet used a number of dialects. This means that some Qur'anic words were used in ways unfamiliar to certain tribes. Later, over the first few centuries of Islam, Arabic vernaculars changed as the language spread outside the Arabian Peninsula. Scholars therefore considered it important to study the vocabulary of the Qur'an to ensure that there was no confusion about the meanings signified by particular words. This is the kind of analysis undertaken by one of the earliest Qur'an scholars, Muqatil ibn Sulayman (d. 150/767), in his *Aspects of the Qur'an*[12] and his other commentaries.

Early scholars made in-depth linguistic analyses of many, if not most, words of the Qur'an. This is the case, for example, in the discussion of a word that occurs in the following passage, which cites the statements of tribal chiefs who rejected the message of one of the ancient prophets:

> *"Does he promise that when you die and become dust and bones*
> *that you will be brought forth again?*
> *Far, far is that which you are promised!"*
>
> (Mu'minun; 23:35–36)

The word that is translated as "far" – *hayhata* – does not seem to have been an everyday kind of word in the vocabulary of the Arabs. For this reason (and, no doubt because scholars generally like to explore all possible nuances of their subjects), one can find extensive discussions of the ten different variants of this word in the Arabic language, along with citations of pre-Islamic poetry to show how the variants are used by the masters of eloquence, for example:

> You recall the past days of youthfulness –
> Far, far, are you from returning to them![13]

Even more interpretations are offered for the meaning of the so-called "disconnected letters" (*al-huruf al-muqatta'a*) that appear at the beginning of twenty-nine suras. These letters are recited as individual letters of the alphabet; the English equivalent transliteration of the beginning of Sura al-Baqara (*Alif Lam Mim*), for example, is

> *A. L. M. This is the book in which there is no discrepancy.*
>
> (Baqara; 2:1–2)

What is the meaning of these letters ("A. L. M.")? Some said that the letters are acronyms for some of God's attributes found in the associated Sura, for example, "Al-Rahman." Others said that the letters are mystical signs with symbolic meaning.[14] Among the many opinions offered, the one I find the most convincing takes into account the essentially oral nature of the revealed Qur'an. In this view, calling out the letters was a way to attract attention to the recitation that followed. Pre-Islamic poets sometimes began their recitations in the same way, the purpose being to draw people's attention to the fact that the poet was commencing his recitation. This view is strengthened by the fact that Qur'anic *tajwid* requires that some of these vowels should be elongated and drawn out, in the way that someone calling out another's name to attract his attention might do (like an English speaker saying "Heeeey Jane!").

Since the same word can be used in different ways, scholars spend a great deal of effort trying to determine a word's particular meaning in a specific passage. To analyze the range of meanings possible within one passage, scholars employ a range of hermeneutical tools, including probing into the roots of words, examining the grammatical structure of the sentences, and comparing the way in which such words are used in other verses.

For example, the imperative form of a verb ("Go!" "Write!" "Spend!") implies a command. However, scholars argued that the normative value of such commands differs, depending on the context. For example, the Qur'an discusses the obligatory Friday communal prayer in the following verses:

> O you who believe, when you are called to prayer on the Friday (lit. the "day of congregation"), hurry to the remembrance of prayer and cease all business. That is better for you if you only knew. Then when the prayer is finished, disperse throughout the land and seek the bounty of God and remember God frequently so that you will prosper.
>
> (Jumu'a; 62:9–10)

In this passage, the verbs "hurry," "cease," "disperse," and "seek" are all in the imperative form. However, scholars understand only "hurry" and "cease" to create an obligation (*farida*), while "disperse" and "seek" imply permission (*nadb*), not obligation. That is, believers must make a sincere effort to get to the Friday prayer on time and must not engage in business after the call to prayer is made. On the other hand, believers are not required to leave the mosque and go to work when the prayer is finished. If they like, they can go home for a nap, have lunch, stay in the mosque and study, etc.

The question arises, how do scholars distinguish which verbs imply obligation and which imply permission if all of them are expressed in the imperative form? Clearly, it is only by bringing some other factors to the text that it is possible to make such a distinction. As we will discuss shortly, the Sunna of the Prophet, the consensus of the scholars, and other considerations are brought in to the interpretive process to help understand the true implications of any Qur'anic verse.

Given that so many variables are considered relevant to the analysis of any Qur'anic passage, it is not surprising that scholars will arrive at different conclusions. Nevertheless, as we read the various opinions offered by scholars about the meanings and applications of certain

Qur'anic terms, we may feel somewhat disconcerted to note how often early scholars offered different interpretations of the same terms or verses, with no indication of the means by which they arrived at their positions.

One reason for the absence of supporting proofs in many early books may be that, particularly in the early centuries of Islam, books were seldom "authored," but were mostly collections of opinions gathered by students of the scholars. The justifications for many interpretations, therefore, may have been given orally, but did not always find their way into early texts. At the same time, we also hear that in the early centuries of Islam, some scholars criticized others for explaining the meaning of the Qur'an according to their "opinion," *bi'l-ray*, without giving explicit proofs for their reasoning. For their part, it seems that these scholars felt confident in their own abilities to understand much of what the Qur'an was saying. After all, the Qur'an declares that it is:

> – *a book whose verses are explained in detail;*
> *an Arabic Qur'an for a people who understand.*
>
> (Fussilat; 41:3)

The reliability of reason as a tool for assessing the truth seems to be implied in the Qur'an's insistence that humans contemplate and reflect upon its verses. Yet, it is easy to convince oneself that one is offering a reasonable interpretation, when, in fact, one is rationalizing one's desires. The Qur'an offers the sobering example of Iblis, who disobeyed God because it seemed illogical to him that a creature made of a noble substance like fire would have to bow to a creature made from the earth:

> *(God said to Iblis): "What prevented you from prostrating (in front of Adam) when I ordered you?" He replied: "I am better than him. You created me from fire and him from clay."*
>
> ('Araf; 7:12)

It is this fear of self-deception and an arrogant exaltation of human logic over divine revelation that led to the increasing formalization and standardization of exegetical techniques, subject to approval and scrutiny by the developing scholarly community. At the same time, reason, intuition, and common sense, among other things, continued in various forms to play a role in interpretation, as did personal authority. As we shall see, the Shi'ites developed a doctrine of the unique ability of the Imams to understand the meaning of the Qur'an, Sufism generally supported the idea that the spiritually elect could obtain a superior understanding of the deeper meaning of the Qur'an, and the Mu'tazilites argued that human reason was created by God as a sufficient tool for determining the correct implication of a multivocal text.[15] For its part, the Sunni community distinguished itself by relying on two major interpretive tools to fix the meaning of the Qur'an and its normative implications: the Sunna of the Prophet Muhammad and the consensus (*ijma'*) of the scholars. Indeed, Sunni identity is constructed on these two pillars, as declared in the formal name of the Sunnis: *Ahl al-Sunna wa'l-Jama'a*: "The People of the Sunna and Community."

All interpretive communities shared a similar challenge to develop a coherent system whereby multiple sources of varying authority could be used to interpret the Qur'an and apply its norms to the lives of Muslims. In the following pages, we will consider some of these sources and interpretive tools, beginning with a source external to the Qur'an.

Intertextuality: The Isra'iliyyat

The Isra'iliyyat are extra-Qur'anic stories about the prophets and pre-Islamic peoples mentioned in the Qur'an. The Qur'an mentions at least twenty-five prophets, including the ancient prophets – Adam, Noah, Hud, and others – Ibrahim and his sons, Isma'il and Isaac, and the Israelite prophets, Jesus, John, and Mary,[16] the Arabian prophets – Salih and Hud – as well as others. The Qur'an invokes these prophets and holy figures as exemplars of piety and courage, who, in many cases, met with significant opposition from their people whom they were calling to righteousness. At times, a reference to one of these figures is introduced with the words, "and recall when . . . ," implying that the listener already knows the basic story. In most cases, this story can be found in other suras. For example, in one sura, the Qur'an makes brief mention of a number of prophets in succession, not giving much detail about their stories. All that is said about Mary, for example, is this:

> And (remember) the one who guarded her chastity, then we breathed into her from our spirit and made her and her son a sign to the worlds.
>
> (Anbiya'; 21:91)

However, another sura which was given the name "Mary" expands upon these references to Mary's special status as a chaste devotee of the temple, her angelic visitation, and her delivery and birth of Jesus:

> Make mention of Mary in the Book: how she withdrew from her family to a place in the east.
> She placed a veil between them; then we sent to her our spirit, who came to her in the form of a person.
> He said, "Verily, I am a messenger from your Lord to give to you a holy son."
> She said, "How am I to have a son, when no man has touched me and I am not unchaste?"
> He said, "Thus it will be. Your Lord says, 'That is easy for me, and We will make him a sign to the people as a mercy from Us. It is a matter decreed.' "
> So she conceived him and withdrew with him to a remote place.
> When the pains of childbirth drove her to (grab onto) the trunk of a date-palm, she cried, "Ah, would that I have died before this or become a thing long forgotten!"
> Then she heard from beneath the tree, "Do not despair! Your Lord has placed a stream beneath you.
> And shake the tree trunk towards you so fresh, ripe dates will fall to you.
> Then eat and drink and rest your eyes. If you see any person say, 'I have made a vow of abstinence to the Merciful, and I will not speak to anyone today.' "
>
> (Maryam; 19:16–26)

The stories of these and other prophets in the Qur'an are thematically complete and coherent. Their main message is that God has always sent prophets or pious men and women to call others to the worship of the one God and to act with righteousness. From Christian and Jewish perspectives, however, the stories are missing many of the details included in biblical narratives of the same figures. The Qur'an, for example, does not mention Mary's marriage to Joseph, or the flight into Egypt. In relating the story of Noah, the Qur'an mentions the ark, but does not mention the details of its construction or the composition of its inhabitants.

We do not know if the Prophet Muhammad and early Muslims knew of these biblical stories, but the Qur'an seems to assume that the listener has general knowledge of the figures involved. This knowledge may have come from the biblical tradition, but it is also likely that the pre-Islamic Arabs had their own oral traditions about these figures. We recall that the Arabs had many stories about their ancestor Abraham; as we saw earlier, the Prophet Muhammad himself related some of these stories to his Companions.

In addition, Christians and Jews who converted to Islam also brought their knowledge of both canonical and oral narratives of the prophets. Muslim scholars were then confronted with the question of whether these stories could be drawn upon to provide additional context to the Qur'anic stories, or if they should be rejected. The decision rested on the same concern for epistemological certainty that entailed when sifting prophetic hadith or other non-Qur'anic material. The Qur'an does recognize the divine origin of other scriptures:

> *Allah! There is no god but He, the Living, the Self-Subsistent.*
> *He sent down to you the Book in truth, confirming what you have*
> *and he sent down the Torah and the Gospel before this as a guide to*
> *people, and He sent the Criterion.*
>
> (Al 'Imran; 3:3)

On the other hand, the Qur'an states that much of the original message of the earlier revelations has been changed or lost:

> *Because (the Children of Israel) broke their covenant, we cursed*
> *them and made their hearts hard. They take words out of context*
> *and forget some of that which was sent to them. You will not cease*
> *to find deceit appearing among them, except for some of them.*
> *But bear with them and pardon them. Surely God loves those who*
> *are kind.*
>
> (Ma'ida; 5:13)

Muslim scholars took this and other verses to mean that the scriptures used by Jews and Christians were not fully reliable sources of revealed knowledge. At the same time, many scholars were reluctant to completely reject the extant scriptures, given the possibility that they still contained a significant amount of material originating in earlier revelations. Lacking any other tools for source-criticism, many scholars decided that if a Bible story contradicted a Qur'anic narrative or a fundamental Islamic doctrine, it would be rejected. If the biblical material was in agreement with the Qur'an and Islamic principles, it could be considered potentially corroborating revealed knowledge. If the biblical material offered information that was neither supported nor contradicted by the Qur'an and Islamic principles, it could be referenced, but should not be considered a normative source.

Although this might seem to have been a balanced way to use biblical material to supplement the Qur'anic narratives of the prophets, in fact their use was problematic on a number of levels. In the first place, not only biblical material but also extra-scriptural narratives were frequently cited. These stories most likely originated in Christian and Jewish oral traditions and *midrashim*, and the connection of these traditions to revealed knowledge is tenuous at best. Most of these stories have little probability of originating in revelation and, in many cases, clearly conflict with general Qur'anic principles, if not specific narratives.

For example, in his *tafsir*, Tabari relates a story from "some people from the Companions of the Prophet" (an exceedingly vague reference that probably means no more than that it is an "old" story) that when Adam was first created, he wandered alone and lonely around Paradise. Then, one day, he awoke to find a woman standing by his head. He said, "Who are you?" The woman replied, "Your wife."

This story, which could have originated in the Bible, in the oral tradition of the People of the Book, or even in ancient Arabian narratives, seems relatively harmless. However, what follows in Tabari's *tafsir* is a series of narratives that put the blame for sin on Adam's wife, and link the physical suffering of menstruation and childbirth to what is recharacterized as Eve's sin. This clearly contradicts the Qur'anic narrative, which shows that Adam and his wife both sinned, and both were forgiven by God for their transgressions.

Indeed, the Isra'iliyyat that most undermine Qur'anic values are those related to women. Barbara Stowasser notes that these misogynistic stories "were accepted and propagated by the consensus (*ijma'*) of the learned doctors of law and theology until eighteenth-century premodern reformists began to question their authoritative status. Since the nineteenth century, Islamic modernists have denied the authenticity and doctrinal validity of what they viewed as medieval extraneous interpretative 'lore,' while re-emphasizing the Qur'anic notion of the female's full personhood and moral responsibility."[17]

The movement to delegitimize Isra'iliyyat as a source for *tafsir* has not been accepted by all Muslims. This is not necessarily because these Muslims want to retain the misogynistic narratives found in *tafsirs*, but because they find other value in many of the stories of the prophets. Among other things, these stories support and complement popular traditions that identify sacred sites linked to prophets in Jordan, Syria, Palestine, and elsewhere in the Middle East. Perhaps we could see the attachment to Isra'iliyyat as an attempt by these Muslims to retain a broader sense of sacred space and revelation than those who have a more exclusivist approach to Islamic identity. At the same time, the challenge remains for those who wish to assign some authority to these narratives to establish a coherent methodology for weeding out those stories that conflict with Qur'anic principles and values. As we shall see in the following section, the Isra'iliyyat are not the only texts external to the Qur'an whose value and authority are contested. A more critical and important source is the corpus of prophetic hadith.

Providing Context: The Sunna, Hadith, and Occasions of Revelation

Before there was such a thing as a Sunni or a Shi'ite (these sectarian or communal affiliations would take a few centuries to develop), it is evident that many, if not most, Muslims believed that they would have the greatest chance of understanding the true import of the Qur'an if they could determine how the Prophet Muhammad, who was divinely guided, understood and implemented the revelation. For the first generation of Muslims, the Prophet Muhammad was not only the transmitter but also the interpreter of the Qur'an. The Qur'an repeatedly orders the believers to follow and obey the Prophet:

> Say: if you love God then follow me and God will love you and forgive your sins; indeed God is All-Forgiving; Compassionate.
> Say: Obey God and the Messenger. If they turn away, then God does not love those who disbelieve.
>
> (Al 'Imran; 3:31–32)

For the Companions, the Prophet's actions and teachings exemplified and explained the Qur'an. The Prophet's wife 'A'isha is reported to have said that the Prophet's "character was the Qur'an."[18] Islam as we know it would not exist without the detailed information the Sunna provides to implement general Qur'anic commands. For example, the Qur'an repeatedly commands believers to "establish prayer," but gives little detail on how this is to be done. As Imam al-Shafi'i (d. 204/820), one of the most influential early jurists, explained:

> The Prophet specified that daily prayers shall number five, that the number of cycles in the noon, afternoon and evening prayers shall number four repeated twice in the towns and that the cycles at the sunset prayer are three and the dawn prayer two. He decreed that in all the prayers there should be recitation from the Qur'an, audible in the sunset, evening and dawn prayers, and silent in the noon and afternoon prayers. He specified that at the beginning of each prayer, the *takbir* should be said and at the end, the *taslim*, and that each prayer consists of *takbir*, recitation, bowing and two prostrations after each inclination but beyond that, nothing is obligatory [only recommended]. He decreed that the prayer made on a journey can be shorter, if the traveler so desires, in the three prayers that have four cycles, but he made no change in the sunset and dawn prayers.... [19]

As al-Shafi'i notes, it is only through the instruction of the Prophet that Muslims can perform the basic rituals of prayer, fasting, and pilgrimage that the Qur'an requires of them.

The most frequently performed rituals and commonly occurring public actions of the Prophet were witnessed by many people; for this reason, there are not significant differences among Muslims about how to perform these actions. Some practices, however, were done less frequently or were not always performed by the Prophet in the same way. For example, it seems that sometimes the Prophet prayed with his arms at his sides, while at other times he prayed with his arms folded across his chest. Those who prayed with the Prophet at various times imitated the gestures they saw him making, and continued to do so after they left his presence. Individual Companions transmitted these variants of ritual practices to the next generation of believers in different lands, giving rise to regional variations in practices.

The Companions closest to the Prophet Muhammad played an important role in providing information about the context of these practices to their peers who had enjoyed less interaction with the Prophet, and to later generations of Muslims. Among the Companions most important in this respect are the Prophet's wives, especially 'A'isha and Umm Salama, the Prophet's cousins, 'Abdullah ibn al-'Abbas and

'Ali ibn Abi Talib, 'Abdullah ibn 'Umar (the son of 'Umar ibn al-Khattab), and two Companions who had lived much of the time in the Prophet's mosque of Medina, 'Abdullah ibn Mas'ud and Abu Hurayra.

These and other Companions transmitted the Prophet's understanding and implementation of the Qur'an in two ways: by explicit report, i.e., hadith, and implicitly, by offering an explanation they knew to be in keeping with the Prophet's understanding, or by embodying the Prophet's practices. Clearly, the explicit reports leave less room for doubt or ambiguity. However, the Companions often offered opinions without explicitly attaching them to the Prophet. Many later scholars decided that as long as a Companion was known to have been upright and close enough to the Prophet to know his opinions, we should assume they were conveying at least the spirit of the Prophet's message. Exegesis "by tradition" (tafsir bi'l-athar) therefore normally included statements of the major Companions as well as statements by the Prophet.

Some situations mentioned in the Qur'an occurred infrequently enough that even prominent Companions were unclear about their meaning. For example, in connection with the pilgrimage to Mecca, the Qur'an states:

> Verily Safa and Marwa are among the sacred rites of God. So whoever makes the major or minor pilgrimage (Hajj or 'Umra) to the House will bear no sin if he circles between them. Anyone who performs an act of goodly piety – indeed God will show them thanks.
> (Baqara; 2:158)

Because the Muslims were barred by the Quraysh from performing the pilgrimage until a few years before the Prophet's death, not everyone had the opportunity to witness his performance of the rites and rituals involved. Some of these individuals understood the Qur'an to be saying that the sa'i, the "running" between hills of Safa and Marwa (in imitation of Hajar's righteous exertion), was not a required ritual of the Hajj. Indeed, the wording of the verse seems to imply that the ritual is an acceptable, but not obligatory, action. However, this apparent meaning of the verse was deemed incorrect by the Prophet's wife 'A'isha, who provided context for the revelation. 'A'isha said that the verse had been revealed in connection with some Companions who felt that the ritual was a sinful practice because it had been done during the pre-Islamic period.[20] The Qur'anic revelation, there-fore, removed any stigma associated with the *sa'i*, while the Sunna further indicated that the *sa'i* was the practice of the Prophet.

Here, the "occasion of revelation" (*asbab al-nuzul*) of the verse gives a different kind of context than the Sunna. Whereas the Sunna shows the way the Prophet put general principles and specific commands of the Qur'an into practice, the occasions of revelation give context for Qur'anic statements for which there may or may not be correlating information from the Sunna. Without the background of the occasions of revelation, the normative value of many Qur'anic statements could be misunderstood if the verses are read in a literal fashion.

In another example, there is a report that some early Muslims understood the following verse to permit believers to consume alcohol:

> *No harm falls upon those who believe and do good works for what they have consumed as long as they are conscious of God and believe and do good works and then are conscious of God and believe and then are conscious of God and do good. Verily, God loves those who do good.*
>
> (Ma'ida; 5:93)

The claim that this verse permits a sincere believer to consume any-thing he wishes was contested by one of the Companions, who said, "If they had known the occasion of revelation they would not have said that; (the occasion) is that when wine was forbidden [by Qur'an 5:90], people used to say, 'What about those who were killed in the path of God [before this prohibition] and died after they had been drinking wine which is an abomination?' Then this verse was revealed."[21] The point of this verse, then, is not that the sacred law is waived for those who have faith and do good works, but that those who are ignorant of the law will not be punished for lack of compliance with it. What this story shows is that a decontextualized reading of the Qur'an can lead to a grave misunderstanding of its meaning.

Using the Sunna to contextualize the Qur'an, however, is not a simple exercise. One of the greatest challenges is to weigh the epist-emological value of all hadith that purport to provide that Sunnatic context. Although the majority of scholars have agreed with al-Shafi'i that the Prophet's Sunna is essential to understanding the Qur'an, they have differed on the extent to which they have considered various types of hadith to be reliable records of the Sunna. Some hadith were narrated by many people from the earliest generations; such "wide-spread" (*mutawatir*) hadith are certainly reliable, but they are rare. Some hadith were narrated by only one person in a generation. These "solitary" (*ahad*) hadith are generally accepted by scholars like al-Shafi'i and Ahmed ibn Hanbal, if all the narrators are trustworthy and reliable, but other scholars cast a more skeptical eye towards using these narrations to bind the Qur'an in any way. How could one justify limiting or specifying the meaning of a Qur'anic verse, which is certainly from God, with a hadith narrated by a single, fallible narrator? Even those who accepted such hadith had to weigh their value against other legal principles to ensure that they could be reconciled with all the relevant proofs.

Since the early modern period, many Muslim reformers have taken a strong stance against using hadith to restrict or interpret the Qur'an.[22] Intellectuals from Sayyid Ahmed Khan in nineteenth-century India to Khaled Abou El Fadl in late twentieth-century America have expressed outrage at the use of weak and spurious hadith by Muslim preachers to undercut what they consider to be fundamental Qur'anic values, like an openness to learning and the dignity of women. Even some hadith accepted by classical scholars as "authentic" convey negative messages, these reformers have argued. While it is true that the early hadith scholars were sincere and vigorous in their attempts to separate false reports from those that were accurate, they were not infallible. According to these reformers, Muslims have to use their God-given reason, as well as their knowledge of Qur'anic values, to reexamine the corpus of hadith.

Whether we are talking about prophetic hadith, traditions and interpretations of the Companions or Isra'iliyyat, the question of how much external context can be brought into Qur'anic exegesis is of vital importance. Given that there is so much controversy on this subject, one might be tempted to suggest that all external sources should be excluded when interpreting the Qur'an. After all, no other document or narrative matches the epistemological certainty of the Qur'an.

Indeed, almost every scholar will say that the best *tafsir* of the Qur'an is the Qur'an itself. However, as we have discussed earlier when we looked at the importance of dialect and grammar in understanding the meaning of the Qur'an, language, even sacred language, is not transparent, but must be understood. We cannot help but rely on external sources – such as grammatical texts, dictionaries, and poetry – to understand the very meaning of the words of the Qur'an. Further, as we shall see now, even if we took only the verses of the Qur'an as a source of Islamic norms, we would still be left with the difficulty of trying to reconcile apparently conflicting commands and prohibitions.

Deriving Norms from the Qur'an

To get a better understanding of the challenges involved in deriving norms from the Qur'an alone, we can examine some of the considerations that must be brought in when analyzing verses that have legal content. *Fiqh* (literally, "understanding") is the art and science of making these kinds of legal and ethical judgments. As we continue to discuss Qur'anic exegesis in this chapter, we will give more attention to such issues than to those topics that are mostly theological in nature. This focus does not necessarily reflect the amount of attention *tafsirs* give to legal and ethical issues, but rather, the greater interest such issues attract on the part of contemporary interlocutors with the Qur'an.

The following passage, which lists eight categories of alms recipients, is illustrative of the challenges involved in relying on the Qur'an alone as a source of Islamic norms. Here, scholars must determine which terms are being used in a technical or restricted fashion:

> *Alms are only for the poor, and the needy, and those who work with alms, and those whose hearts are to be joined in affection, and for the captive, and the debtor, and in the path of God, and the wayfarer. This is a command from God; and God is All-Knowing and Wise.*
>
> (Tawba; 9:60)

A number of questions are raised by this passage. For example, there are two separate words, *fuqara'* and *masakin*, that generally mean "the poor" or "the needy" – what is the difference between the two terms? Who are "those whose hearts are to be joined in affection"? What is the definition of a "wayfarer"? What about the debtor – is any debtor eligible for alms? What if he had fallen into debt doing something unlawful, like gambling – can he still receive alms?

Many of these issues are analyzed in *tafsirs* that focus on the laws derived from the Qur'an, like al-Qurtubi's *Ahkam al-Qur'an* (although more details, including how to apply these principles administratively, are found in legal texts).[23] Here we learn that the distinction between "poor" and "needy" is that one of the two terms (and scholars differ on which one) signifies what might be called the "structurally poor," that is, people who were born into a poor family, while the other signifies the "fallen poor," that is, people who have become poor due to an unforeseen tragedy, like the death or disability of the family bread-winner. "Those whose hearts are to be joined in affection" referred originally to the Quraysh and other tribal leaders who needed some kind of gift when they made allegiance to the Prophet to show that they had not lost status by joining the Muslim community. When he became caliph, 'Umar ibn al-Khattab declared this category void, arguing that the Muslim community was now powerful enough that it did not need to offer such incentives. Some later scholars argued that this category could be applied to those who wanted to embrace Islam, but needed financial support to join the Muslim community, perhaps because their families would cut off their sources of support if they converted. As for the debtor, scholars discussed the relevance of repentance to his eligibility for alms, many arguing that it would be unreasonable to continue to pay the debts of an unrepentant gambler, but that someone sincerely trying to make a new start should be given assistance.

In addition to finding ambiguity in single passages of the Qur'an, jurists were also faced with apparent conflicts between verses. These conflicts were often resolved by limiting the application of one of the texts. For example, some texts were deemed to be general, while others applicable only to a specific group of people; some texts were deemed unrestricted, while others restricted to a certain situation.

In his *Principles of Islamic Jurisprudence*, Mohammad Hashim Kamali provides many examples of the ways in which jurists reconciled various proofs from the Qur'an and Sunna. For example, scholars analyzed two related Qur'anic verses on the subject of witnessing in the following manner:

> One of these (verses), which requires the testimony of two witnesses in all commercial transactions, is conveyed in absolute terms, whereas the second is qualified. The first of the two texts does not qualify the word "men" when it states "and bring two witnesses from among your men" (Baqara; 2:282). But the second text on the same subject, that is, of witnesses, conveys a qualified command when it states "and bring two just witnesses [when you revoke a divorce]" (Talaq; 65:2). The ruling in both of these texts is the same, namely the requirement of two witnesses, but the two rulings differ in

respect of their causes. The cause of the first text, as already noted, is commercial transactions which must accordingly be testified to by two men; whereas the cause of the second ruling is the revocation of (a pronouncement of divorce). In the first verse [the] "witnesses" are not qualified, but they are qualified in the second verse. The latter prevails over the former. Consequently, witnesses in both commercial transactions and the revocation of a pronouncement of divorce must be upright and just.[24]

Another way Sunni scholars reconciled apparent conflicts between verses was through the principle of "abrogation" (*naskh*). Scholars argued that some verses of the Qur'an had been "abrogated" by later verses, basing their argument on the verse:

> *We do not abrogate nor cause to be forgotten any verse (aya) but that we bring something better or similar to it. Do you not know that God is over all things All-Powerful.*
>
> (Baqara; 2:106)

The need for abrogation (*naskh*) was explained by the fact that different norms were needed for the different circumstances Muslims faced over the twenty-three-year period of revelation. For example, Qur'an 2:142–144 orders the facing of the Ka'ba in prayer, abrogating an earlier practice to pray in the direction of Jerusalem. Scholars suggest that the initial practice of facing Jerusalem was necessary as long as the Muslims were surrounded by the polytheistic rituals performed at the Ka'ba; facing Jerusalem, in that context, was a sign of their faithfulness to the monotheism of Abraham. However, once the Muslims established themselves in Medina, where they were removed from the polytheistic Meccan culture, they were ordered to turn once again towards the Ka'ba, with the expectation that it would soon be purified of its idols. From this time forward, the Ka'ba would be the *qibla* of the Muslims.

The principle of abrogation has always had critics, on both theoretical and ethical grounds. They argue that the "verses" Qur'an 2:106 mentions as abrogated are verses from previous scriptures (like the Torah), not Qur'anic verses. Indeed, if we turn to the textual context in which abrogation is mentioned, we see that it occurs within a passage referring to the beliefs of the People of the Book. Further, some scholars have argued that there is no consistent standard for abrogation and that every case of abrogation can be explained by other means. For example, in the case we discussed above – the change in the *qibla* from Jerusalem to Mecca – the Qur'an abrogated a Prophetic practice, not a Qur'anic injunction; there was no previous revelation ordering the Muslims to pray towards Jerusalem.

Even those who accepted the principle of abrogation disagreed about the number of verses affected, ranging from five to one hundred and twenty. The latter, exceedingly high number was initially claimed by some scholars living under the rule of the 'Abbasids, who donned the mantle of religion in a particularly aggressive way to promote their military and political policies. These scholars argued that all previous Qur'anic rulings urging kindness, friendship, and reconciliation among Muslims and non-Muslims were abrogated by the following words:

> . . . *and fight the polytheists all together as they fight you all together, and know that God is with those who are conscious of God.*
> (Tawba; 9:36)

According to this understanding, the final position of the Qur'an is that the Islamic state should exercise perpetual military dominance over all non-Muslims. Later scholars found this argument cynical and preposterous and argued that earlier scholars who propounded this view had let their religious authority be appropriated by state interests. These scholars argue that the verse in question addresses the specific historical situation of the Prophet, when the Quraysh were trying to destroy the Muslim community of Medina. The "polytheists" here are not all non-Muslims, but only the Quraysh who had joined to attack the Muslims. Once again, the importance of understanding the historical context of the revelation and the extent to which that context is relevant to deriving norms becomes apparent.

Turning to another topic, it is clear that a basic challenge for Muslims throughout history has been to find ways to keep the Qur'an relevant to constantly changing conditions. To this end, scholars have found ways to extend particular rulings to new situations and to derive general principles and values from the Qur'an as a whole.

One tool used by most legal schools to derive norms from the Qur'an is analogical reasoning (*qiyas*).[25] This allows the rules of the Qur'an to be continually adapted to new circumstances. When confronted with a new case not addressed in the Qur'an or Sunna, the jurist looks for a similar case in those sources. If he is able to find a case that shares a relevant attribute, then the ruling from the original case can be transferred to the new case.[26] For example, the Qur'an prohibits grape-wine (*khamr*). Although there are some hadith that discuss the prohibition of intoxicants generally, some scholars might consider those hadith to be less than certain. These scholars can turn instead to analogical reasoning and argue that any substance – like alcohol spirits – that can cause intoxication as does grape-wine is similarly prohibited.

Specific rulings in the Qur'an can also yield general legal principles which can then be applied to other situations. For example, Islamic law knows of a distinction between a personal obligation (*fard 'ayn*) and a communal obligation (*fard kifaya*). Al-Shafi'i cites the Qur'anic verse which yields this rule:

> It is not right that all the believers deploy together. If a group from each contingent does not deploy, they can devote themselves to understanding their religion in order to exhort their armies when they return so they might take heed.
>
> (Tawba; 9:122)

Al-Shafi'i explains the implication of the verse for Islamic jurisprudence:

> (God) made it known that going into battle was obligatory on some, not on all, [just] as knowledge of the law is not obligatory on all but on some, except for the fundamental duties which should be known to all people. But God knows best.... In a like manner are other duties, the fulfillment of which is intended to be collective; whenever they are performed by some Muslims collectively, those who do not perform them will not fall into error. (But) if all men failed to perform the duty so that no able-bodied man went forth to battle, all of them, I am afraid, would fall into error.... So far as I have been informed, the Muslims have continued to act as I have stated, from the time of the Prophet to the present. Only a few men must know the law, attend the funeral service, perform the jihad and respond to greeting, while others are exempt. So those who know the law, (perform the jihad), attend the funeral service, and respond to a greeting will be rewarded, while others do not fall into sin since a sufficient number fulfill the [collective] duty.[27]

Since the distinction between individual and collective duty is derived from a Qur'anic verse, this principle can then be used in the application of other obligations specified in the Qur'an.[28]

As we can see, Qur'anic rulings and principles have been extended by scholars to ensure that the revelation remains relevant to new situations and circumstances. Scholars have also recognized that while it is important to analyze individual verses for their vocabulary, syntax, grammar, rhetorical style, and cultural and historical references, the Qur'an will be left in disjointed pieces if one does not have a broader framework that goes beyond these particularities. To this end, scholars have invoked general principles and universal values found in the Qur'an to connect, reconcile, and balance divergent rulings obtained through deductive reasoning from particular Qur'anic texts. In the early centuries of Islam, legal scholars referred to concepts such as *istihsan* (setting aside a particular ruling if it will have a negative impact), *istislah* (choosing a ruling that benefits people), and *ma'ruf* (what is "fair" or "reasonable") to empower them to set aside a judgment arrived at through narrow legal reasoning for the sake of another judgment that is more in keeping with the overall spirit and values of the Qur'an.

A more comprehensive and holistic framework for assessing legal rulings was fully developed by the middle period of Islamic history. Imam al-Ghazali, once again, emerges as an influential figure in Sunni Islam with his convincing and emphatic demonstration that all rulings found in the Qur'an and Sunna aim to promote a limited number of universal goals. Other scholars, including, most famously, Abu Ishaq al-Shatibi (d. 790/1388), joined al-Ghazali in arguing that the primary purpose of Islam was to promote and preserve five or six fundamental values: religion, life, property, intellect, family, and honor.[29] Theoretically, any exegesis or ruling that contravenes these "goals of the Shari'a" (*maqasid al-Shari'a*) must be set aside.

Reference to the goals of the Shari'a have become more frequent since the advent of modernity, when Muslim scholars have been trying to find a consistent and holistic approach to legal reasoning that can replace, to some extent, the narrower, technical, and case-by-case deductive approach of much traditional legal reasoning. According to many contemporary scholars such as Mohammad Hashim Kamali, this approach is more consistent with the message of the Qur'an:

> A cursory perusal of the Qur'an would be enough to show that the Qur'an pays much greater attention to values and objectives such as justice and benefit, mercy and compassion, upright character and *taqwa*, promotion of good and prevention of evil, affection and love within the family, charity,

camaraderie and other redeeming values. The Qur'an may thus be said to be goal-oriented and focused on the structure of values that have a direct bearing on human welfare. The Qur'an is for the most part concerned with the broad principles and objectives of morality and law, rather than with specific detail and technical formulas that occupy the bulk of the *usul* [juridical] works.[30]

While emphasizing the importance of the goals of the Shari'a, Kamali also stresses that they in themselves are not a methodology, but rather "serve the purpose of opening up the avenues of *ijtihad*." After all, to determine whether a ruling furthers or hinders a goal of the Shari'a, scholars must assess the "benefit" (*maslaha*) of the ruling. This assessment is, to a large extent, an empirical determination. Who is qualified to make such an assessment? Is it only scholars of the Qur'an and other religious scholars? In any case, this new legal thinking will only be productive if it occurs within an interpretive framework that is consistent, and within a context that can be accepted as legitimate and authoritative. At this point, it is therefore necessary to consider the way in which authority has been constructed in an Islamic exegetical and legal context and what challenges entail for arriving at authoritative rulings in a modern context.

Constructing Authority

Given the numerous factors that had to be taken into consideration when deriving norms from the Qur'an, it is not surprising that jurist-scholars (*mujtahids*) often arrive at different conclusions. Sunni scholars generally have accepted this outcome as acceptable, citing the reported statement of the Prophet, "Every *mujtahid* (lit., one who 'exerts himself') hits his mark; if he is correct, he gets two rewards, if he is incorrect, he gets one reward." This hadith indicates that the goal of the jurist is to obey and be rewarded by God by exerting himself to the utmost (by exercising *ijtihad*) to find the correct ruling. In God's assessment, there is an objectively "correct" ruling, and the jurist is motivated to find that ruling with the knowledge that his reward is greater if he discovers it. On the other hand, if the jurist tries his best but makes a mistake, he will still be rewarded for the effort. Thus, jurists do not refrain from making judgments out of fear of punishment if they are mistaken. In sum, the hadith inspires jurists with the motivation to study and examine cases on a deeper level, the confidence to go forward with a well-reasoned judgment, and the humility to recognize that there is a possibility they could have made a mistake. This attitude was summed up in the juristic aphorism, "Our school is correct, but may be wrong; the school of those who disagree with us is wrong, but it may be right." Finally, it was the practice of Sunni scholars to conclude their legal judgments with the words, "But God knows better (*wa Allahu 'alam*)." What this means is that the scholar should be confident in his judgments, but not so arrogant as to preclude the possibility that he had made an error. The word *shari'a*, which is used by scholars to indicate divine law, literally means, "the path to the water," and therefore signifies not so much an outcome as a methodology and the intention to seek the "sacred waters" of guidance.

Despite their internal differences, Sunni scholars shared a general methodology and core body of judgments that generally distinguished them as an interpretive community from the Shi'ites, Mu'tazilites, and others. Where there was this broad scope of agreement, Sunni scholars claimed "consensus" (*ijma'*) and considered departures from this consensus to place one outside the bounds of "The People of the Sunna and the Community." (We should note that Shi'ite scholars developed a type of consensus that was authoritative for their community as well, so much of what I have to say below applies to some extent to Shi'ites).

Although it played an important role in providing some sense of cohesion within the Sunni community, the number of opinions for which a broad consensus could be claimed was always relatively small. There was most agreement upon basic theological issues, and less agreement on juridical issues because of the many different levels of context and interpretive tools used to understand the meanings of, and extract rulings from, the Qur'an. In addition, Sunni scholars differed among themselves about the conditions they set for establishing consensus. The Hanbalis accepted the authority of the consensus of the Companions only, with Ahmed ibn Hanbal arguing that any other claim of consensus was impossible to verify. For their part, the Maliki school accepted only the consensus of the scholars of the early community of Medina as authoritative. Because the number of cases for which a true consensus could be claimed were limited, scholars instead often projected their opinions as authoritative if they were supported by "the majority" (al-jumhur). Here, as with consensus, the only opinions that mattered were those of qualified scholars.

The authority of scholars in classical Islam was supported, displayed, and transmitted through institutions of religious learning – the seminary (madrasa), the "cathedral mosques," the ijaza system, etc. These institutions provided not only a locus from which religious authority could be projected, but also a substantial framework within which the great diversity of Sunni thought could be expressed and organized. To this extent, I suggest that "tradition" was a stabilizing element in premodern Muslim societies to the extent that it was manifest in actual institutions and practices rather than just a body of ideas transmitted over the centuries. This does not mean that premodern Muslim societies were always peaceful and stable. Scholars regularly came into conflict with one another and with political authorities. At the same time, as a group, the scholars exercised a certain authority within designated institutions; thus, their corporate identity superseded any internal dissent, and ensured that there was a place for "scholars" in every Muslim society.

However, when these institutions were disrupted, destroyed, and disconnected, first under colonialism and then when they were placed under the bureaucratic order of separate modern nation-states, Sunnism underwent a radical transformation and experienced a significant blow to its sense of a unified community. This is one of the reasons why scholars from the early modern period until today have tried to find an institutional mechanism to revive a form of consensus that could be relevant to society. The late twelfth-/eighteenth-century Indian reformer Shah Wali Allah Dihlawi, for example, argued that consensus was never intended to be universal, but was authoritative in a town or locality when it was comprised of "the ulema and men of authority."[31] Later, Muhammad Iqbal (d. 1938 CE) suggested that consensus could be institutionalized by forming a legislative assembly from representatives of the different schools of law. In the mid-twentieth century, the shaykh of al-Azhar, Mahmud Shaltut, pointed out that such a body would be authoritative only if all constituents were granted freedom of opinion and were protected from the arbitrary exercise of political power. Here, the efficacy of consensus is wedded to the process of ijtihad – the continual exertion of the intellect to search for new information or previously unexamined factors that could contribute to different judgments or perspectives.

Figure 5.2   American Hamza Yusuf, who studied the classical tradition of Islamic law, teaches in the Kairaouine Mosque and University in Morocco. Founded in the third/ninth century, it is the oldest continuously operating institute of higher learning in the world. (Peter Sanders)

Modernity: Making the Words "Reasonable"

In this chapter, we have merely provided an overview of developments in Qur'anic exegesis. The reality is that there have always been multiple, parallel traditions of interpretation and intellectual thought in Muslim societies, and that diversity continues until today. Similarly, when we speak about "Muslim societies," we are grouping together communities, nations, and empires that are highly diverse in their political, historical, and cultural identities. Because of this diversity, Muslims encountered modernity in a myriad of ways and over a period stretching from the late eighteenth century until, in some remote lands, the late twentieth century. As we further consider the Muslim encounter with modernity, we can therefore highlight only a few of the important themes, tensions, and developments that characterized this encounter.

In our discussion of Islamic legal reasoning, we have already seen that as Muslim societies approached modernity, a number of tendencies present in classical thought became increasingly important. These include: a reduction of the importance or complete rejection of the notion of abrogation; a wider contextualization of the Qur'anic revelation; an increasing reliance on general principles over particular rulings; a cautious attitude towards the use of Isra'iliyyat; greater attention to the role of prophetic hadith used to limit or restrict the meaning of the Qur'an; and a redefinition of the meaning of "consensus" both to allow greater societal participation in the process of consensus building and to allow each generation to reconsider (through *ijtihad*) the decisions made by scholars of the past.

The concern with stimulating the process of *ijtihad* is closely linked with the desire for reform. Reform and renewal have been predominant themes of modernity, although we must stress that the desire for societal reform did not originate in the modern era. As John Voll has shown, premodern developments set the stage for the success of later reformist movements. Voll points out, for example, that Sufi brotherhoods since the twelfth century "provided the organizational framework for a variety of social movements." By the late sixteenth century – the time of the "great Sultanate empires" of the Ottomans, the Safavids, and the Moghuls – the structures of Sufi brotherhood "provided the potential for mobilizing large numbers of people," and brotherhoods "were at times the basis for movements of revolt."[32]

Figure 5.3   "The Qur'an is our constitution" was the slogan of some Iraqis who participated in the Constitutional referendum of 2005. (Ghaith Abdul-Ahad/Getty Images)

Later, Sufism, especially where it exhibited tendencies towards syncretism in religion and worldly disengagement, itself became a target for reform and renewal. The Salafiyya movement, taking its leadership from Jamal al-Din al-Afghani (d. 1897 CE), Mohammed Abduh (d. 1905 CE), and Rashid Rida (d. 1935 CE), has been particularly critical of these tendencies in Sufism. The Salafiyya were also critical of much of the religious and political establishment in general for having "adapted" to customs they considered contrary to Islamic law and ethics. All of this occurred, says Voll, before there was any significant impact upon the Muslim world by the West:

> Although there was already some impact from the modernizing West, that was not the primary or most visible challenge that aroused the reforming spirit. Just before the time of European dominance, a reformist-revivalist tradition had been established in the mold of the fundamentalist style of Islamic experience, and that tradition created an underlying theme for the modern Islamic experience.[33]

By "fundamentalist," Voll means a tendency to reject many aspects of the Islamic tradition that had developed over the centuries, and "return to Islam" as it had been practiced by the Prophet and his community. For these reformers, Muslim societies were weak because, over the centuries, they had taken a deviant path; thus, the solution was to return to the pure Islam of the Prophet's time. Muslims had to abandon, in Voll's words, all "accommodation" of norms, customs, and paradigms that originated from any other place.

One of the most powerful spokesmen of this tendency was the Egyptian writer Sayyid Qutb (d. 1966 CE), who was executed by the authoritarian ruler Nasser (in whose jails Qutb and many others were tortured – no doubt contributing to his radicalization). In his infamous book *Milestones* (*Ma'alim fi'l-tariq*), Qutb lists "idolatrous societies" in places like India, Japan, and the Philippines which, like pre-Islamic Arabian society, are *jahili*. He also lists many reasons why all "Jewish and Christian societies" are *jahili*, including because they give "their priests and rabbis . . . authority to make laws." Then Qutb goes on to say:

> All the existing so-called "Muslim" societies are also *jahili* societies. We classify them among *jahili* societies not because they believe in other deities besides God or because they

worship anyone other than God, but because their way of life is
not based on submission to God alone. Although they believe
in the Unity of God, still they have relegated the legislative
attribute of God to others and submit to this authority, and
from this authority they derive their systems, their traditions
and customs, their laws, their values and standards, and
almost every practice of life.[34]

It is not surprising that the radical successors to Qutb are sometimes
characterized as "neo-Khawarij" by Muslims who experience their intolerance, violence, and, perhaps most relevant to our focus on the Qur'an,
the radicals' literalistic and decontextualized readings of the Qur'an.

It is important to recognize, however, that textual literalism is not
necessarily connected with intolerance, political radicalism or violence. On the positive side, the insistence of the Salafiyya on comparing
societal practices with the practices of the early Muslim community
allowed for the abandonment of some unjust customs, like the exclu-
sion of women from the mosque. On the other hand, this approach can
degenerate into a simplistic and literalist reading of the Qur'an and
the Sunna. In particular, fundamentalist readings often diminish the
relevance of historical context for understanding the true meaning
of the Qur'an and the Prophet's Sunna. Such readings also give little
attention to the need to reconcile particular rulings with general
principles and values articulated in the Qur'an and the Sunna. Finally,
literalistic readings can efface the role of the human interpreter.
Decrying "man-made" institutions, literalists seem unaware of their
own roles as human interpreters when they select particular passages
to justify their positions.

At the same time, we must also recognize that many Muslims who
practice what might be called a "liberal" reading of the Qur'an can be
as intolerant of other opinions as their ideological opponents. Intolerance is rooted in the belief that one's own reading is obviously correct,
whether that reading is based on a literalistic approach to the text or
on a conviction that (one's own) reason is such a perfect instrument
for assessing truth, justice, and fairness that interpretations in conflict
with that assessment are dismissed out of hand. This attitude is not
just intolerant, but, in contemporary scholar Khaled Abou El Fadl's
words, "authoritarian." He says, "Authoritarianism is the act of 'lock-
ing' or captivating the Will of the Divine, or the will of the text, into
a specific determination, and then presenting this determination

as inevitable, final, and conclusive."[35] In our final chapter, we will further address this question of the proper approach to Qur'anic interpretation.

Not all of the heirs of the nineteenth-century Salafiyya movement went in the direction of scriptural literalism and a simplistic call to the past. Many modernists were focused primarily on the need for Muslim societies to progress materially through greater literacy and the acquisition of scientific knowledge. All groups, however, were deeply concerned with European imperialism.

From the beginning of the nineteenth century until the middle of the twentieth century, many Muslims experienced violent incursions and colonial occupation by European forces of their lands. The impact on the political, social, economic, and cultural sectors of these societies was profound. As we have previously mentioned, religious institutions were radically restructured, and, in many places, completely destroyed. Western domination of Muslim lands did not cease with the end of colonialism, and the concern for Muslim independence from foreign interference remains strong in many areas. Indeed, one could see the desire for self-determination, and the power to achieve it, as one of the highest priorities of many Muslim thinkers since the nineteenth century.

From the beginning of the colonial period, the technological superiority of the European invaders was an immediate and readily apparent threat. For this reason, many Muslim reformers wanted to understand how the Europeans could have so completely surpassed Muslims in technical knowledge, when Muslims had been at the forefront of scientific thinking centuries earlier. Many reformers blamed poorly educated and "superstitious" religious leaders for the ignorance of the Muslim masses. The desire to encourage "rational" thinking in Muslims led some scholars to reinterpret Qur'anic statements they considered to be in conflict with scientific thinking. Abduh, for example, suggested that the jinn mentioned in the Qur'an could be understood as microbes.

In the twentieth century, a number of Muslim scientists and scholars moved from defending the harmony of the Qur'an with science to showing how many modern scientific discoveries are referenced or implicit in the Qur'an. In his book *The Bible, the Qur'an and Science*, for example, Maurice Bucaille argues that the divine origin of the Qur'an is proven by the scientifically accurate descriptions found within its pages.[36]

More generally, many Muslim reformers have argued that the Qur'an places a great deal of emphasis on the acquisition of knowledge. To withdraw from the world in spiritual contemplation and asceticism, they argue, is a violation of the message of the Qur'an. This sentiment is captured in the following words by M. Shamsher Ali, Chairman of "the Committee on Scientific Indications in the Holy Qur'an" in Dhaka, Bangladesh, who writes:

> The question which disturbs the minds of the young boys and girls of today is: why in spite of the strongest Qur'anic urges present from the beginning (*Iqra Bisme Rabbika al-lazi Khalaq* ["Read in the name or your Lord who created – "]) to the end of the Qur'anic verses, about two third [*sic*] of the Muslim Ummah remain illiterate, economically poor and backward in science and technology? This is indeed, a very vital question which needs to be addressed to in a very serious manner. The answer to this may be in the fact that although we recite the Holy Qur'an, many of us cannot comprehend its meaning because of lack of knowledge. Allah Himself has proclaimed that the Holy Qur'an is for "a people who think."[37]

It is certainly true that the Qur'an urges humanity to learn about the material world, as a way to learn about the power and majesty of the Creator. At the same time, it seems that some contemporary Muslims sometimes have a rather utilitarian approach to the Qur'an, using it to promote particular development policies or political agendas rather than primarily as a source of moral and spiritual guidance.

A pressing problem for many postcolonial Muslim states (like many postcolonial non-Muslim states in Africa and Asia) is their inability to develop stable, democratic governance systems. As a result, so-called "Islamic" parties and rulers have assumed authoritarian stances and have tried to justify their power by manipulating religious discourse and symbols. Opposition to government policies is characterized as "apostasy" or "heresy" and freedom of speech is stifled. Many political activists who assume power in these regimes have little understanding of the breadth and depth of classical Islamic scholarship, and resort to fundamentalist readings of the Qur'an.

On the other hand, a number of serious scholars in the twentieth century have developed new approaches to the Qur'an and pushed the limits of contextualization to a point that many Muslims consider unorthodox. In his teachings and controversial book *The Second Message of Islam*, Sudanese scholar Mahmoud Taha (d. 1985 CE), for example, not only rejected abrogation but also argued in direct opposition to that doctrine that earlier Qur'anic revelations superseded the later ones. In particular, Taha argued that it is the Meccan verses of the Qur'an that contain the universal message of Islam, while the Medinan revelations are culturally specific applications of the original message. According to Taha, this means that later generations of Muslims are not bound by detailed rules found in the Medinan revelations.

Mahmoud Taha was not just a theologian but a reformist leader often opposed to the state, who was tragically executed for sedition in a highly politicized and unfair trial. His controversial ideas have not gained a wide following, although they have become more well known due to the efforts of his student, and later respected legal scholar, Abdullahi an-Na'im. At the same time, Taha's contention that traditional Qur'anic exegesis and jurisprudence did not give enough consideration to the context of the Prophet's community and the universal values of the Qur'an has been shared by other modern scholars. A number of these scholars, including Fazlur Rahman (d. 1988 CE) of Pakistan and Nasr Abou-Zayd of Egypt, were forced to leave their home countries because of accusations that their ideas were heretical. Others, like Mohammed Arkoun, have developed and promoted their ideas primarily in European secular circles.

It is evident that the issue of free speech and freedom of opinion, when that speech or those opinions contradict notions of orthodoxy, is a particularly challenging one for many Muslim societies. Preservation of religion is the most important goal of the Shari'a, but what does that preservation mean? The Qur'an clearly states,

> *There is no compulsion in religion.*
>
> (Baqara; 2:256)

What does this statement mean? Does freedom of religion entail the freedom to reject religion, and even further, to question, insult, and belittle religion? Some contemporary scholars – certainly a minority at this time – believe it does. Most Muslims, however, understand the preservation of religion in the traditional sense to mean promoting Islam and promoting respect for the sacred in general. At the same time, they want to uphold the principle of freedom of speech. What is clear is that this will continue to be a topic of extensive and vigorous discussion among Muslims in contemporary society.

Leaving aside the issue of how notions of orthodoxy or heresy are constructed, the challenge remains for sincere Muslims to arrive at a consistent methodology that determines how much context is relevant to an interpretation and when it is proper to set aside specific rulings for general principles. One has to acknowledge the risk of overcontextualizing the Qur'an and relying too heavily on the general principles it expresses. This could lead to a complete relativizing of the content of the Qur'an, so that its explicit norms would apply only to the era of its revelation. Nevertheless, the line between relevant context and self-interested or careless relativization is not easy to discern. We will finish this chapter with an exploration of an issue that illustrates this dilemma.

In pre-Islamic Arabia, women did not have a right to inheritance. The fact that the Qur'an gave women a fixed share of their relatives' estate was therefore significant progress. At the same time, the Qur'an generally gives males twice the share of their female counterparts. For example, a son receives twice the share of his sister from their father's estate. This discrepancy is explained by some scholars as a mechanism to put more wealth into the hands of males who are legally required to provide maintenance (*nafaqa*) for their families. Not only is a man legally responsible for providing for his wife and children, but he also must provide for his mother, sister or other close female relative if any one of them is in need. In addition, a man is required to give a valuable gift (*mahr* or *sadaq*) to his wife upon marriage as a sign of his commitment to provide for her throughout their married life. In many Muslim societies, this is a significant gift of money, jewelry or property. The greater inheritance share of males, therefore, although not equal, is considered equitable because of their greater financial responsibility within the nuclear and extended family.

Some Muslims have questioned whether this system of wealth distribution within the family meets Qur'anic objectives in modern societies, which differ drastically from premodern societies in terms of their economic and social structures. Is it fair that men are solely responsible for supporting needy relatives and funding household expenses, when many women now earn a good income – sometimes even more than their husbands? At the same time, because there is no transnational authority that can compel the payment of maintenance from a man in one country to his female relatives in another, many women are not receiving the support to which they have a right – while their son or brother (who, in the age of globalization, has immigrated to a wealthier country to seek his fortune) might return to the home country to claim his greater share of the inheritance upon the death of their father. Some argue that because the objective of Qur'anic wealth distribution is to ensure equity among men and women, it makes more sense in contemporary societies to simply require the same financial obligations and give the same financial benefits to men and women.

Others argue that there is no clear evidence that equity is the only objective of maintenance and inheritance laws. This latter group suggests that the Qur'an also aims to support the role of the man as primary breadwinner to free women from this burden so they can act as primary caretakers of their children and other family members in need (the elderly, the ill, etc.). Requiring women to provide equal financial support to the family would lessen their ability to provide such care. To this end, the obligation of men to provide full support for women furthers a primary goal of the Shari'a, which is the pre-servation of the family. Thus, injustices created by new social and economic circumstances should be rectified by means other than bypassing the Qur'anic rules for wealth distribution. For example, liens can be placed on men's inheritance for maintenance past due.

As we can see, then, context and general principles can reasonably be brought to the Qur'anic text in significantly different ways. Once again, a key issue that remains is how to arrive at an authoritative opinion. Some believe that it is safest to rely on the consensus of past scholars, since they were pious people who were closer to the time of revelation. Others argue that humanity has increasing opportunities in each generation to expand their knowledge and understanding, and so we must be open to reconsidering all views, even those for which consensus was claimed in the past. In the final chapter, I will suggest some parameters which I believe are necessary, although perhaps not sufficient, guidelines for Muslims to follow. One of the most important considerations, I will argue, is that no approach can succeed if it is not rooted in self-awareness and spiritual development – individually, and collectively.

Notes

1   Tabari, *History*, vol. 10, translated by Fred M. Donner as *The Conquest of Arabia* (1993), 105–134.
2   Bukhari, "*Kitab al-Tafsir*," 969.
3   A detailed analysis of these reports is offered by E. L. Petersen in '*Ali and Mu'awiya in Early Arabic Tradition* (Copenhagen, 1964).
4   Tabari, *History*, vol. 17, translated by G. R. Hawting as *The First Civil War* (1996), 8.
5   Tabari, *History*, 17:103.
6   Tabari, *History*, 17:129–130.
7   Tabari, *History*, 17:219–222.
8   Abu'l-Qasim Jarallah Al-Zamakhshari, *Al-Kashshaf 'an haqa'iq al-tanzil wa 'uyun al-aqawil fi wujuh al-ta'wil*, 4 vols. (n.p: Dar al-'Alimiyya, n.d.).
9   Zamakhshari, 1:628; 4:46.
10   Abu Ja'far Muhammd ibn Jarir al-Tabari, *Jami' al-bayan fi tafsir al-Qur'an*, 30 vols. in 12 bks. (Cairo: Dar al-Hadith, 1987).
11   Fakhr al-Din Muhammad ibn 'Umar al-Razi, *Al-Tafsir al-Kabir*, 32 vols. (Beirut: Dar Ihya' al-Turath al-'Arabi, 1980).
12   Muqatil ibn Sulayman al-Balkhi, *Al-Ashbah wa'l-naza'ir fi'l-Qur'an al-Karim*, ed. 'Abdallah Mahmud Shihatah (Cairo: al-Hay'a al-Misriyya al-'Amma li'l-Kitab, 1975).
13   Abu 'Abdallah Muhammad ibn Ahmed al-Ansari al-Qurtubi, *Al-Jami' li ahkam al-Qur'an*, ed. 'Abd al-Razzaq al-Mahdi, 20 vols. in 10 bks. (Beirut: Dar al-Kitab al-'Arabi, 2001), 12:112–113.
14   Keith Massey, "Mysterious Letters," *EQ* 3:471–477.
15   Sabine Schmidtke, "Mu'tazila," *EQ* 3:466–471.
16   Most Sunni scholars denied that women could be prophets, basing their argument primarily on their understanding of Qur'an 12:109, 16:43, 21:7. The Zahiri scholar Ibn Hazm rejects this interpretation and argues convincingly that there were female prophets – and that Mary was among them. 'Ali ibn Ahmed ibn Hazm, *Al-Fasl fi'l-milal wa'l-ahwa' wa'l-nihal*, 5 vols. (Cairo: Muhammad 'Ali Subayh, 1964), 5:17–19.
17   Barbara Freyer Stowasser, *Women in the Qur'an: Traditions and Interpretation* (New York: Oxford University Press, 1994), 28.
18   Ahmed ibn Hanbal, *Musnad Ahmed* (Riyadh: International Ideas Home for Publishing and Distribution, 1998).
19   Muhammad ibn Idris al-Shafi'i, *Islamic Jurisprudence: Shafi'i's Risala*, translation by Majid Khadduri of *al-Risala* (Baltimore: Johns Hopkins University Press, 1961), 158–160.
20   Suyuti, 1:122.

21 Suyuti, 1:121.
22 See Brown's *Rethinking Tradition* (cited Chapter 2, note 6).
23 I discuss this topic with reference to some of the important early sources in my essay "Status-Based Definitions of Need in Early Islamic *Zakat* and Maintenance Laws," in *Concepts of Poverty and Charity in Middle Eastern Contexts*, eds. Michael Bonner, Mine Ener, and Amy Singer (Albany: State University of New York Press, 2003), 31–51.
24 Mohammad Hashim Kamali, *Principles of Islamic Jurisprudence* (Cambridge: Islamic Texts Society, 1991), 115. This passage has been corrected for typos and Arabic words have been translated to facilitate understanding.
25 The Zahiris were a notable exception.
26 For more details see Wael B. Hallaq, *A History of Islamic Legal Theories: An Introduction to Sunni Usul al-Fiqh* (Cambridge: Cambridge University Press, 1997), 83–107.
27 Shafi'i, 86–87.
28 And, perhaps, expanded to include those collective actions which Muslims are obliged to undertake with others, as I argue in my essay, "The Axis of Good: Muslims Building Alliances with Other Communities of Faith," published online at macdonald.hartsem.edu/articles.htm#mattson.
29 Two important studies of Imam al-Shatibi's thought are: Muhammad Khalid Masud, *Shatibi's Philosophy of Islamic Law* (Islamabad: International Islamic University, 1995) and Ahmed al-Raysuni, *Imam al-Shatibi's Theory of the Higher Objectives and Intents of Islamic Law* (Herndon, VA: International Institute of Islamic Thought, 2006).
30 Kamali, *Issues in the Legal Theory of Usul and Prospects for Reform* (Kuala Lumpur, Malaysia: International Islamic University, Malaysia), 2002.
31 Kamali, *Principles*, 90.
32 John Obert Voll, *Islam: Continuity and Change in the Modern World*, 2nd ed. (Syracuse: Syracuse University Press, 1994), 28.
33 Voll, 30.
34 Sayed Qutb, *Milestones* (Cedar Rapids, IO: Unity Publishing, n.d.), 82–83.
35 Khaled Abou El Fadl, *Speaking in God's Name: Islamic Law, Authority and Women* (Oxford: Oneworld, 2001), 93.
36 Maurice Bucaille, *La Bible, Le Coran et la science: les Ecritures saintes examinées à la lumière des connaissances modernes*, 2nd ed. (Paris: Seghers, 1976).
37 M. Shamsher Ali, *Scientific Indications in the Holy Qur'an (written by a Board of Researchers under Research Programme of 1985–1990)* (Dhaka: Islamic Foundation Bangladesh, 1990), xii.

6

Conclusion: Listening for God

As we discussed in the last chapter, scholars of the Qur'an – those who have studied the sacred book and its commentaries – play an important mediating role in Muslim societies. Their authority to represent the meaning of God's words derives from their specialized knowledge that is organized and transmitted through the customs and institutions of the scholarly class – the *ijaza* system, the *madrasa*, and the mosque study circle. As Jacob Neusner notes, most adherents of the world's religions rely on scholars and revered leaders to interpret their sacred texts for them:

> Even now, when literacy is widespread but not ubiquitous, it is not clear that most practitioners of [the major world religions] "read" the sacred texts of their religion in any systematic or disciplined way. More typically, religious intellectuals and vir-tuosi read, understand, interpret, mediate, and exemplify the texts in the life of a religious community.... These "living" texts become models of behavior – of ethics, piety, learning, compassion, and discipline. People who practice those religions turn to these "living texts" to learn what to do and what their religion teaches.[1]

Here Neusner emphasizes that it is not just knowledge but exemplary behavior that, in the minds of the faithful, gives any individual the authority to speak on behalf of the Divine. This is particularly true in Islam which, despite its development of sophisticated institutions of religious education and formation, never embraced a system of ordination.

Certainly religious specialists – formally trained scholars and preachers – have dominated religious discourse in Muslim societies.

However, these specialists have never been able to claim a monopoly on religious knowledge and authority. Indeed, a brilliant scholar or imam who is a poor communicator might have little influence in his society, while a charismatic, self-taught preacher might gather a large following. In addition, we have seen that the rigid and destructive literalism of the Khawarij in the first century of Islam demonstrated an important lesson to the Muslim community, and that is that a person could master the text of the Qur'an while at the same time acting in complete opposition to its spirit. Knowledge, without good character, does not confer much authority. Finally, it is also true that ordinary Muslims often have little sustained contact with religious experts, and simply seek guidance from someone who appears to them to be living a righteous life. The most significant religious authority in the lives of many Muslims, in fact, is a parent, a wise elder of the community or even a friend who seems to have internalized the spirit of the Qur'an, despite having little of the knowledge possessed by the scholars. Consciously or unconsciously, many individuals will recognize good character and practical wisdom as indications that someone has attained a true understanding of the Qur'an.

The medieval poet and mystic Rumi (d. 672/1273) wrote:

> The interpretation of the sacred text is true
> if it stirs you to hope, activity and awe;
> and if it makes you slacken your service,
> know the real truth to be this:
> it is a distortion of the sense of the saying, not a true interpretation.
> This saying has come down to inspire you to serve –
> that God may take the hands of those who have lost hope.
> Ask the meaning of the Qur'an from the Qur'an alone,
> and from that one who has set fire to his idle fancy and burned it away,
> and has become a sacrifice to the Qur'an, bowing low in humbleness,
> so that the Qur'an has become the essence of his spirit.
> The essential oil that has utterly devoted itself to the rose,
> You can smell either that oil or the rose, as you please.[2]

Here, Rumi presents the spiritual guide as the one who has immersed himself so deeply in the Qur'an that he becomes like an essential oil – completely infused with God's word. This is why the Sufi Sheikh is capable of guiding others, who may or may not be able to study the meaning of the Qur'an themselves. The emphasis here, then, is not so much on correct methodology as on a positive outcome: a true interpretation – and a true interpreter – inspires, awes, and motivates, whereas a false interpretation – and a false interpreter – enervates and demotivates.

We have seen earlier that the Qur'an itself indicates that a sound "heart" is needed to grasp the meaning of revelation. There is disagreement, however, about whether the Qur'an also indicates that it has deeper or hidden meanings that can by attained only by certain individuals by virtue of their unique knowledge or heightened spiritual state. There is one verse that is particularly important in this debate:

> It is He who has sent down the Book to you. In it are definitive verses (muhkamat) that are the foundation of the Book, and others are ambiguous (mutashabihat) . . .
>
> (Al 'Imran; 3:7)

Here, the Qur'an indicates that it is comprised of two kinds of verses: those that are "definitive" or "concise," and those that are "ambiguous" or "allusive." Now, what is particularly problematic in understanding the implication of these words is that the continuation of the verse can be read in two different ways, depending how one punctuates the phrases. According to one reading, the Qur'an indicates that a special group of people know the meaning of these ambiguous verses:

> As for those who have some deviation in their hearts, they follow the ambiguities therein, seeking discord and seeking interpretations. And none knows its interpretations except for God and those firmly grounded in knowledge.
> They say, "We believe in it. All of it is from our Lord."
> And none will take heed of this except for those who have insight.

However, according to another reading, only God knows the meaning of the verses:

> As for those who have some deviation in their hearts, they follow the ambiguities therein, seeking discord and seeking interpretations. And no one knows its interpretations except for God.
> And those firmly grounded in knowledge say, "We believe in it. All of it is from our Lord."
> And none will take heed of this except for those who have insight.

The latter reading demands skepticism towards those who would claim to have special "insight" into the hidden meanings of the Qur'an; indeed, such people could be considered among those with deviating hearts, and hence are incapable of grasping the truth of God's word. The former meaning, in contrast, seems to demand a search for those individuals (*"those firmly grounded in knowledge"*) who can give insights into the meaning of the Qur'an that are not accessible to the majority.

Sufism has placed particular emphasis on the flashes of insight that God can bestow upon those with hearts truly open to guidance. The great synthesizer of traditional Sunnism and Sufism, Imam al-Ghazali, argued that the goal of those who read the Qur'an should be to rid themselves of obstacles that prevent a deeper understanding of its "wonders of the secrets." Among these obstacles, al-Ghazali says, is the belief "that Qur'anic verses only have those meanings which have been transmitted by tradition from Ibn 'Abbas, Mujahid and other exegetes, and that meanings going beyond them are interpretations of the Qur'an by personal opinion (*tafsir bi'l-ra'y*)." Al-Ghazali refers to a statement of 'Ali which indicates that God gives some people an understanding of the meanings of the Qur'an that are not accessible to others.[3] Al-Ghazali asserts that the great early Qur'an commentators like Ibn 'Abbas and Mujahid offered their own understandings of many words and verses, the proof of this being the fact that they often gave different explanations and presented multiple interpretations for the same word or verse.

Al-Ghazali agrees that proffering one's personal opinion of the Qur'an is not permitted, but what he understands by this is that it is sinful to deliberately interpret the Qur'an in a way one knows to be in contradiction to its true meaning. Further, it is not permitted for one ignorant of the external meaning of the Qur'an to offer his own opinion about what it means. He says, "One who claims to possess understanding of the deep meanings of the Qur'an, without being prudent of its outward exegesis, is comparable to a man who claims to reach the upper part of a house without crossing its door, or claims to understand the meaning of the Turks when they speak, although he does not understand the Turkish language."[4]

Al-Ghazali explains that another obstacle to reaching a deep understanding of the Qur'an is rigid adherence to a particular school of thought. This rigidity leads one who is reading the Qur'an to reject flashes of insight that could allow him to reach a deeper understanding of the meaning of the Qur'an:

> This is a person whose belief has shackled him from going beyond [the transmitted meaning]. So it is not possible that any idea

other than that in which he has believed should come to his mind. If a distant flash of "lightning" is seen and one of the meanings which is opposite to the meaning he has heard appears to him, then the Satan of purely following a school of thought dogmatically attacks him severely saying, "How can this meaning come to your mind, seeing that it is contradictory to the meaning in which your forefathers believed?" So he considers the new meaning as a deception from Satan, and he remains at a distance from it and guards himself against the like of it.

For a reason similar to this, the Sufis have said that knowledge is a veil, and by this knowledge they have meant those beliefs which most people have been firmly holding either by dogmatically following an authority or by mere reliance on casuistic sentences written by partisans of schools of thought and passed to them. As for the real knowledge which is the uncovering of the actual condition of the thing known, and which is a vision by the light of spiritual insight, how can it be a veil, seeing that it is the ultimate object of desire?[5]

Thus, for the Sufis, epistemological certainty cannot be attained by academic study alone, rather, true understanding – *ma'rifa* – is a gift from God that is the fruit of a spiritual struggle. The aim of the Sufi path, then, has been to allow those who have already gained such insight and mastered the spiritual disciplines to assist others on the path to true knowledge.

There is no doubt that gnosticism sometimes leads to esoteric interpretations quite at odds with the apparent meaning of verses. Some mystics have taught that certain esoteric meanings are suitable for understanding and implementation by the spiritually elect alone, and that the average believer should be taught and compelled to follow the law according to an objective and exoteric hermeneutics. On the other hand, many Sufis, like al-Ghazali, denied that any valid understanding of the Qur'an could conflict with the apparent meaning of the verses. Al-Ghazali stressed that the deeper insight God gives to certain individuals is utterly different than personal opinion; such interpretations must be based on true knowledge that comes from God. These interpretations provide a deeper, complementary meaning to the divine words that, after all, originate with the infinite God, and therefore are endlessly productive of meaning.

Esoteric interpretations have, perhaps, been found among the Shi'ites to an even greater extent than among the Sunnis. This is because the Shi'ites explicitly embraced the concept of a post-Prophetic guide early in their formation, with the belief that the descendants of the Prophet Muhammad – the 'Alid Imams – had been granted a unique ability to grasp the inner meaning of the Qur'an. Justification for this belief was sought in statements attributed to the Prophet, as well as Qur'anic verses.

Mahmoud Ayoub explains that the Shi'ites identify *"those firmly rooted in knowledge"* as the Imams who are "the true vicegerents of the prophet and heirs to the knowledge of all prophets from Adam to Muhammad." Shi'ites remain, like Sunni Muslims, committed to the doctrine of the finality of the prophethood of Muhammad, so they do not consider the Imams to be prophets. The Imams are not "recipients of *wahy* (direct revelation); yet as people spoken to (*muhaddathun*) by angels, they are recipients of a special non-Qur'anic kind of revelation. Their mission is not a legislative one, which is the special prerogative of an apostle (*rasul*) sent by God with a new sacred law (*shari'a*). Rather, the Imams receive the true and full meaning of the prophetic revelations, which includes the correct exegesis of legal precepts, knowledge of the concealed (*ghayb*), and elucidation of the Qur'an's references to past history and prophecies of future events."[6]

Sunni scholars reject the Shi'ite doctrine of the special status of the Imams on theological grounds; nevertheless, it is a sociological reality that great reverence for descendants of the family of the Prophet has been widespread in Sunni communities, particularly, but not exclusively, in the premodern era. Sunnis who claim descent from the Prophet commonly use the honorific *Sayyid* and *Sayyida* ("Lord" and "Lady") before their name, and are considered a kind of nobility in many Muslim societies.

If we take into consideration the considerable influence of both Sayyids and Sufi Sheikhs, we recognize that there has long been a dynamic tension in Sunnism between the charismatic power of these religious figures and the bureaucratized authority of the scholarly class. At the same time, together, scholars, preachers, Sufi Sheikhs, and Sayyids comprise a religious sector that provides vital services to communities that go beyond spiritual support and religious services. In particular, they have founded, developed, and supported a large sector of charitable institutions. In addition, religious leaders often use their prestige to mediate between political powers and ordinary people.

On the other hand, there is the risk that the deference ordinary people are sometimes expected to show to religious leaders and Sayyids can make it difficult to hold the latter accountable for any mis-behavior.[7] Early modern reformers, who were keen to bureaucratize the religious sector, were particularly concerned about this. But even before modernity, there was a strain of Muslim popular and folk culture that related tales of the religious classes using their charisma and social capital to exploit the underprivileged, and to avoid account-ability for their actions.[8] A strong strain of what could be called "anti-clericism" has therefore always existed alongside the reverence shown to "saints," Sayyids, and charismatic religious leaders. In the end, what is clear is that in the religious sector, as in the political sector, it is critical that institutions are accountable to the greater community. It is only with such accountability and oversight that any sector of Muslim society can carry and transmit the values their community ascribes to the Qur'an.

Ordinary people will never demand such accountability, however, if they do not have a certain level of confidence in their convictions and courage to articulate them. This is why we need not only to study the history of the dominant leaders and institutions in Muslim soci-eties, but also to search for the voices of marginalized individuals and groups – to see how they articulated and maintained their faith when they had little power. It is for this reason that Abu Dharr, whose opposition to the Umayyads we discussed earlier, serves as an inspir-ation for those fighting the status quo. But here we need to exercise some caution. We cannot simply romanticize the voice of protest – after all, Abu Dharr was claimed as an inspiration not just by pious reformers but also by Arab communists.[9] Further, the Khawarij were a marginalized protest movement – but they were ruthlessly violent and intolerant. Indeed, there is a lesson in that history as well: some-times groups are marginalized for good reason, and no person, no matter how noble his stated cause, is immune from error or the temptations of arrogance and power.

Nevertheless, due heed must be paid to the small voices (or inner voices) that sometimes challenge the interpretations offered by those who are considered to be speaking authoritatively. Like Khawla, whom we met at the beginning of this book, many Muslims have a strong internal conviction that God is just and fair, and that any Qur'anic interpretation that conflicts with their sense of justice and fairness, even if it is considered authoritative, demands, at the very least, further scrutiny. To this end,

Figure 6.1 The Qur'anic imperative to seek justice inspires Illinois Muslims affiliated with the Inner-City Muslim Action Network to lobby at the state capital for better laws for the socially marginalized. (IMAN)

stories like the following can encourage ordinary Muslims to feel confident enough to voice their reservations or discomfort with certain interpretations of the Qur'an.

Zaynab bint Mu'ayqib was a woman of Medina, who, along with thousands of others, went out to attend the funerals of two great men – one a religious scholar and one a poet – who died on the same day at the beginning of the second century of Islam.[10] Zaynab was among a large group of women who were gathering behind one of the coffins. A prominent Sayyid, Abu Ja'far Muhammad ibn 'Ali ("al-Baqir" – who would be identified by the Shi'ites as their fifth "Imam"), tried to approach the coffin. Blocked by the crowds of women who would not part to let him through, Abu Ja'far began to snap his cloak at them saying, "Enough, you companions of Joseph!" (The "Joseph" referred to here is Joseph the son of Jacob, whose long and moving narrative merits a complete Sura in the Qur'an. In the Qur'anic story, the mistress of the imperial house and the women of the court admire Joseph's beauty, placing him in an awkward and morally compromising situation.)

In response to Abu Ja'far's insult, Zaynab called out, "O son of the Messenger of God, you are correct that we are the companions of Joseph – and we treated him better than you!" After the funeral was over, Abu Ja'far sent someone to bring Zaynab to him. The narrator of the story says that Zaynab arrived "as though she were a spark of fire." Abu Ja'far asked what she had meant when she said that "(We) women are better than (you) men." Before she responded, Zaynab "asked for immunity" from Abu Ja'far. This is an interesting request, because Abu Ja'far held no political office or authority. However, it is clear that he was so revered among the people of Medina that he was, to some extent, a power unto himself. Abu Ja'far granted immunity to Zaynab, so she responded to him: "We women, O Son of the Messenger of God, invited (Joseph) to the delights of food and drink, and to enjoy and be comfortable. But you men threw him in the well, sold him for a miserable price and locked him in prison – so which of us was more tender and kind to him?"[11]

When Abu Ja'far used the Qur'an to dismiss the women who got in his way, Zaynab knew this was not fair. Her knowledge was not based on an academic study of the Qur'an, nor on the claim that she had any special spiritual status that gave her unique insight to the meanings of the Qur'an. Zaynab, rather, had confidence in her intuitive sense of fairness which allowed her to tell Abu Ja'far how she perceived misogyny in his words (for his part, Abu Ja'far is said to have expressed admiration at Zaynab's spirited defense). As a woman, Zaynab also had a different perspective than Abu Ja'far on the Qur'anic story of Joseph. In her eyes, the story clearly shows a male propensity for violence and acquiring power at any cost.

In his book *What is Scripture?*, Wilfred Cantwell Smith suggests that, in fact, the intuitive sense of what is just and fair is the ultimate arbiter of Qur'anic meaning for all sincere Muslims.

> If you yourself are a Muslim writing a commentary; or are a Sufi *pir* master instructing your *murid* disciple; or are a conscientious jurisconsult deciding a tricky point of law; or are a modern Cambridge-educated Muslim reflecting on contemporary life; or are a twelfth-century Shirazi housewife practicing your private devotions in the solitude of your home; or are a left-wing leader of the ninth-century slave revolt of the Zanj protesting against what seem to you the exploitation and hypocrisy of the establishment – in all such cases the correct interpretation of a particular Qur'an verse is the best possible

interpretation that comes to you or that you can think up. I do not mean that you concoct it cunningly or contrive it irresponsibly. On the contrary: you are constrained by the very fact of your esteeming this as the word of God to recognize as the most cogent among all possible alternatives that interpretation that in your judgment is the closest to universal truth and to universal goodness. You choose not what is the best for you, but what in your judgment is the closest to what is good and true absolutely, cosmically. (Your sense of what it signifies may inhibit acting on what you would prefer, or are strongly impelled to do.)[12]

But this begs the question, what is the origin or source of a sense of "universal goodness" or "universal truth" in an individual? If it is true that God created human beings with an innate sense of right and wrong (*fitra*), it is also true that the Qur'an and the Sunna teach that this inner sense can be corrupted by persisting in sin, and that one can easily be led astray by one's selfish desires. It is for this reason that revelation is a theological necessity – to help guide us back to what is right. But how do we attain a true understanding of revelation if we are already emotionally and spiritually wounded people?

Figure 6.2   After decades of suppression, the Muslims of China, including "female Imams," are once again able to teach their religion. (Ronna Syed)

If we return to the first story we related in this book – the story of Hajar – we find a way out of this dilemma. The spiritual matriarch of Islam shows us that we must first trust in God, and then struggle, using all the means God has given us, to find the pure waters of Divine knowledge. Hajar found the holy water only because she was confident that God would provide for her, and then exerted all her energy and resources to find her provisions.

Thus, in the first place, we must use all the intellectual resources God has given us to attempt to understand the true meaning of the Qur'an. God gave Hajar two legs which she used to run back and forth between the mountains, and two eyes with which she looked for a source of water. God gave Muslims, individually and collectively, sight, hearing, and intellect to put at the service of studying the linguistic and historical context of the Qur'an. It is impossible for any one individual to master all these aspects of Qur'anic learning, even in a lifetime of study. A serious effort to understand the Qur'an, therefore, necessarily includes a deep engagement with the extensive scholarly tradition of Islam.

This is something that many modern activists and commentators on the Qur'an have lacked. Indeed, many of the most influential Muslims (for better or worse) who made claims about the Qur'an in the twentieth century were not trained as religious scholars. Sayyid Qutb was a writer who captured the attention of Arabic readers with his articulation of widely felt frustration with arrogant and repressive Middle Eastern rulers in his extensive commentary *In the Shade of the Qur'an*. Abul Ala Mawdudi (d. 1979), founder of Jamaat-e-Islami in pre-partition India and prolific commentator on the Qur'an, was a journalist. With the success of the argument that the doors of *ijtihad* should open and that consensus should be expanded to include the voices of non-specialists, writers like Qutb and Mawdudi did not feel restrained by their lack of scholarly credentials to make claims about the meaning of the Qur'an.

In his characteristically blunt fashion, Fazlur Rahman, an influential twentieth-century scholar of the Qur'an, decried the inability of many activist-oriented Muslims to develop a relevant, coherent, and systematic approach to the interpretation and application of the Qur'an:

> The traditionalist ulema, if their education has suffered from a disorientation toward the purposes of the Qur'an, have nevertheless built up an imposing edifice of learning that

invests their personalities with a certain depth; the neoreviv-
alist is, by contrast, a shallow and superficial person – really
rooted neither in the Qur'an nor in traditional intellectual
culture, of which he knows practically nothing. Because he
has no serious intellectual depth or breadth, his consolation
and pride both are to chant ceaselessly the song that Islam is
"very simple" and "straightforward," without knowing what
these words mean. In a sense, of course, the Qur'an is simple
and uncomplicated, as is all genuine religion – in contradistinc-
tion to theology – but in another and more meaningful sense a
book like the Qur'an, which gradually appeared over almost
twenty-three years, is highly complicated – as complicated as
life itself.[13]

While activists and revivalists are limited by their superficial understanding of classical Islamic learning, staunch traditionalists must be
aware of the severe limitations of the inherited tradition. Our search
for the true meaning of the Qur'an and its application to our lives
cannot be a narrow, partisan following of a particular school of
thought, for it is certainly possible that groups, like individuals, can
engage in self-interested exegesis. In a previous study of slavery and
social status in Islamic law, I argued that such a tendency is evident
in the deliberations of early Muslim scholars.[14] Only a truly open-
minded, critical engagement with the diverse schools of thought and
approaches to the Qur'an will be sufficient to claim the exercise of due
diligence.

The second necessary condition for understanding revelation is
the proper intention – to sincerely wish to be guided by God. This
does not mean that non-Muslims and even atheists cannot contribute
to the factual body of knowledge useful to contextualizing the Qur'an;
but you cannot attain what you do not set out to find. The meaning
of the revelation can only be accessed by those who believe that
ultimate meaning is beyond the limited understanding of any human
being and who sincerely turn to the Qur'an for the purpose of finding
that meaning. However, attaining the state of humility that is characteristic of a sincere intention is not easy. How many individuals are
confident of the purity of their intentions and the soundness of their
hearts, yet clearly are deceiving themselves?

We all have emotional scars, spiritual disabilities, and stubborn
desires that make us less than perfect mirrors for God's divine light.
This is why we need to live our faith in community with others – so

they can help illuminate our flaws and support us in our spiritual growth. But our growth will be limited unless our communities reflect the diversity of human experience. Parochialism has been an inescapable reality for much of humanity since we first inhabited the earth. In our era, for most people who are not impoverished, parochialism is a choice. It is possible in an age of niche marketing and virtual communities, when we have email list-serves, webpages, radio and TV channels catering to narrow, special interests, to limit our contact to those who reflect our own perspectives and experiences and who do not challenge us to expand our frames of analysis. To do this violates the teaching of the Qur'an that diverse communities were created by God precisely for the purpose of mutual knowledge, which itself must lead to greater self-knowledge:

> O people! Indeed We created you from a male and a female, and made you into tribes and nations so that you might know each other. The most noble of you in the sight of God is the one who is most God-fearing. Indeed, God is All-Knowing, Completely Aware.
> (Hujarat; 49:13)

After the Prophet Muhammad died, it became the responsibility of the Muslim community to interpret and apply the meaning of the Qur'an to their lives. It would be an awesome task:

> If We had sent down this Qur'an upon a mountain, you would have seen it humble itself and split open out of fear of God. Such are the parables we set forth to humanity, so they might reflect.
> (Hashr; 59:21)

According to the Qur'an, it is the collective responsibility of humanity to find ways to fulfill their role as stewards of creation and vicegerents of God on earth. We will make mistakes, but according to the Qur'an, God has a purpose in putting us flawed creatures in charge of the earth:

> When your Lord said to the angels, "I am going to put a vicegerent on the earth," they said, "Will you put on (the earth) someone who will cause corruption there and shed blood, while we celebrate your praise and sanctify you?" He said, "I know what you do not know."
> (Baqara; 2:30)

Fear, whim, greed, pride – how many potential barriers exist to block our understanding of the true meaning of God's words! Certainly we need to be exceedingly cautious about claiming to have grasped the true meaning of the Qur'an. How much better would it be if we stopped making declarations for a while and humbly, earnestly, tried to listen to God?

Still, there are times when we need to make judgments and take action. We should have confidence in the full power of God to guide us to a correct understanding, but always, always, with the humility to acknowledge that *wa Allahu 'alam*: "But God knows better."

Notes

1 Jacob Neusner, *Sacred Texts and Authority* (Cleveland: Pilgrim Press, 1998), xv.
2 *The Pocket Rumi Reader*, ed. Kabir Helminski (Boston: Shambhala Publications, 2001), 171; I have made minor changes to the translation.
3 Muhammad Abul Quasem, *The Recitation and Interpretation of the Qur'an: al-Ghazali's Theory* (London: Kegan Paul International, 1982), 66.
4 Abul Quasem, 94. I have made minor changes to his translation.
5 Abul Quasem, 70–71.
6 Mahmoud M. Ayoub, "The Speaking Qur'an and the Silent Qur'an: A Study of the Principles and Development of Imāmī Shī'ī *tafsīr*," in *Approaches to the History of the Interpretation of the Qur'an*, ed. Andrew Rippin (Oxford: Clarendon Press, 1988), 186–187.
7 Leslie Peirce, " 'The Law Shall not Languish': Social Class and Public Conduct in Sixteenth-Century Ottoman Legal Discourse," in *Hermeneutics and Honor: Negotiating Female "Public" Space in Islamicate Societies*, ed. Asma Asfaruddin (Cambridge, MA: Harvard University Press, 1999), 151.
8 Francis Robinson, "Knowledge, its Transmission, and the Making of Muslim Societies," in *The Cambridge Illustrated History of the Islamic World*, ed. Francis Robinson (Cambridge: Cambridge University Press, 1996), 219–221.
9 'Abd al-Hamid Judah Sahhar, *Abu Dharr al-Ghifari, al-ishtiraki al-zahid, sahib Rasul Allah: masdar bi bahth al-ishtirakiyya fi'l-islam* (Cairo: Maktabat Misr, 1978); Muhammad 'Ali Al-Suri, *Abu Dharr al-Ghifari: al-ishtiraki al-mutarid* (Beirut: al-Mu'assassa al-'Arabiyya li'l-dirasat wa'l-nashr, 1979).

10   'Ikrima, the client of 'Abdullah ibn al-'Abbas, and Kuthayyir 'Izza; they died ca. 105/723. Muhammad ibn Sa'd, *al-Tabaqat al-Kubra*, 8 vols. (Beirut: Dar al-Kutub al-'Ilmiyya, 1958), 5:224.

11   'Umar Kahhala, *A'lam al-Nisa' fi 'Alimay al-'Arab wa'l-Islam*, 4 vols. (Beirut: Mu'assasat al-Risala, 1977), 2:116–117.

12   Wilfred Cantwell Smith, *What is Scripture? A Comparative Approach* (Minneapolis: Fortress Press, 1993), 72–73.

13   Fazlur Rahman, *Islam and Modernity: Transformation of an Intellectual Tradition* (Chicago: University of Chicago Press, 1982), 137.

14   Ingrid Mattson, *A Believing Slave is Better than an Unbeliever: Status and Community in Early Islamic Society and Law* (University of Chicago doctoral dissertation, 1999), 113–123. Also, Amal Ghazal has shown how one of the most prominent defenders of traditionalism, Yusuf al-Nabhani, was a vocal opponent of the abolition of the slave trade; her research is found in her unpublished paper, "Debating Slavery: Abolition between Muslim Reformers and Conservatives," presented at the York University (Toronto) "Conference on Slavery, Islam and Diaspora," October 24–26, 2003.

Glossary

'Abbasid	Islamic dynasty which ruled from Baghdad 132/750–655/1258
adhan	Call to prayer
'Alim/'Ulama'	"Learned" person/s; Islamic scholar/s
Ansar	"Helpers"; the Medinan Muslims who hosted and helped settle the Meccan Muslims into their city
Ash'ari	School of orthodox Sunni theology named after Abu'l-Hasan al-Ash'ari (d. 323/935)
aya/ayat	"Sign/s"; verse/s of the Qur'an
batin	"Interior"; the inner, hidden or esoteric meaning of the Qur'an
dhikr	"Remembrance" of God; the Sufis of Islam emphasize group and individual audible chanting of the names and attributes of God.
fiqh	"Knowledge"; Islamic legal rulings
fitra	Innate knowledge of God
hadith	"Report"; report about the Prophet Muhammad
hafiz	"Preserver"; someone who has memorized the Qur'an
Hajj	Pilgrimage to Mecca that every Muslim must undertake once in a lifetime if he or she is physically and financially able.
harf/ahruf	Variant reading/s of the Qur'an
hijra	Emigration undertaken by Muhammad and his followers in 622 CE from Mecca to the city of Yathrib, known thereafter as "Medina" – "The City (of the Prophet)." This event marks the beginning of the Islamic calendar.
ijaza	Certificate of mastery of a subject

ijtihad	"Exertion"; utmost exertion of the intellect to arrive at a sound ruling
iltifat	"Turning"; a sudden unexpected shift from one pronoun to another
isnad	Chain of transmitters
Jahiliyya	Period of "ignorance" or "impetuousness" before Islam
Jibril	Gabriel
Juz'	One-thirtieth portion of the Qur'an
Ka'ba	"Cubic" temple located within the Sacred Mosque of Mecca
kalam	"Speech"; also signifies speculative theology
Khalifa (Caliph)	"Successor" to the Prophet; leader of the Muslim community
khatma	"Completion"; complete recitation of the Qur'an from beginning to end
Khawarij	"Secessionists"; originally supporters of 'Ali ibn Abi Talib who became his violent opponents. The term was later applied to other radical and militant opposition groups
lawh mahfudh	"Preserved tablets"; celestial locus of Qur'an
ma'rifa	Gnostic "understanding"
mihna	"Test"; the inquisition established by the 'Abbasid caliph al-Ma'mun in 218/833
mihrab	Niche in mosque wall indicating the *qibla*
minaret	Tower from which the *adhan* is called
mu'adhdhin	Person who calls the *adhan*
Mu'allaqat	Master poems "hanging" on the Ka'ba before Islam
muhaddith	Hadith scholar
Muhajirun	"Emigrants"; the Meccan Muslims who emigrated to Medina
muhkamat	Unequivocal verses; opposite of *mutashabihat*: ambiguous verses
Mujahid/ Mujahidun	"Those who struggle"; usually used in reference to those who serve in a just war.
muqri'	Master-Reciter
murid	Sufi disciple
mushaf	Pronounced *mus-haf*; manuscript of the Qur'an
mutakallim	Speculative theologian
Mu'tazilite	Proponent of the Mu'tazili school of Islamic theology that emerged in the second century of

Islam. The Mu'tazilites employed Greek logic and rational philosophy to develop a distinctive Islamic ontology and political theory. Considered "unorthodox" by Sunni Islam after the third century, Mu'tazilism has regained some popularity in the modern period.

nabi/anbiya   Prophet/s

naskh   Abrogration of rulings

Ottomans   Turkish Islamic dynasty, ruled for six centuries until 1922

pir   (Hindi) spiritual master

qari/qurra'   Qur'an reciter/s

qasida   Epic Arabic poem

qibla   Direction towards the Ka'ba; hence, the direction which a Muslim must face while performing *salat*

qira'a/   Particular recitation/s of the Qur'an
   qira'at

qiyas   Analogical reasoning

Quraysh   The tribe to which the Prophet Muhammad belonged; the leading tribe of Mecca at the rise of Islam

rak'a/rak'at   Cycle/s of prayer consisting of standing, bowing, and prostration

Ramadan   Name of the twelfth month of the Islamic calendar; month during which the annual obligation of fasting (*sawm*) is undertaken

rasul/rusul   Messenger/s (of God)

Sabab/Asbab   Occasion/s of revelation
   al-Nuzul

Sahabi/   Companion/s of the Prophet Muhammad
   Sahaba

Salafi/   Sometimes derogatory term for Muslims who reject
   Salafiyya   the necessity of following the classical legal schools but instead rely on (often literal) direct readings of the Qur'an and prophetic hadith, believing this to be the methodology of the first few generations of righteous Muslims, the *salaf al-salih.*

salat   "Ritual prayer"; prayer requiring ritual purity that must be performed in the direction of the *qibla* at certain times in an established manner of standing, bowing, and prostration.

Sayyid/ Sayyida	"Lord/Lady"; title given to descendants of the Prophet Muhammad
shahid	"Witness"; a "martyr" who is killed because of his faith or fighting for a just cause
shari'a	"Path to the water"; the divine norms including law and ethics; Islamic jurisprudence
Sheikh/ Sheikha	lit. "Elderly Man/Woman"; term of respect for an elder or religious scholar
Sira	The biography of the Prophet Muhammad
Sufism	Islamic discipline of spirituality; a "Sufi" is one who submits him or herself to such a discipline.
Sunna	"The way"; guidance from the Prophet Muhammad
Sura/Suwar	"Enclosure/s"; chapter/s of the Qur'an
tafsir	"To explain"; Qur'an commentary, exegesis
tahara	Purity
tajwid	"Making beautiful"; art of reciting Qur'an
ta'wil	"To return to the source"; term often used as a synonym of *tafsir* but can also be used to signify esoteric interpretation in particular
Umayyad	First Islamic dynasty, ruled 41/661–132/750 from Damascus, Syria
Wahhabi	Derogatory term applied to followers of Arabian revolutionary theologian Muhammad ibn 'Abd al-Wahhab (d. 1792 CE)
wahy	Divine "inspiration"
zahir	"Exterior"; the apparent or literal meaning of the Qur'an

Bibliography

Studies

Abbott, Nabia. *The Rise of the North Arabic Script and its Quranic Development.* Chicago: University of Chicago Press, 1939.

Abbott, Nabia. *Studies in Arabic Literary Papyri.* 3 vols. Chicago: University of Chicago Oriental Institute Publications; vols. 75–77, 1957–1972.

Abd-Allah, Umar Faruq. "One God Many Names," Nawawi Foundation paper. Published online: www.nawawi.org/downloads/article2.pdf.

Abdel Haleem, Muhammad A. S. *English Translations of the Qur'an: The Making of an Image.* United Kingdom: SOAS, 2006.

Abdel Haleem, Muhammad A. S. "Grammatical Shift for the Rhetorical Purposes: Iltifat and Related Features in the Qur'an," *Bulletin of the School of Oriental and African Studies,* LV, 3 (1992): 407–432.

Abdel Haleem, Muhammad A. S. "Qur'anic Orthography: The Written Representation of the Recited Text of the Qur'an," *Islamic Quarterly* 38, 3 (1994): 171–192.

Abdel Haleem, Muhammad A. S. *Understanding the Qur'an: A Study of Themes and Style.* I. B. Tauris, 2001.

Abou El Fadl, Khaled. *Speaking in God's Name: Islamic Law, Authority and Women.* Oxford: Oneworld, 2001.

Abu Zayd, Nasr Hamid. *Al-Khitab wa'l-ta'wil.* Casablanca: al-Markaz al-Thaqafi al-'Arabi, 2000.

Abul Quasem, Muhammad. *The Recitation and Interpretation of the Qur'an: al-Ghazali's Theory.* London: Kegan Paul International, 1982.

Adhami, Abdullah. *Ithaf al-Munawwarat bi Tabyin Ijazat al-Qari'at.* New York: Sakeenah Books, forthcoming.

Ahmed, Shahab. "Ibn Taymiyyah and the Satanic Verses," *Studia Islamica* 87 (1998): 67–124.

Arkoun, Mohammed. *Lectures du Coran.* Paris: G.-P. Maisonneuve et Larousse, 1982.

Arkoun, Mohammed. *The Unthought in Contemporary Islamic Thought*. London: Saqi Books, 2002.

As-Said, Labib. *The Recited Koran: A History of the First Recorded Version*. Princeton, NJ: Darwin Press, 1975.

Atiyeh, George N., ed. *The Book in the Islamic World: The Written Word and Communication in the Middle East*. Albany: State University of New York Press, 1995.

Austin, Allan D. *African Muslims in Antebellum America: Transatlantic Stories and Spiritual Struggles*. New York: Routledge, 1997.

Ayoub, Mahmoud M. *The House of 'Imran*, vol. 2 of *The Qur'an and its Interpreters*. Albany: State University of New York Press, 1992.

Ayoub, Mahmoud M. "The Speaking Qur'an and the Silent Qur'an: A Study of the Principles and Development of Imami Shi'i *tafsir*." In *Approaches to the History of the Interpretation of the Qur'an*, ed. Andrew Rippin, 177–198. Oxford: Clarendon Press, 1988.

Azami, M. M. *The History of the Qur'anic Text: From Revelation to Compilation: A Comparative Study with the Old and New Testaments*. Leicester: UK Islamic Academy, 2003.

Azami, M. M. *Studies in Early Hadith Literature*. Indianapolis: American Trust Publications, 1978.

Bar-Asher, Meir M. *Scripture and Exegesis in Early Imami Shiism*. Jerusalem: Magnes Press (Hebrew University), 1999.

Barlas, Asma. *"Believing Women" in Islam: Unreading Patriarchal Interpretations of the Qur'ān*. Austin: University of Texas Press, 2002.

Beeston, A. F. L. "Judaism and Christianity in Pre-Islamic Yemen." In *L'Arabie du sud: histoire et civilisation*, ed. Joseph Chelhod, 271–278. Paris, 1984.

Berkey, Jonathan P. *The Formation of Islam: Religion and Society in the Near East, 600–1800*. Cambridge: Cambridge University Press, 2003.

Blair, Sheila and Jonathan M. Bloom. *The Art and Architecture of Islam: 1250–1800*. New Haven, CT: Yale University Press, 1994.

Blair, Sheila and Jonathan M. Bloom, eds. *Images of Paradise in Islamic Art*. Hanover, NH: Hood Museum of Art, 1991.

Bloom, Jonathan M. *Minaret: Symbol of Islam*. Oxford Studies in Islamic Art VII. Oxford: Oxford University Press, 1989.

Bonner, Michael. *Jihad in Islamic History: Doctrines and Practice*. Princeton, NJ: Princeton University Press, 2006.

Boullata, Issa J. *Literary Structures of Religious Meaning in the Qur'an*. Richmond, Surrey, UK: Curzon Press, 2000.

Böwering, Gerhard. *The Mystical Vision of Existence in Classical Islam: The Qur'anic Hermeneutics of the Sufi Sahl at-Tustari (d. 283/896)*. Berlin: Walter de Gruyter, 1980.

Bowman, John. "Holy Scriptures, Lectionaries and Qur'an," in *International Congress for the Study of the Qur'an, Australian National University, Canberra,*

8–13 May 1980, ed. A. H. Johns, 29–37. Canberra: Australian National University, 1981.

Boyle, Helen N. *Quranic Schools: Agents of Preservation and Change*. New York: RoutledgeFalmer, 2004.

Bravmann, M. M. " 'Life after Death' in Early Arab Conception," in *The Spiritual Background of Early Islam*, 288–295. Leiden: Brill, 1972.

Brockett, Adrian. "The Value of the Hafs and Warsh Transmissions for the Textual History of the Qur'an," in *Approaches to the History of the Interpretation of the Qur'an*, ed. Andrew Rippin, 31–45. Oxford: Clarendon Press, 1988.

Brookes, John. *Gardens of Paradise: The History and Design of the Great Islamic Gardens*. London: Weidenfeld and Nicolson, 1987.

Brown, Daniel. *Rethinking Tradition in Modern Islamic Thought*. Cambridge: Cambridge University Press, 1996.

Bucaille, Maurice. *La Bible, Le Coran et la science: les Ecritures saintes examinées à la lumière des connaissances modernes*, 2nd ed. Paris: Seghers, 1976.

Bulliet, Richard W. *Conversion to Islam in the Medieval Period: An Essay in Quantitative History*. Cambridge, MA: Harvard University Press, 1979.

The Cambridge Illustrated History of the Islamic World. Ed. Francis Robinson. Cambridge: Cambridge University Press, 1996.

Cook, Michael. *The Koran: A Very Short Introduction*. Oxford: Oxford University Press, 2000.

Diouf, Sylviane A. *Servants of Allah: African Muslims Enslaved in the Americas*. New York: New York University Press, 1998.

Dodd, Erica Cruikshank and Shereen Khairallah. *The Image of the Word: A Study of Quranic Verses in Islamic Architecture*. Beirut: American University of Beirut, 1981.

Donner, Fred McGraw. *The Early Islamic Conquests*. Princeton, NJ: Princeton University Press, 1981.

Donner, Fred McGraw. "From Believers to Muslims: Patterns of Communal Identity in Early Islam," *Al-Abhath* 50–51 (2002–2003): 9–53.

Donner, Fred McGraw. *Narratives of Islamic Origins: The Beginnings of Islamic Historical Writing*. Princeton, NJ: Darwin Press, 1998.

Eickelman, Dale F. "Qur'anic Commentary, Public Space and Religious Intellectuals in the Writings of Said Nursi," *The Muslim World* 88, 3–4 (July–October 1999): 260–269.

El-Awa, Salwa M. S. *Textual Relations in Qur'an: Relevance, Coherence and Structure*. London: Routledge, 2006.

Encyclopedia of Islam. 2nd ed. Eds. P. J. Bearman, Th. Bianquis, C. E. Bosworth, E. van Donzel, W. P. Heinrichs et al. 12 vols. with indexes. Leiden: Brill, 1960–2005.

Encyclopedia of the Qur'an. 5 vols. Gen. Ed. Jane Damen McAuliffe. Leiden: Brill, 2001–2006.

Federspiel, Howard M. *Popular Indonesian Literature of the Qur'an.* Ithaca, NY: Cornell Modern Indonesia Project, 1994.

Gade, Anna M. *Perfection Makes Practice: Learning, Emotion and the Recited Qur'an in Indonesia.* Honolulu: University of Hawai'i Press, 2004.

Gätje, Helmut. *The Qur'an and its Exegesis: Selected Texts with Classical and Modern Muslim Interpretations.* Trans. and ed. Alford T. Welch. Berkeley: University of California Press, 1976.

Ghazal, Amal. "Debating Slavery: Abolition between Muslim Reformers and Conservatives," unpublished paper presented at the York University (Toronto) "Conference on Slavery, Islam and Diaspora," October 24–26, 2003.

Al-Ghazali, Muhammad. *A Thematic Commentary on the Qur'an.* Translation by 'Ashur Shamis of *Al Tafsir al-Mawdu' li suwar al-Qur'an al-Karim.* Herndon, VA: International Institute of Islamic Thought, 1999.

Grabar, Oleg. *The Mediation of Ornament.* Princeton, NJ: Princeton University Press, 1992.

Grabar, Oleg. *The Shape of the Holy: Early Islamic Jerusalem.* Princeton, NJ: Princeton University Press, 1996.

Graham, William A. *Beyond the Written Word: Oral Aspects of Scripture in the History of Religion.* Cambridge: Cambridge University Press, 1987.

Graham, William A. "Scripture as Spoken Word." In *Rethinking Scripture: Essays from a Comparative Perspective,* ed. Miriam Levering, 129–169. Albany: State University of New York Press, 1989.

Gruendler, Beatrice. *The Development of the Arabic Scripts: From the Nabatean Era to the First Islamic Century, according to Dated Texts.* Atlanta: Scholars Press, 1993.

Gwynne, Rosalind. *Logic, Rhetoric and Legal Reasoning in the Qur'an: God's Arguments.* London: RoutledgeCurzon, 2004.

Hallaq, Wael B. *A History of Islamic Legal Theories: An Introduction to Sunni Usul al-Fiqh.* Cambridge: Cambridge University Press, 1997.

Hawting, G. R. and Abdul-Kader A. Shareef, eds. *Approaches to the Qur'an.* London: Routledge, 1993.

Henninger, Joseph. "Pre-Islamic Bedouin Religion." In *Studies on Islam,* ed. Merlin L. Swartz, 3–22. New York: Oxford University Press, 1981.

Hillenbrand, Carole. *The Crusades: Islamic Perspectives.* New York: Routledge, 2000.

Hodgson, Marshall G. S. *The Venture of Islam: Conscience and History in a World Civilization.* 3 vols. Chicago: University of Chicago Press, 1974.

Izutsu, Toshihiko. *Ethico-Religious Concepts in the Qur'an.* Montreal: McGill University Press, 1966.

Izutsu, Toshihiko. *God and Man in the Qur'an: Semantics of the Qur'anic Weltanschauung.* 1964. Reprint, Kuala Lumpur: Islamic Book Trust, 2002.

Kabbani, Muhammad Hisham. *Encyclopedia of Islamic Doctrine.* 7 vols. Mountain View, CA: As-Sunna Foundation of American Publications, 1998.

Kahf, Mohja. "Braiding the Stories: Women's Eloquence in the Early Islamic Era," in *Windows of Faith: Muslim Women Scholar-Activists in North America*, ed. Gisela Webb, 147–171. Syracuse: Syracuse University Press, 2000.

Kamali, Mohammed Hashim. *Issues in the Legal Theory of Usul and Prospects for Reform*. Kuala Lumpur: International Islamic University Malaysia, 2002.

Kamali, Mohammed Hashim. *Principles of Islamic Jurisprudence*. Cambridge: Islamic Texts Society, 1991.

Kamen, Henry. *The Spanish Inquisition: A Historical Revision*. New Haven, CT: Yale University Press, 1997.

Kister, M. J. "Mecca and Tamim (Aspects of their Relations)," *Journal of the Economic and Social History of the Orient* 8 (1965): 117–163.

Lane, Edward William. *An Account of the Manners and Customs of the Modern Egyptians*, "the Definitive 1860 Edition," reprinted from the fifth edition of 1860. Introduced by Jason Thompson. Cairo: American University in Cairo Press, 2003.

Lawson, Todd. "Akhbari Shi'i Approaches to *tafsir*," in *Approaches to the Qur'an*, ed. G. R. Hawting and Abdul-Kader A. Shareef, 173–210. London: Routledge, 1993.

Leaman, Oliver. *An Introduction to Medieval Islamic Philosophy*. Cambridge: Cambridge University Press, 1985.

Leemhuis, Fred. "The Koran and its Exegesis: From Memorising to Learning." In *Centres of Learning: Learning and Location in Pre-Modern Europe and the Near East*, eds. J. W. Drijvers and A. A. MacDonald, 91–102. Leiden: Brill, 1995.

Leepson, Marc. *Flag: An American Biography*. New York: Thomas Dunne Books/St. Martin's Press, 2005.

Lings, Martin. *The Quranic Art of Calligraphy and Illuminations*. London: World of Islam Festival Trust, 1976.

Lings, Martin. *A Sufi Saint of the Twentieth Century: Shaikh Ahmad al-'Alawi, His Spiritual Heritage and Legacy*. 2nd ed. London: George Allen and Unwin, 1961.

Lopez-Morillas, Consuelo. *The Qur'an in Sixteenth-Century Spain: Six Morisco Versions of Sura 79*. London: Tamesis Books, 1982.

Lucas, Scott C. *Constructive Critics, Hadith Literature, and the Articulation of Sunni Islam: The Legacy of the Generation of Ibn Sa'd, Ibn Ma'in, and Ibn Hanbal*. Leiden: Brill, 2004.

Lunde, Paul. "Arabic and the Art of Printing," *Saudi Aramco World* (March/April 1981): 20–35.

MacCulloch, Diarmaid. *The Reformation: A History*. New York: Penguin, 2004.

Mack, Rosamond E. *Bazaar to Piazza: Islamic Trade and Italian Art, 1300–1600*. Berkeley: University of California Press, 2002.

Madelung, Wilfred. *Religious Schools and Sects in Medieval Islam*. London: Variorum Reprints, 1985.

Makdisi, George. *The Rise of Colleges: Institutions of Learning in Islam and the West*. Edinburgh: Edinburgh University Press, 1981.

Marcinkowski, Muhammad Ismail. "Some Reflections on Alleged Twelver Shi'ite Attitudes towards the Integrity of the Qur'an," *The Muslim World*, 91, 1/2 (Spring 2001): 137–154.

Maraqten, Mohammed. "Writing Materials in pre-Islamic Arabia," *Journal of Semitic Studies*, 43, 2 (1998): 287–310.

Masahif Sana'a. Kuwait: Dar al-Athar al-Islamiyya, 1985.

Masud, Muhammad Khalid. *Shatibi's Philosophy of Islamic Law*. Islamabad: International Islamic University, 1995.

Mattson, Ingrid. *A Believing Slave is Better than an Unbeliever: Status and Community in Early Islamic Society and Law*. University of Chicago doctoral dissertation, 1999.

Mattson, Ingrid. "Status-Based Definitions of Need in Early Islamic *Zakat* and Maintenance Laws." In *Concepts of Poverty and Charity in Middle Eastern Contexts*, eds. Michael Bonner, Mine Ener, and Amy Singer, 31–51. Albany: State University of New York Press, 2003.

Mattson, Ingrid. "The Axis of Good: Muslims Building Alliances with Other Communities of Faith." Online at macdonald.hartsem.edu/articles.htm#mattson.

Mawdudi, Sayyid Abul A'la. *Towards Understanding the Quran*. Translation by Khurshid Ahmad of *Tafhim al-Qur'an*. Lahore: Islamic Publications, 1960.

McAuliffe, Jane Dammen. *Qur'anic Christians: An Analysis of Classical and Modern Exegesis*. Cambridge: Cambridge University Press, 1991.

Mir, Mustansir. "The *Sura* as a Unity: A Twentieth-Century Development in Qur'an Exegesis." In *Approaches to the Qur'an*, ed. G. R. Hawting and Abdul-Kader A. Shareef, 211–224. London: Routledge, 1993.

Mir, Mustansir. *Coherence in the Qur'an: A Study of Islahi's Concept of Nazm in Tadabbur al-Qur'an*. Indianapolis, IN: American Trust Publications, 1986.

Modarressi, Hossein. "Early Debates on the Integrity of the Qur'an: A Brief Survey," *Studia Islamica*, 77 (1993): 5–39.

Motzki, Harald. "The Collection of the Qur'an: A Reconsideration of Western Views in Light of Recent Methodological Developments," *Der Islam* (2001): 1–34.

Motzki, Harald., ed. *Hadith: Origins and Developments*. Burlington, VT: Ashgate/Variorum, 2004.

Moynihan, Elizabeth B. *Paradise as a Garden in Persia and Mughal India*. New York: G. Braziller, 1979.

al-Munajjid, Salah al-Din. "Women's Roles in the Art of Arabic Calligraphy." In *The Book in the Islamic World: The Written Word and Communication in the Middle East*, ed. George N. Atiyeh, 141–148. Albany: State University of New York Press, 1995.

Murata, Sachiko. *The Tao of Islam: A Sourcebook on Gender Relationships in Islamic Thought*. Albany: State University of New York Press, 1992.

Murad, Abdal-Hakim. "The Trinity: A Muslim Perspective," lecture given "to a group of Christians in Oxford, 1996," published online at www.masud.co.uk/ISLAM/ahm/trinity.htm.

Nadvi, Mohammed Shihabuddin. *Qur'an, Science, and the Muslims*. Trans. Khalid Irfan and Sayeedur Rahman Nadvi. Bangalore: Furqania Academy Trust, 2001.

Nelson, Kristina. *The Art of Reciting the Qur'an*. Cairo: American University in Cairo Press, 2001.

Neusner, Jacob, ed. *Sacred Texts and Authority*. Cleveland: Pilgrim Press, 1998.

Neuwirth, Angelika. *Studien Zur Komposition der Mekkanischen Suren*. Berlin: De Gruyter, 1981.

Okada, Amina and M. C. Joshi. *Taj Mahal*. New York: Abbeville Press, 1993.

O'Shaughnessy, Thomas J. *Creation and the Teaching of the Qur'an*. Rome: Biblical Institute Press, 1985.

Peirce, Leslie. " 'The Law Shall not Languish': Social Class and Public Conduct in Sixteenth-Century Ottoman Legal Discourse." In *Hermeneutics and Honor: Negotiating Female "Public" Space in Islamicate Societies*, ed. Asma Asfaruddin, 140–158. Cambridge, MA: Harvard University Press, 1999.

Peters, F. E. *Mecca: A Literary History of the Muslim Holy Land*. Princeton, NJ: Princeton University Press, 1994.

Petersen, E. L. *'Ali and Mu'awiyah in Early Arabic Tradition*. Copenhagen, 1964.

The Pocket Rumi Reader. Ed. Kabir Helminski. Boston: Shambhala Publications, 2001.

Poonawala, Ismail K. "Ismā'ili *ta'wil* of the Qur'an." In *Approaches to the History of the Interpretation of the Qur'an*, ed. Andrew Rippin, 199–222. Oxford: Clarendon Press, 1988.

Qadhi, Abu Ammaar Yasir. *An Introduction to the Sciences of the Qur'aan*. Birmingham, UK: Al-Hidaayah Publishing and Distribution, 1999.

al-Qadi, Wadad. "The Impact of the Qur'an on the Epistolography of 'Abd al-Hamid." In *Approaches to the Qur'an*, eds. G. R. Hawting and Abdul-Kader A. Shareef, 285–313. London: Routledge, 1993.

The Qur'an as Text. Ed. Stefan Wild. Leiden: Brill, 1996.

Quraishi, Asifa. "Interpreting the Qur'an and the Constitution: Similarities in the Use of Text, Tradition, and Reason in Islamic and American Jurisprudence," *Cardozo Law Review*, 28, 1 (October 2006): 67–121.

Raby, Julian and Jeremy Johns, eds. *Bayt al-Maqdis*. 2 vols. New York: Oxford University Press, 1992–1999.

Rahman, Fazlur. *Islam and Modernity: Transformation of an Intellectual Tradition*. Chicago: University of Chicago Press, 1982.

Rahman, Fazlur. *Major Themes of the Qur'an*. Minneapolis: Bibliotheca Islamica, 1980.

Rahman, Fazlur. *Prophecy in Islam: Philosophy and Orthodoxy*. Chicago: University of Chicago Press, 1979.

Al-Raysuni, Ahmed. *Imam al-Shatibi's Theory of the Higher Objectives and Intents of Islamic Law*. Herndon, VA: International Institute of Islamic Thought, 2006.

Rippin, Andrew, ed. *Approaches to the History of the Interpretation of the Qur'an*. Oxford: Clarendon Press, 1988.

Rippin, Andrew. "The Function of *Asbab al-nuzul* in Qur'anic Exegesis," *BSOAS*, 51 (1988): 1–20.

Rippin, Andrew, ed. *The Qur'an: Formative Interpretation*. Burlington, VT: Ashgate/Varorium, 1999.

Rippin, Andrew, ed. *The Qur'an: Style and Contents*. Burlington, VT: Ashgate/Varorium, 2000.

Roth, Cecil. *The Spanish Inquisition*. New York: W. W. Norton, 1964.

Rubin, Uri. *Between Bible and Qur'an: The Children of Israel and the Islamic Self-Image*. Princeton, NJ: Darwin Press, 1999.

Ruggles, Fairchild. *Gardens, Landscape and Vision in the Palaces of Islamic Spain*. University Park: Pennsylvania State University Press, 2000.

Sahhar, 'Abd al-Hamid Judah. *Abu Dharr al-Ghifari, al-ishtiraki al-zahid, sahib Rasul Allah: masdar bi bahth al-ishtirakiyya fi'l-islam*. Cairo: Maktabat Misr, 1978.

Salameh, Khader. *The Qur'an Manuscripts in the al-Haram al-Sharif Islamic Museum, Jerusalem*. New York: Garnet/Ithaca Press, 2001.

Saleh, Walid. "In Search of a Comprehensible Qur'an: A Survey of Some Recent Scholarly Works," *Bulletin of the Royal Institute for Interfaith Studies*, 4, 2 (Autumn/Winter 2003): 143–162.

Scientific Indications in the Holy Qur'an (written by a Board of Researchers under Research Programme of 1985–1990). Dhaka: Islamic Foundation Bangladesh, 1990.

Sells, Michael. *Approaching the Qur'an: The Early Revelations*. Ashland, OR: White Cloud Press, 1999.

Shahab, Ahmed. "Ibn Taymiyyah and the Satanic Verses," *Studia Islamica*, 87 (1998): 67–124.

Shahid, Irfan. "Pre-Islamic Arabia." In *Cambridge History of Islam*, 2 vols., ed. P. M. Holt, 1:3–19. Cambridge: Cambridge University Press, 1970.

Simon, R. "Hums et Ilaf, ou Commerce sans Guerre," *Acta Orientalia Academiae Scientiarum Hungaricae*, 23, 2 (1970): 205–232.

Smith, Wilfred Cantwell. *Towards a World Theology: Faith and the Comparative History of Religion*. Maryknoll, NY: Orbis Books, 1989.

Smith, Wilfred Cantwell. *What is Scripture? A Comparative Approach*. Minneapolis: Fortress Press, 1993.

Stetkevych, Jaroslav. *The Zephyrs of Najd: The Poetics of Nostalgia in the Classical Arabic Nasib*. Chicago: University of Chicago Press, 1993.

Stetkevych, Suzanne Pinckney. *The Mute Immortals Speak: Pre-Islamic Poetry and the Poetics of Ritual.* Ithaca: Cornell University Press, 1993.

Stowasser, Barbara. *Gender Issues and Contemporary Quran Interpretation.* New York: Oxford University Press, 1998.

Stowasser, Barbara. *Women in the Qur'an, Traditions and Interpretation.* New York: Oxford University Press, 1994.

Al-Suri, Muhammad 'Ali. *Abu Dharr al-Ghifari: al-ishtiraki al-mutarid.* Beirut: al-Mu'assassa al-'Arabiyya li'l-dirasat wa'l-nashr, 1979.

Surty, Muhammad Ibrahim H. I. "The Qur'an in Islamic Scholarship: A Survey of *tafsīr* Exegesis Literature in Arabic," *Muslim World Book Review,* 7, 4 (1987): 51–65.

Taji-Farouki, Suha. *Modern Muslim Intellectuals and the Qur'an.* Oxford: Oxford University Press, 2004.

Thomas, Evan. "How a Fire Broke Out: The Story of a Sensitive *Newsweek* Report about Alleged Abuses at Guantánamo Bay and a Surge of Deadly Unrest in the Islamic World," *Newsweek,* May 23, 2005.

Versteegh, C. H. M. *Arabic Grammar and Qur'anic Exegesis in Early Islam.* Leiden: Brill, 1993.

Voll, John Obert. *Islam: Continuity and Change in the Modern World.* 2nd ed. Syracuse: Syracuse University Press, 1994.

Von Denffer, Ahmad. *'Ulum al-Qur'an: An Introduction to the Sciences of the Qur'an.* Leicester, UK: The Islamic Foundation, 1983.

Wadud, Amina. *Qur'an and Woman: Rereading the Sacred Text from a Woman's Perspective.* Oxford: Oxford University Press, 1999.

Wansbrough, John. *Quranic Studies: Sources and Methods of Scriptural Interpretation.* Foreword, translations, and expanded notes by Andrew Rippin. Amherst, NY: Prometheus Books, 2004.

Watt, W. M. *Muhammad at Mecca.* Oxford: Oxford University Press, 1953.

Wheeler, Brannon M. *Moses in the Qur'an and Islamic Exegesis.* London: RoutledgeCurzon, 2002.

Whelan, Estelle. "Forgotten Witness: Evidence for the Early Codification of the Quran," *Journal of the American Oriental Society,* 118, 1 (January–March 1998): 1–15.

Whelan, Estelle. "Writing the Word of God: Some Early Qur'an Manuscripts and their Milieux, Part I," *Ars Orientalis,* 20 (1990): 113–136.

Zarabozo, Jamaal al-Din. *How to Approach and Understand the Quran.* Boulder, CO: Al-Basheer Co., 1999.

Primary Sources in Arabic and in Translation

Al-Ansari, Abu Yahya Zakariyya ibn Muhammad. *al-Daqa'iq al-muhkamah fi sharh al-muqaddimah al-Jazariyya fi 'ilm al-tajwid.* Damascus, 1980.

Ashqar, 'Umar Sulayman. *The World of Jinn and Devils*. Translation by Jamaal al-Din M. Zarabozo of *'Alam al-jinn wa'l-shayatin*. Denver, CO: al-Basheer Publications and Translations, 1998.

Al-Azraqi, Abu'l-Walid Muhammad ibn 'Abdullah. *Ta'rikh Mecca*. Ed. Rushdi Malhas. Mecca: Dar al-Thaqafa, 1965.

Al-Balkhi, Muqatil ibn Sulayman. *Al-Ashbah wa'l-naza'ir fi'l-Qur'an al-Karim*. Ed. 'Abdallah Mahmud Shihatah. Cairo: al-Hay'a al-Misriyya al-'Amma li'l-Kitab, 1975.

Al-Bukhari, Abu 'Abdullah Muhammad ibn Isma'il. *Kitab al-Jami' al-Sahih*. Riyadh: Dar al-Salam, 1998.

Al-Dani, Abu 'Amr 'Uthman ibn Sa'id. *Al-Muqni' fi rasm masahif al-amsar* (with *Kitab al-Naqt*). Ed. Hasan Sirri. Alexandria, Egypt: al-Tawzi' marakaz al-Iskandariyya li'l-kitab, 2005.

Al-Dhahabi, Abu 'Abdullah Muhammad ibn Ahmed. *Ma'rifat al-qurra' al-kibar 'ala'l-tabaqat wa'l-a'sar*. 2 vols. Beirut: Mu'asassat al-Risalah, 1984.

Al-Ghazali, Abu Hamid Muhammad. *The Faith and Practice of al-Ghazali*. Translation by W. Montgomery Watt of *al-Munqidh min al-dalal* and *Bidayat al-hidaya*. 1953. Reprint, Oxford: Oneworld, 1994.

Al-Ghazali, Abu Hamid Muhammad. *Inner Dimensions of Islamic Worship*. Selections from *Ihya 'ulum al-din* translated by Muhtar Holland. Leicester, UK: The Islamic Foundation, 1983.

Al-Ghazali, Abu Hamid Muhammad. *The Ninety-Nine Beautiful Names of God: al-Maqsad al-asna fi sharh asma' Allah al-husna*. Trans. David B. Burrell and Nazih Daher. Cambridge: Islamic Texts Society, 1992.

Al-Hamdhani al-'Attar, Abu'l-'Ala' al-Hasan ibn Ahmed. *Ghayat al-ikhtisar fi qira'at al-'asharat 'a'immat al-amsar*. Jiddah, 1994.

Al-Harawi, 'Ali bin Abi Bakr. *A Lonely Wayfarer's Guide to Pilgrimage*. Translation by Josef W. Meri of *Kitab al-Isharat ila ma'rifat al-ziyarat*. Princeton, NJ: Darwin Press, 2004.

Al-Husayni, al-Hajjah Hayat 'Ali. *Mulaq al-mufid fi 'ilm al-tajwid*. Damascus, 1997.

Ibn Anas, Malik. *Al-Muwatta* [compilation of Yahya ibn Yahya al-Laythi]. Trans. 'A'isha 'Abdarahman and Ya'qub Johnson. Norwich, UK: Diwan Press, 1982.

Ibn al-Anbari, 'Abd al-Rahman ibn Muhammad. *Nuzhat al-alibba fi tabaqat al-udaba'*. Ed. Attia Amer. Stockholm: Almqvist and Wiksell, 1963.

Ibn Ghalbun, Tahir ibn 'Abd al-Mun'im. *Tadhkirah fi'l-qira'at*. Ed. 'Abd al-Fattah Buhayri Ibrahim. Cairo: al-Zahra' li'l-'ilam al-'arabi, 1990.

Ibn Habib, Muhammad. *Kitab al-Muhabbar*. Hyderabad, 1942.

Ibn al-Hajjaj, Muslim. *Sahih*. 18 vols. Published as *Sahih Muslim bi sharh al-Nawawi*. Beirut: al-Dar al-Thaqafa al-'Arabiyya, 1929.

Ibn Hanbal, Ahmed. *Musnad Ahmed*. Riyadh: International Ideas Home for Publishing and Distribution, 1998.

Ibn Hazm, 'Ali ibn Ahmed. *Al-Fasl fi'l-milal wa'l-ahwa' wa'l-nihal.* 5 vols. Cairo: Muhammad 'Ali Subayh, 1964.

Ibn Hisham, 'Abd al-Malik. *The Life of Muhammad: A Translation of Ishaq's Sirat Rasul Allah.* Trans. Alfred Guillaume. Oxford: Oxford University Press, 1955.

Ibn al-Jazari, Abu'l-Khayr Muhammad ibn Muhammad. *Ghayat al-Nihayah fi tabaqat al-qurra'.* Ed. G. Bergstraesser. 2 vols. Cairo, 1932.

Ibn al-Jazari, Abu'l-Khayr Muhammad ibn Muhammad. *Al-Nashr fi'l-qira'at al-'ashr.* 2 vols. Damascus, 1926.

Ibn Jubayr, Muhammad ibn Ahmed. *The Travels of Ibn Jubayr, being the chronicle of a mediaeval Spanish Moor concerning his journey to the Egypt of Saladin, the holy cities of Arabia, Baghdad the city of the caliphs, the Latin Kingdom of Jerusalem, and the Norman kingdom of Sicily.* Translation by R. J. C. Broadhurst of *Rihlat Ibn Jubayr.* London: Jonathan Cape, 1952. Arabic text: *Risalat Ibn Jubayr fi Misr wa Bilad al-'Arab wa'l-'Iraq wa'l-Sham wa Saqliyya 'asr hurub al-Salibiyya.* Ed. Husayn Nassar. Cairo: Maktabat Misr, 1992.

Ibn Khaldun, 'Abd al-Rahman Muhammad ibn Muhammad. *The Muqaddimah: An Introduction to History.* Translation by Franz Rosenthal of *Al-Muqaddimah.* Abridged and ed. N. J. Dawood. Princeton, NJ: Princeton University Press, 1967.

Ibn Mujahid, Abu Bakr Ahmed ibn Musa. *Kitab al-sab'a fi'l-qira'at.* Ed. Shawqi Dayf. Cairo: Dar al-Ma'arif, 1979.

Ibn Qayyim al-Jawziyya, Muhammad ibn Abi Bakr. *Al-Tibb al-Nabawi.* Ed. 'Abd al-Ghani 'Abd al-Khaliq. Beirut: Dar al-Kutub al-'Ilmiyya, 1957.

Ibn Qayyim al-Jawziyya, Muhammad ibn Abi Bakr. *The Legal Methods in Islamic Administration.* Translation by Ala'eddin Kharofa of *al-Turuq al-hukmiyya fi'l-siyasa al-shar'iyya.* Kuala Lumpur: International Law Book Services, 2000.

Ibn Qutayba, Abu Muhammad 'Abdullah ibn Muslim al-Dinawari. *al-Ma'arif.* Beirut: Dar al-Kutub al-'Ilmiyya, 1987.

Ibn Sa'd, Muhammad. *al-Tabaqat al-Kubra,* 8 vols. Beirut: Dar al-Kutub al-'Ilmiyya, 1958.

Ibn Sallam, Abu 'Ubayda al-Qasim. *Fada'il al-Qur'an.* Ed. Wahbi Sulayman Ghawaji. Beirut: Dar al-Kutub al-'Ilmiyya, 1991.

al-Juwayni, Imam al-Haramayn 'Abd al-Malik ibn Yusuf. *A Guide to Conclusive Proofs for the Principles of Belief.* Translation by Paul E. Walker of *Kitab al-irshad 'ila qawati'l-'adilla fi usul al-i'tiqad.* Reading, UK: Garnet, 2000.

al-Juwayni, Imam al-Haramayn 'Abd al-Malik ibn Yusuf. *Kitab al-Waraqat* in the text of Jalal al-Din Muhammad ibn Ahmed al-Mahalli's *Sharh al-waraqat fi 'ilm usul al-fiqh.* Cairo: Muhammad 'Ali Subayh, 1965.

Kahhala, 'Umar. *A'lam al-Nisa' fi 'Alimay al-'Arab wa'l-Islam.* 4 vols. Beirut: Mu'assasat al-Risala, 1977.

Laqani, Ibrahim ibn Ibrahim. *Jawharat al-Tawhid.* Cairo, 1967.

Al-Misri, Ahmad ibn Naqib. *Reliance of the Traveller: A Classical Manual of Islamic Sacred Law*. Translation of and commentary on *'Umdat al-Salik* by Nuh Ha Mim Keller. Rev. ed. Evanston, IL: Sunna Books, 1994.

al-Nasa'i, Ahmed ibn Shu'ayb. *Fada'il al-Qur'an*. Ed. Faruq Hamadah. Casablanca: Dar al-Thaqafah, 1980.

al-Nawawi, Yahya ibn Sharaf. *Etiquette with the Quran*. Translation by Steven (Musa) Woodward Furber of *al-Tibyan fi adab hamalat al-Qur'an*. Illinois: Starlatch Press, 2003.

Al-Qurtubi, Abu 'Abdallah Muhammad ibn Ahmed al-Ansari. *Al-Jami' li ahkam al-Qur'an*. Ed. 'Abd al-Razzaq al-Mahdi. 20 vols. in 10 bks. Beirut: Dar al-Kitab al-'Arabi, 2001.

Qutb, Sayyid (Sayed). *In the Shade of the Quran*. Translation by M. A. Salahi and A. A. Shamis of *Fi dhilal al-Qur'an*. London: MWH, ca. 1979.

Qutb, Sayyid (Sayed). *Milestones*. Translator not named. Cedar Rapids, IO: Unity Publishing, n.d.

Al-Razi, Fakhr al-Din Muhammad ibn 'Umar. *Al-Tafsir al-Kabir*. 32 vols. Beirut: Dar Ihya' al-Turath al-'Arabi, 1980.

Sabiq, al-Sayyid. *Fiqh al-Sunna*. 3 vols. Beirut: Dar al-Kitab al-'Arabi, n.d.

Al-Shafi'i, Muhammad ibn Idris. *Islamic Jurisprudence: Shafi'i's Risala*. Translation by Majid Khadduri of *al-Risala*. Baltimore: Johns Hopkins University Press, 1961.

Al-Shatibi, al-Qasim ibn Firruh. *Hirz al-amani wa wajh al-tahani fi'l-qira'at al-saba'*. Medina, 1989.

Al-Sijistani, Abu Bakr ibn Abi Daud. *Kitab al-Masahif*. Ed. Muhammad ibn 'Abduh. Cairo, 2002.

al-Suyuti, Jalal al-Din 'Abd al-Rahman ibn Abi Bakr. *al-Itiqan fi 'ulum al-Qur'an*. Ed. Fawwaz Ahmed Zamarli. 2 vols. Beirut: Dar al-Kitab al-'Arabi, 1999.

Al-Tabari, Abu Ja'far Muhammd ibn Jarir. *Jami' al-bayan fi tafsir al-Qur'an*. 30 vols. in 12 bks. Cairo: Dar al-Hadith, 1987.

Al-Tabari, Abu Ja'far Muhammd ibn Jarir. *The History of Prophets and Kings*. Translation of *Ta'rikh al-rusul wa'l-muluk*. Multiple translators. 39 vols. Series Ed. Ehsan Yar. Albany: State University of New York, 1985–1998.

Al-Tahawi, Abu Ja'far Ahmed ibn Muhammad. *Al-'Aqida al-Tahawiyya*; text found in: 'Ali ibn 'Ali ibn Abi'l-'Izz, *Sharh al-Tahawiyya fi'l-aqida al-salafiyya*. Cairo: Zakariyya 'Ali Yusuf, 196–?. I have used the translation of the text by Iqbal Ahmad Azami on the website www.masud.co.uk/ISLAM/misc/tahawi.htm.

Al-Zamakhshari, Abu'l-Qasim Jarallah. *Al-Kashshaf 'an haqa'iq al-tanzil wa 'uyun al-aqawil fi wujuh al-ta'wil*. 4 vols. N.p: Dar al-'Alimiyya, n.d.

English Translations of the Qur'an

Muslims say that "the Qur'an can never be translated" because any translation is not the original revelation; only the meaning of the Qur'an can be translated. Translations of the Qur'an seem flat to most Arabic speakers, because the translator has to choose one of many complementary meanings possible. It is therefore recommended to compare a few translations to get some sense of the nuances of the words. Here are some of the most commonly used and available translations.

Abdel Haleem, Muhammad A. S. *The Qur'an: A New Translation*. Oxford: Oxford University Press 2005. A scholarly translation by one of the preeminent contemporary Qur'anic scholars.

'Ali, 'Abdullah Yusuf. *The Meaning of the Holy Qur'an: New Edition with Revised Translation, Commentary and Newly Compiled Comprehensive Index*. Beltsville, MD: Amana Publications, 1409 AH/1989 CE. A widely used translation with many useful notes. A unique feature is 'Ali's poetic introductions to each section.

Arberry, A. J. *The Koran Interpreted* (combined in one volume). 1955. Reprint in 1 vol. New York: Macmillan, 1969. Older English that yields some nice phrasing but some words are translated oddly or even inaccurately.

Asad, Muhammad. *The Message of the Qur'an*. Gibraltar, Spain: Dar al-Andalus, 1980. A straightforward translation inclined towards a "modern" approach.

Cleary, Thomas. *The Qur'an: A New Translation*. Burr Ridge, IL: Starlatch Press, 2004. A contemporary, fluid translation.

Helminski, Kabir. *The Book of Revelations: A Sourcebook of Selections from the Qur'an with Interpretations by Muammad Asad, Yusuf Ali, and Others*. Bristol: Book Foundation, 2005. This is not a complete translation of the Qur'an, only a collection of selections, with explanation and titles that beautifully capture the essence of the passages selected. It is possibly the best introduction to the Qur'anic message available in the English language.

al-Hilali, Muhammad Taqi-ud-Din and Muhammad Muhsin Khan. *The Noble Qur'an: English Translation of the Meanings and Commentary*. Madina, Saudi Arabia: King Fahd Complex for the Printing of the Holy Qur'an, 1419 AH/1998 CE. A translation notorious for placing ideologically biased parenthetical comments in the translation.

Pickthall, Muhammad Marmaduke. *The Meaning of the Glorious Koran: An Explanatory Translation*. 1930. Reprint, New York: New American Library, 1970. An older translation that tries to capture some of the beauty of the oral Qur'an.

Index of Qur'anic Citations and References

Index